Contents

KU-481-719

Contents

943
·08
77

Sebastian Cobler

Law, Order and Politics
in West Germany

Translated by Francis McDonagh

Penguin Books

Penguin Books Ltd, Harmondsworth,
Middlesex, England
Penguin Books, 625 Madison Avenue,
New York, New York 10022, U.S.A.
Penguin Books Australia Ltd, Ringwood,
Victoria, Australia
Penguin Books Canada Ltd, 2801 John Street,
Markham, Ontario, Canada L3R 1B4
Penguin Books (N.Z.) Ltd, 182–190 Wairau Road,
Auckland 10, New Zealand

Die Gefahr geht von den Menschen aus first published 1976
This revised and edited translation, with new Foreword and Conclusion,
published in Penguin Books 1978

Copyright © Rotbuch Verlag, 1976
This translation copyright © Penguin Books Ltd, 1978
Foreword and Conclusion copyright © Sebastian Cobler, 1978
All rights reserved

Made and printed in Great Britain by
Cox & Wyman Ltd, London, Reading and Fakenham
Set in Intertype Times

Except in the United States of America,
this book is sold subject to the condition that
it shall not, by way of trade or otherwise, be lent,
re-sold, hired out, or otherwise circulated without
the publisher's prior consent in any form of
binding or cover other than that in which it is
published and without a similar condition
including this condition being imposed on the
subsequent purchaser

In 1963, before he began his work of improving the techniques of ideological repression, Werner Maihofer wrote:

In a development exactly parallel to that of the medieval inquisition into heretics and dissidents, political criminal law in the modern authoritarian state is going beyond its classical function of defence against threats to the internal and external security of the state to become an instrument of political inquisition into all heretics and dissidents, into any subject who outwardly, or even merely inwardly, opposes the Credo imposed by the party in power and asserted as universally binding. In this way political justice in all authoritarian states has become an instrument used under the cloak of outward legality to remove or at least intimidate political opponents, using techniques of ideological pressure and ideological terror against anyone who does not voluntarily and inwardly submit to the creed imposed by the party ideology, or at least conform to it, without attracting attention, in all he does and does not do.

In such authoritarian states the light of publicity must be shunned not just by the man or woman who contravenes the constitution or the laws of the land, but even by anyone who does not agree with the public 'political line', who does not, wherever it is required of him in words or actions, join in accepting the official political creed. A state of this sort will therefore, sooner or later, as we saw in the National Socialist state, become ever more ready to use the classical state security offences, treason and high treason, not just against the real enemies of the state but also against opponents of its own policies, the 'enemies' of the party, against those who merely doubt the ideology which is set above all doubt, declared sacrosanct and identified with the welfare of the state ... A return of even the faintest traces of this evil must frighten anyone who is serious about the defence of our free system, and open the eyes of all those of us who know to what it once led, to the dangers which lurk here. We

7

shall only avoid those dangers by a firm resolve to turn back from the path taken since 1951 with the amendments to the criminal law, by retracing those ill-considered steps, already far too many, in a wrong direction which are taking us inevitably further and further from the social order which we are so determined to defend, our liberal democratic constitutional state. – (W. Maihofer, 'Staatsschutz in Rechtsstaat', a lecture given in 1963 at the Evangelical Academy of Arnoldshain/Taunus, published in *Veröffentlichungen der Evangelischen Akademie in Hessen und Nassau*, No. 53, pp. 4–5, 14–15.)

Foreword to the English Edition

This study of internal political developments in the Federal Republic of Germany appeared in German in 1976. The publication of the English edition has been overshadowed by a rapid succession of events each more amazing than the last: paramilitary police interventions against opponents of atomic power stations in many places; the assassination of Federal Attorney-General Buback, the state's senior prosecutor; the murder of the banker Ponto; a nationwide police alert during the demonstration by more than 50,000 citizens against the 'fast breeder' reactor in Kalkar; the kidnapping and murder of Hanns Martin Schleyer, the president of the Federation of Employers' Organizations, and his bodyguards. Other events in the year were the effectual subordination of the press to the government by a week-long news blackout and the total isolation for the same period of over a hundred prisoners facing charges in political cases – justified by the notion of a 'supra-legal state of emergency'; the West German government's cynical poker-playing with the lives of ninety-one people in a Lufthansa aircraft hijacked to Mogadishu; and finally the mysterious deaths of Gudrun Ensslin, Andreas Baader and Jan-Carl Raspe, the members of the 'Red Army Faction' held in the prison of Stuttgart-Stammheim.

In the course of these events and in their aftermath the police apparatus and the secret service surveillance system have been extended by measures which, though their proclaimed purpose is to deal with a handful of political desperadoes, mean further massive inroads into civil rights. As is customary in West Germany, they reduce political conflict to problems of law and order.

Foreword to the English Edition

This comes out particularly clearly in a confidential decision
by the Federal Ministry of the Interior on the attitude it should
adopt towards the International Russell Tribunal on the situation of human rights in West Germany. A leaked ministerial
paper details a series of measures to obstruct or prevent the
work of the Tribunal. These include 'informative' press campaigns by the Federal Government's Information Office and a
newly formed 'inter-ministerial working party' to deal with 'unjustified foreign criticism of the rule of law in the Federal Republic', infiltration of the jury with government supporters who
would work for an 'acquittal', and a refusal of entry to the
foreign members of the Tribunal. Public sessions were to be
banned on the ground that they constituted a 'threat to public
safety and order' under the very laws which the tribunal was to
investigate in connection with the question of censorship, primarily § 90a StGB, 'defamation of the state', a relic of Germany's authoritarian past. In other words, the discussion of
censorship will itself be censored. The Interior Ministry document is a revealing example of the police ignorance and arro-
gance which passes for policy in West Germany. It shows that a
stage has already been reached in which merely investigative
activity such as that of the Tribunal is treated as crime, and
shows the means which the leaders of 'the most liberal state in
German history' are ready to employ if need be to achieve this
end.

As though all the fuses had blown, a witch-hunt is being
organized against left and left liberal intellectuals which recalls
the period of McCarthyism in the USA in the 1950s. Any attempt to differentiate or to analyse the real significance of the
measures taken by the government under the banner of 'anti-
terrorism' is branded as 'sympathizing with terrorism'; language
is controlled, feelings prescribed, ideas banned and confessions
demanded. A 'state of intellectual siege' seems to have been
imposed. For example, openly expressed doubt of the official
government view that the Stammheim prisoners committed
suicide is prosecuted as 'defamation of the state', and all 1,500
participants in the funeral of the three prisoners were checked

10

by the police. General grief at the deaths of Buback and Schleyer was officially expected, while remarks about their activities as Federal Attorney-General and president of the Federation of Employers' Associations, and references to Schleyer's SS past, were punished as approval of the shots fired at them.

The list of the measures carried out or merely suggested in this climate of suspicion, incitement and denunciation is depressing. In addition to unashamed public calls for lynch justice, martial law, the liquidation of prisoners and the death penalty,[1] both government and opposition put forward bills for the 'protection of communal peace'. The proposals range from an unlimited extension of police powers and the intimate coordination of the police and secret service, through a tightening of the law on demonstrations and assembly, refinement of data processing, i.e. the electronic shadowing of citizens, alterations in criminal procedure in favour (naturally) of the prosecution, to the demand for political offenders to be placed in 'secure confinement', a proposal described by the conservative lawyers' association as 'smelling of concentration camps'.[2]

Irrespective of which of these proposals are in fact implemented – in the case of the death penalty, for example, this is at present totally inconceivable – even raising such proposals prepares the ground for others, which can then be introduced fairly smoothly. One example is the so-called 'contact ban' law, which in a summary procedure legalized the solitary confinement to which many prisoners in West Germany are subjected. Of this law, an extreme right-wing paper commented that its effect was 'to legalize a grave infringement of the rights of the accused which is normally a criterion of dictatorships', though it speedily added, 'in this situation an exercise of power by the legally constituted state was unavoidable'.[3]

Apart from a few observations on this 'contact ban' in the last chapter, I felt it unnecessary to give a detailed description of all the other 'exercises of power by the legally constituted state' which are currently being prepared and which have been briefly described above. They reveal no new aspects of the methods and organization of the West German state security system, but merely complement the fundamental thesis of this book, that the politically isolated and disastrous activities of a few desperadoes – in the literal sense of the word – serve as a welcome pretext for sealing off a whole society against any possibility of the growth of a political extra-parliamentary opposition.

Introduction: The Uneasy Sense of Danger

In West Germany today an almost insane fear marks the daily invocations of 'internal security' and 'internal peace' which pour in an incessant stream from the executive, press and judiciary. The simultaneous massive expansion of the state security apparatus prompts the questions: what do they really expect? what are they waiting for?

More than any other previous government, the SPD and FDP have spent more resources in this area than in areas where the term 'threat to security' might justly be used, such as unemployment and social policy. Short-term economic management and labour market policies have proved useless, and the Social Democratic receivers have been forced to wind up the reforms to which they alone still clung and which they hoped would provide 'protection' against 'dissatisfaction and social tensions'.[1] All this is hastening the collapse of the values, standards and attitudes which until now have given the existing system at least ideological coherence through slogans such as 'more freedom', 'more welfare' and 'more social security', which could continue to arouse hopes to allay immediate disappointments. All this is threatening not to work much longer. True, the government can still point to a relatively secure 'industrial peace', but it is clearly no longer able to judge how long it will last. All the greater is the urgency with which government and opposition are pressing on with the development of the most comprehensive possible system of surveillance and security – 'modern state security must include practically all areas of social life'.[2]

With the effect of advance warning, intimidation and punishment, rules are ostensibly being made for an exceptional case

13

which as a result threatens to become the rule. In the view of the minister of justice it is possible to disagree 'about whether this makes the situation better. At least it prevents it from getting worse, and compared with the situation which would otherwise occur, that is a better, and preferable, situation.' Old instruments are disinterred and sharpened up, a variety of devices combined to 'make action against crime better, tougher and more accurate'.[3] This book examines those parts of this action taken by the state as part of state security, what is suggestively known as the 'protection of the constitution'. 'The danger to the community comes from organized people,' ran the preamble to the draft produced in 1950 for a political criminal law, the most important provisions of which owed much to the Nazis' penalization of opinions. As well as this tradition, the function of the modern state security system was copied from the Nazis, retaining the motto of the thirties, 'advanced state security'. The whole range of measures, as we shall see, is inspired by two ideas: fear of people acting in solidarity, and the need to bring forward every form of surveillance and defence into the area of ideas and opinions, discussion and alternative publicity. In trials of demonstrators, squatters and occupiers of building sites, in charges of 'defamation of the state' or breach of the peace', in *Berufsverbote* or action to preserve 'industrial' or 'communal peace' – resistance is labelled terror. Criticism, information and protest are punished as 'subversion', and publicity if necessary reduced to what is officially published. The question of violence, we are told, has already received a final answer in the Basic Law – for example: 'It is hardly possible to imagine attacks or other actions against the basic order with which the security service would have to deal which might be performed out of conviction and still be worthy of respect.'[4]

But it is not just opposition, but names too, which draw scorn, names which symbolize ideas of freedom and the struggle for it. It is enough to remember the fuss created by the SPD state governments of the time to prevent the naming of the universities of Düsseldorf and Oldenburg after Heinrich Heine and

14

Carl von Ossietzky. In the latter case, Social Democrat minister of science Grolle even moved in 300 emergency police to remove the title 'Carl von Ossietzky University'. Students who protested with jeers were beaten.[5] In other words the names of people whom there is no longer any need to persecute must be erased from memory, while the others, the new 'enemies', are officially labelled and publicized because they are still around. This is where we hear of people whose behaviour is 'socially harmful' or 'dangerous to the community', who are 'ill-disposed towards the state', 'reject the state', are 'prejudicial to the state,' 'despise the state', 'defame the state', 'subvert the state', 'endanger the state', are 'hostile to the state', 'a threat to the state', etc. None of these terms is anywhere legally defined, and their use should therefore not be grounds for any legal disadvantages, but they are nevertheless accompanied by sanctions and negative attitudes. On the other side from the 'enemies of the state' stand the 'decent people', those who, 'with a positive, accepting national consciousness',[6] 'accept – and not just in words – the state and its ruling constitutional order', 'see and acknowledge the high positive value [of the constitution], who are worth fighting for'. Their 'attitude to the state and constitution is more than just formally correct', not 'uninterested, cool, inwardly distanced'. They are 'ready to support their state', and 'feel at home in this state, which they have to serve, now and at all times'[7] for, ultimately, they are interested 'in this liberal state of ours which we love'.[8]

When language is strained in this way, phrases inevitably crop up which involuntarily give the real problem its true name. In the Bundestag Ernst Benda complained about the 'opponents of the emergency'[9] – of course he meant to refer to opponents of the emergency legislation – and there has also been a striking increase in references to an 'increase in security offences' and 'political crimes'.[10] One has to examine the language of secret service and ministry officials, prosecutors and judges, the forms in which they think and speak, to find the sources of their actions. One has to do it also to show that their ideas and statements are dominated by double standards, criminal fantasy and projections with which they try to make their surroundings resemble themselves.[11]

References to 'enemies' within and the dangers they present are used to deal with existing tensions and attitudes, which can be seen to be created when there is talk of security. Attention is directed away from the real causes of these fears – economic and social distress. There is no attempt to talk people out of their fear; it is used, cultivated, though from a different angle. Fears diverted in this way do not go away, but are exploited to justify the introduction of security measures.

Tightening up state security in this way, in times of crisis and by exploiting a sense of crisis, is a well-tried technique. Many examples can be cited from the past. We may recall the anti-socialist law of 1878, the pretext for which was an attempt on the life of Kaiser Wilhelm,[12] the 'Draft for a Law to Combat the Acts of Violence of Anarchism' of 1898, the 'Reich President's Order of 29 August 1921' issued three days after the murder of Matthias Erzberger, which laid down penalties for 'incitement to disobey the laws' and the production and distribution of 'periodical publications' containing 'agitation for the violent change or abolition of the constitution'.[13] A similar 'Order for the Protection of the Republic' was issued on 24 June 1922, the day of Walter Rathenau's murder. This order penalized, among other acts, the 'approval and rewarding of violence',[14] a provision which, in spite of numerous attempts, it had never before been possible to make part of the criminal code and which was made more severe as late as the beginning of 1976 in the shape of the revised § 140 StGB as part of the 'communal peace' law. And finally we may recall the burning of the Reichstag and its legal consequences; the Korean War, which had to do duty as the reason for the new criminal code hastily passed in 1951; and lastly the events of recent years and the laws based on them, all of which are laid at the door of the Red Army Faction.

'In this country we may expect with complete certainty,' said Max Weber about Germany in 1918, that those who have interests in the old order and the independent bureaucracy will use any outbreak of syndicalist putsches, however trivial, to play on the unfortunately still very weak nerves of the petty bourgeoisie ... After the war similar speculations will recur on a larger scale. Whether the German nation has reached political maturity will then be shown by the reaction to this. We must despair of our future if [the speculations] succeed, however much so many of our experiences show this to be possible.[15]

With greater or lesser hesitation, such speculations have also constantly appeared in the Federal Republic, as the history of its state security system shows.[16] It is precisely the most recent actions of a group of people who regard and describe themselves as 'urban guerrillas' which have provided government propaganda with a convenient pretext for accelerating the introduction of laws to restrict freedom of expression and the rights of defence lawyers, etc., which for the most part had been prepared long before. If these actions of the Red Army Faction – as these people call themselves – had not taken place, the government could have invented none better. This makes it incredible that even left-wing groups should have reacted to the kidnapping of the CDU politician Lorenz in spring 1975, and the murders of Federal Attorney-General Buback and employers' president Schleyer, by continuing to propagate the nonsense that the government measures were directly connected with these events. These statements may be convenient, but they are also confusing. They deflect the discussion into the tedious argument of left-wingers who admire the right and so regard the 'security' measures as *ad hoc* and likely to be short-lived.

In that case, what 'anarchist terror attacks' made the Federal Government apply in 1951 for a ban on the KPD, which was granted by the Constitutional Court in 1956? What urban guerrilla activities are responsible for the continuous militarization of the police since the fifties, or the enlargement of the Federal Border Guard, the security service and the detective force? What acts of violence produced the decisions of the Criminal Division of the High Court or the emergency legislation announced in 1954 and passed in 1968?

Interior minister Genscher dispelled all conjecture in 1972 during a session of the Bundestag which saw the passing of new laws on weapons and imprisonment, the new law on the Federal Border Guard, the new laws on the Federal Criminal Investigation Bureau and the secret service, together with the necessary amendments to the constitution. 'I have reason to say,' he remarked,

that this overall conception of Federation and states is not, as you can occasionally read in the newspapers, the result of concern at the acts of terror of recent months, but the result of lengthy, very thorough, objective and dispassionate discussion by interior ministers from all the democratic parties, who have faced up to their overall responsibility for the internal security of this country.[17]

The preparation of a solid long-term general plan has been a constant demand of all state security authorities:

Any crime policy worthy of the name and with any prospect of success must have a structure, i.e. assessment, system and reaction, which will last for a considerable period ... It requires the qualities of permanence, reliability and excellence. It must retain the same basic organization for many years, and not be constantly tampered with to fit current political ideas ... A series of different reactions to crime resulting from spectacular events and designed to make an immediate impact on public opinion, should be avoided.[18]

It is this context which this book seeks to describe, the preventive character of the 'internal security' measures introduced and carried out since 1949. These were and are not spontaneous reactions to day-to-day political events, but designed to forestall the threat of spontaneous mass action – 'advanced state security' in a slightly different sense as well.

Worry about such political developments and conflicts and the need to take precautions against them were a feature of the debates on 'internal security' since the fifties and of the various measures taken.

'Everyone regards it as obvious,' said justice minister Heinemann, that – at least in large concerns – there should be consideration and planning in advance of what each person has to do if an emergency occurs. Not to do this would be gross dereliction of duty. So too, every state must consider how it would fulfil its responsibilities if the normal operation of its functions were disrupted.[19]

Crucial elements, therefore, are the call for 'security reserves' and the search for possible 'gaps' in the system of state security which have to be closed in time to prevent 'disruption' from occurring at all.

As early as 1958, the then interior minister, Gerhard Schröder, raised two questions in a policy speech:

are our security organs up to the demands made on them under present conditions? And the second question: are our security organs capable of standing up to heavier tests of their capacity than those of the present?[20]

It must be remembered that in 1958 the Red Army Faction was not even an idea. Only two years had passed since the Federal Government had removed their only radical political opponents with the ban on the KPD, and the Federal prosecutors and the High Court in Karlsrühe had begun to deal with the supporters and members of the stricken KPD in a way which bears full comparison with the Stammheim trial, but carried out then on a massive scale.

Even in this situation, when 'the phase of legal uncertainty (associated with the communist national enemy) which existed for a time during the summer months has now fortunately been ended by the Karlsrühe judgments', and 'these judgments will in fact produce a profound calming effect on the internal situation',[21] even then Schröder warned of possible dangers to the state: 'Under present conditions the national security services are, with some gaps, more or less up to their task ... but for more serious situations our security organs are not adequate.' Schröder therefore suggested 'undertaking operations on the Basic Law', and passing 'satisfactory emergency legislation'.

But this is not all. He called for all appropriate measures to be taken promptly to prevent such 'more serious situations'.

19

Interestingly, he put forward a list of suitable measures, some of which are only now being implemented. He suggested the expansion of the emergency police and the Federal Border Guard, that

most valuable of the Federal Government's security instruments for special police operations . . . The Federal Government regards it as of great importance that the training and equipment of the Federal Border Guard should be adequate to the particular complex demands for which it is the security instrument as well as being a security reserve.

He suggested a uniform national law on the use of firearms by the police, and the strengthening of 'personal contact between the people and the police' through a constable, 'possibly with a bicycle, who maintains close contact with the local people', which would create 'trust through personal acquaintance'. He stressed the need for 'greater involvement of the public as a whole in crime-solving', and called for more effective 'ways and means' of issuing *Berufsverbote* to 'deny the national enemy access to their oases. Legislative proposals for this are being prepared.' He also called for an increase in the powers of the security service, whose 'powers to pursue the enemy are too narrow rather than too wide', quite apart from the fact that its achievements in 'exposing the national enemy' were not given appropriate recognition:

In my opinion the name that was chosen [Office for the Protection of the Constitution] is not a happy one. The duties of the offices concern state security. I do not believe that the term 'state security' can be suspect because at a particular time in the past state security was associated with revolting methods. I think that one day we can confidently go back to that name.[22]

Note: all these suggestions were made in 1958.

1970: the emergency laws had long ago been passed, and interior minister Genscher recalled that ways needed to be found for calling in the Federal Border Guard at times when it might not yet be possible to declare an emergency: 'we want to remedy this defect by an amendment to the Federal Border

Guard Law,'[23] he explained. He justified the law which filled the relevant gap by claiming that 'the security situation in the Federal Republic of Germany and its anticipated development make it necessary to have in reserve an additional security potential which can be called in at any time'.[24]

Koschnick, the mayor of Bremen, urged haste on his fellow SPD members to protect 'communal peace': 'Dear Comrades, give us a chance to find a way which will make it possible to take in hand the defence of our own state, now, while we have time and not when the next explosion is upon us.'[25] For when

the liberal democratic constitutional order is threatened, its defence may depend on hurried action which brings together all the available forces ... This job must be done in quiet times. If the hurricane is already blowing and shaking the house, it's too late to fix the roof.[26]

In short, the measures in the field of 'internal security' have been, as it were, tailored to allow for growth. They must do for today, but also 'fit' if domestic political conflict increases.[27]

These measures were flanked by a press and judiciary which helped to prepare for them and establish them. *Bild* was not the only paper to take to heart the appeal made by Federal Attorney-General Buback in an interview with it at the beginning of 1976. Buback said that 'the most important task of the mass media' was to act 'as a mediator between the security authorities and the citizens of this country'.[28] And Buback's court, the Federal High Court, was always reliable. When political justice could not find in the existing laws the scope needed to neutralize political opponents or consolidate a political situation, it never hesitated to create it, secure in the expectation, usually justified, that the new laws would follow. 'The reliability of the law is today under threat over a large area ... The stability and continuity of the law must be re-emphasized. This does not exclude changes and adaptations of the law.'[29]

This adaptation of the state security laws to changed political requirements and the improvement of the resources available to implement them is described in the rest of this book. I have

21

tried, by using the relevant sources, to reconstruct the positions and thinking of those who decided on these measures. The book therefore begins not with an abstract analysis of recent or forth-coming security measures, but with a description of the political situation they are designed to meet. The strengthening of the security system and the circumstances in which it is taking place show who in the Federal Republic is worried by whom – the 'drive for security comes from the uneasy sense of danger'.[30]

1. The Crisis of Legitimacy in the State

The scope and completeness of the state security provisions in the Federal Republic must be seen against the background of the militant anti-communism which has dominated the domestic politics of the country since its foundation. Action has to be taken in advance to fight, and if possible eliminate, problems with which other European governments are already grappling – the spark might jump. After the end of the illusion of reform, the SPD/FDP government is now trying to win itself an international reputation with an exemplary policy of repression. Interior Minister Maihofer raved about his government's goal of an 'international interior policy', and the first steps in this direction have already been taken.[1] The Federal Government shows itself aware of its role in Europe: the resources devoted to maintaining the 'watch on the Rhine' are explained by the special significance which the political stability of West Germany has for European capitalism as a whole. 'The German people,' we were told in 1950, only five years after the capitulation, 'has perhaps been given the last opportunity in history of making a contribution to the preservation of the Western world. A German legislature possesses a great responsibility'[2] – and, one might add, great experience, for what other European state can offer more in this field, or has a longer training in the taming and suppression of freedom, or has a comparable lack of bourgeois democratic tradition?

Nevertheless the others have to make their contribution. 'Consciousness of the mutual dependence of our destiny is sharper than ever,' declared the President,[3] explaining that this imposed obligations on Germany's NATO partners to ensure that a further development of the crisis did not lead to 'social tensions and political instability'.[4] The alliance would have to 'develop beyond its role as a defence community and see itself as an all-embracing political community of the free states of the Western World, united by a common destiny'. Measures would have to be adopted 'to maintain the social and constitutional structures in which Western liberal democracy developed. All these aspects of security policy [should] force the NATO countries to make plans to avert and deal with crises.'[5]

The fear that these 'liberal structures' might not stand has grown. Shocked into alertness by the present unexpectedly serious and persistent recession in the Federal Republic, which was thought to be immune to crises, West German politicians contemplate the disappearance of the whole basis for the 'maintenance of public order'. The foundations on which this order rests were listed by the former minister of the interior, Schröder, in a policy speech to the police trade union: 'an economy with a high level of employment, with good working conditions and pay and satisfactory social and welfare provisions' and 'a conviction among the citizens of the legitimacy of the state's authority'.[6]

1. Illusions of Reform and Crisis Cosmetics

The 'threat to internal security' denounced by Schröder in 1958 is today a reality. As economic difficulties increased, and inflation and unemployment rose, the market economy whose virtues had been sung for so many years declined in attractiveness and plausibility, and a glossy image of growth and stability shattered. But with no picture, the frame too begins to crack. 'For this reason,' urged Kohl, the CDU leader, 'it is up to all of us to take the necessary steps to check the first signs of any crisis of legitimacy in our state.'[7]

At first the government tried to contain the problem with appeals to endurance. As late as 1973, a half-page press advertisement from the Federal Press and Information Office stated:

In spite of the oil crisis we shall still have secure jobs tomorrow – if

24

everyone is sensible. In the last few years fear of an economic crisis and unemployment have made many people feel insecure. But the judgment of the independent committee of experts in its special study is that 'there is no ground for panic or a feeling of crisis'. This is also the Federal Government's view of the position.[8]

With the diligent assistance of these experts a scoreboard was subsequently set up in Bonn to show the development of unemployment and short-time working. At first these were merely mentioned in passing, then, as concealment became impossible, made light of, until today, the public is expected to get used to about one million unemployed as a yearly average with which 'we' will have to live in the future. 'The position at the moment' became simply 'the position', in other words a permanent instrument of pressure and discipline.

Particularly sinister is the growth of unemployment among the young. In the next few years this problem can be expected to worsen considerably; there will be hundreds of thousands of young people without even an opportunity for training.[9] It is in this area that unemployment thought of as periodic and unusual becomes structural.

As the government's means of influences diminish, conspiracy and concealment are reinforced. How else are we to assess the Chancellor's New Year broadcast for 1975? After announcing a 'realistic assessment of our situation', he went on to mention first in the list of difficulties 'the Communist terrorists of the Baader–Meinhof group' who 'have unsettled us' – before inflation, before unemployment and short-time.[10] On the morning of New Year's Eve, 1974, citizens found a government advertisement in their newspapers assuring them that 'the recovery is coming. By summer we shall be over the hill' – though the government prudently neglected to specify the year in which the summer would be so good. Then, the same evening, in the New Year address just mentioned, Schmidt insisted that the Social Democratic Party regarded itself as still committed to progress: 'Twelve months from today things will look different – better.'[11] The Chancellor ended his message with the assurance, 'all in all, we are on the right road. All of us can feel this' – a piece of contempt which the unemployed had to listen to again a year later:

At home we have sought to spread the unavoidable burdens over as many shoulders as possible ... We have consolidated our achievements and given the economy the breathing space it needed ... The result is a climate of firm confidence in the country ... This can be felt and recognized even by those who are most seriously affected by the recession. I mean the unemployed.[12]

Hollow phrases, which betray a man running out of breath but still trying to whistle in the dark.

Even if the attempt to 'restart' the economy were to succeed, the next difficulties and burdens are already programmed – 'some time', according to Apel, minister of finance, 'we have to tell the truth.'[13] This truth is harsh: 'Apel: Higher Taxes when Recession Over'; [14] 'Schmidt: More Taxes in the Next Boom'.[15] Following unemployment and short-time working, tax increases when things once again take an 'upturn'. But as to whose taxes were to be increased, and who things would start looking up for, the Government left no doubt. Federal economics minister Friedrichs insisted in the cabinet that Apel's tax increases should not be a burden on businessmen's profits – 'We must make it clear that this discussion is not about profits taxes', an idea rejected by Schmidt and Apel as 'a malicious insinuation'.[16]

The principle of the welfare state was defined: social security was not made for the workers, but the workers for social security; or, in the plain language of minister Rohde, 'without the support of employees' organizations no reform programme can be carried out.'[17]

As well as the previously announced tax increases, workers were to be asked for a further measure of support, restraint in wage demands – 'people in the factories must be prepared for this now. The moment is right for education.'[18] Apel's simultaneous appeal, 'Don't kill the recovery by saving,'[19] characterizes the classical dilemma of capitalist economies.

Finally, the much trumpeted reforms meanwhile entered what

in SPD language is called 'a stage in which the main task is to consolidate our achievements'.[20] The meaning of the jargon was clear: 'Apel: No More Reforms for Many Years'; 'Schmidt to Abandon Reforms'.[21] The fact that the list of reforms which were now to be abandoned officially consisted mainly of those which had aroused most political controversy indicates that the economic recession reflected a political one.

But not only reforms were abandoned. The 'achievements' which Schmidt wanted to see consolidated were also undone. What Apel denied ('There will be no dismantling of the welfare state')[22] his cabinet collegue Friedrichs announced plainly: the limit of what the Federal Republic could do in welfare had been reached, for a time at least.[23] Consequently, at the end of 1975, there was passed a 'Law for the Improvement of the Budgetary Structure', which concealed behind its harmless sounding title a multiplicity of measures to reduce welfare provision, and cut into the much praised 'welfare net'. The long-term social and political consequences of these interventions (structural and not just conjunctural) in a worsening of the welfare position can still not be predicted.[24] The claim of an advertising campaign by the social security ministry – 'Our social policy has not stopped'[25] – just needed to be understood correctly, for who would want to deny that regression is also movement?

While still Chancellor, Brandt had called for a bright gloss to be brushed over the first signs of the crash: 'The Government's policies are not being sold well enough,'[26] so admitting that the claims about reforms were no more than slogans. In its national paper, *Vorwärts*, the party was insistently warned 'against public discussions of social policy, against explaining to the voters, except in election campaigns, the possibilities and limits of economic policy'.[27] They were throwing sand in the people's eyes to stop it getting into their own machine.

It could happen, all the same. The declared aim of the reform programme, 'to transform social conditions in such a way that the basis for Communist positions is removed',[28] was not achieved – on the contrary. With its promises of reforms, the

27

SPD had made its supporters conscious of faults familiar from daily experience, and of specific remedies. This was what had made the Social Democrats more attractive than the other parties. But this had also generated and aroused hopes, demands and expectations which – unlike normal election slogans – were associated with tangible, practical, measureable, realizable results. These results had now not only not been produced; the situation which was to have been improved had got worse. Without social reforms, Willy Brandt had warned, 'regression, growing tensions and radicalization' could be expected.[29] This is all the more likely since in West Germany – in contrast to other countries – 'social harmony' has been straightforwardly purchased by constant references to the very welfare provisions which are now having to be withdrawn as things get 'rough'. They simply cannot stand the load they were once expected to bear. This may mean that all the years of talk about a 'secure social safety net' for periods of crisis are threatening to become a liability when a start has to be made on dismantling this celebrated 'safety net'. As the Chancellor said,

If our coalition cannot work its way out of the difficulties in which we are caught, Germany will indeed face the social disturbances, social conditions and political consequences we have seen in other countries for the past two or three years.[30]

The position was put even more clearly by sociologist and SPD deputy Egon Lutz:

If high figures for long-term unemployed were to result in unemployment becoming permanent, if 600,000 or even fewer 'unfortunates' were relegated to the sidelines, it would be bad, very bad. We should then be contributing to laying a charge which would exceed the critical mass and blow our society sky-high more surely than even the most single-minded anarchist.[31]

He is right: 'open people's struggles' exist only in the heads of a few sectarian political groups, but a growth of distrust and discontent, surfacing in more than just individual or isolated protests or breaches of rules, is as visible as the increases of strikes for better wages and working conditions. Nor, in view of the appeals from Bonn for restraint, can even these, local and purely industrial though they are, simply be dismissed as 'economistic'. 'If conflicts about the distribution of wealth become more bitter,' prophesied the *Frankfurter Allgemeine* for the immediate future, 'this will have the inevitable consequence that more and more of the weak will go to the wall, where they may eventually no longer be prepared to tolerate the system that lives off the majority.'[32]

2. The Decay of Political Values and Ideological Rearmament

The 'system which lives off the majority' is not, for all that, on the point of collapse. Nevertheless, Schröder's second criterion for the 'maintenance of public order', the 'conviction among the citizens of the legitimacy of the state's authority', is beginning to waver. In past crisis periods ideological values – success, property, security and authority – could be appealed to and relied on, but they are losing their force. This loss of political values which accompanied the losses in productivity became a constant theme of security debates: 'To a greater degree than we can tolerate, internal stability and therefore internal security are endangered by an intellectual and political weakness. There is no longer a sufficiently clear sense of the values which constitute our liberal democracy.' The symptoms included 'a continual loss of authority affecting traditional institutions such as the state, the family, the schools and the church'.[33]

Particularly among the workers, who were commonly supposed to accept these 'traditional values and institutions', the opposite could be observed; in industry, boycotts, sabotage and 'crimes' against products of their own making were multiplying. 'Ideas such as honour and loyalty have declined in value . . . On the other hand there has been a marked growth in the distribution of periodicals and leaflets with a subversive content.'[34] A well-known public opinion research group gave the Union of West German Employers' Associations the results of a study of 'German Workers' Sense of Values', which found that embourgeoisement, i.e. satisfaction, among workers existed only in the dreams of a few sociologists. 'Values' such as 'thrift', 'order', 'modesty', 'politeness' and 'respect for the property of others' were said to have suffered a marked, and sometimes rapid, decline in the recent past. Bourgeois illusions, such as the view that effort is worth while, achievement means success, or property deserves respect, found no echo among workers. Almost two fifths of young workers wanted a life without work, and only 30 per cent were happy in their work in 1972, compared with 42 per cent in 1962. Of the 49 per cent who in 1964 had still believed that wealth in the Federal Republic was fairly distributed, only 38 per cent were left in 1971. The number was going – would you believe it? – further down.[35]

In contrast there was a clear rise in the number of those who had ceased to believe in justice, and were seeing to re-distribution themselves. 'Crimes against property' and thefts of foodstuffs were increasing disproportionately, and theft alone constituted 65·6 per cent of all crimes. The advice of CDU deputy von Weizsäcker on the social situation, 'Citizens must learn to look after themselves again,'[36] was being followed on a massive scale. For the individual thief, this 'contempt for the property of others' may be unconnected with any political associations such as the idea of alienation, but by its massive scale, and against the background of the current economic and political situation, such action does take on political significance. The shrill commentaries of those with respectable values to lose point to the fear that this might be 'an anticipation of the morality of the future', 'the first step towards what is to come'.[37] Questions are beginning to come into the open such as, 'Doesn't the crisis in the end only benefit the Communists?' and 'Isn't [unemployment] just creating a street-mob from which well-dressed passers-by are no longer safe? Are we moving towards raging crime and, worst of all, towards political radicalism?'[38]

The harsh penalties for 'attacks on property', and the preventive detention established in 1972 for those suspected of 'relapsing into theft' (§ 112a StPO) have not been able to reduce what is officially called 'hostility to law' – 'in addition to dislike

30

of lawyers we find a total lack of respect for the independence of judges, which, after all, is one of the main foundations of the liberal constitutional state'.[39]

The foundations are still there, and the façade, but the gloss is off, and cracks are appearing.

This is the source of the worry felt by those in power that discontent may grow, that infringements of the norm may themselves become the norm. They fear that hopelessness may no longer be felt as helplessness, that receptive discontent may turn into political activity, and the existing cracks become a breach, a breach in any sort of confidence in the Government, its competence and authority. The results would be independent action and self-help. This is one of the nightmares of Herold, the head of the Federal Criminal Investigation Bureau, since in his opinion this is the aim of all 'enemies of the state', 'the deliberate creation of an opposing power over against this state, or the denial of the state's monopoly of force'.[40] The Social Democratic Research Minister, Matthöfer, knew what he was doing when he singled out the Battelle Institute for the task of investigating the motives and potential of the inhabitants of Wyhl – the village in Southern Germany where farmers have for years been occupying a site in order to prevent the construction of a planned nuclear power station. It is well known that the Institute specializes in counter-insurgency, the technique of preventing revolts based on the social sciences.

The investigation found that one main cause of such protest and resistance campaigns was the direct material interests of the participants, which had been neglected, overlooked or damaged by the state. There was a fundamental breakdown of trust between state and citizens. Politicians were making a serious mistake, said the report, if they suspected that such campaigns were the work of minorities or outsiders, and not those directly affected. Similar findings were produced by a study of 'The Causes of Unconventional Political Behaviour in the Federal Republic', according to which as many as 10 per cent of West Germans were prepared to take part in vigorous forms of direct action, such as occupations of factories and offices,

31

'wildcat' strikes, traffic obstruction and independent reduction of rent and taxes.[41]

Of course such figures must be treated with caution, but the statements quoted about the motives for this sort of activity are not only accurate, but also relevant to the present situation of economic depression and disappointed hopes for reforms. The demands which have been made in recent years by a number of social movements in West Germany – of school and university students and apprentices, i.e. independent works' struggles, not kept in check by the unions, campaigns against nuclear power stations, in defence of the environment, neighbourhood campaigns, and so on – have not always, perhaps very rarely, produced immediate material results, but they have allowed those involved to gain and absorb a wealth of political experience, and have so created an important basis for new movements. They have also caused considerable irritation in the established power structure. This unsettling effect has a continuous action, because the ability to absorb claims and deflect resistance has disappeared with the failure of the reform strategies. Instead, the likely result, and fear, is an extension of these local movements.

In the relevant reflections of the guardians of the state the RAF can always have a role in everyday politics. 'Terrorist activities,' according to Ernst Benda, the president of the Constitutional Court,

are simply a particularly dramatic expression of the attacks on law and order. The general picture is extremely serious. Even if these activities of criminal organizations are completely crushed, we shall still have cause for concern and vigilance ... The danger comes from groups in society whose aims are hostile to the constitution, and is reinforced by a slowly spreading irritation with the constitution among the population. In older people this discontent takes the form of indifference, in many younger people that of scepticism, open rejection or a romantic espousal of the ideals of other social systems.[42]

If those in power said openly what their studies of the material basis of the discontent, rejection and opposition have shown them, they would have to admit the collapse of their policies, which in all probability would only hasten the bankruptcy. They therefore take refuge in a new distortion. It is not the absence of reforms, not disappointed hopes, which are responsible for this process, but too many concessions, a 'bout of liberalization',[43] a 'tendency to undermine the inherent legitimacy of the state'.[44] As a remedy they recommend an 'overall political conception', a combination of moral and material rearmament:

Internal security is not just a matter of power and its use; internal security has first and foremost an intellectual, moral and political dimension. It calls for intellectual and political leadership ... We need intellectual mobilization of our people. [This means] that we must ensure the predominance of the scale of values embodied in our constitution, which we have made the foundation of this state, in economic, cultural, social and political affairs ... This excludes the idea of opposition between classes,[45]

– and naturally even more class-conscious action.

The same context includes reference to the 'intellectual security of the state',[46] which is said to be threatened by the administering of 'psycho-social poison', carried out by (among others) 'state teachers at state schools', by a 'considerable number of sympathizers who have their hands on important levers in government and society' and who are attempting 'to confuse the natural feelings and the natural discernment of citizens'.[47]

Censorship of radio programmes, the press, literature, films and plays is regarded, like the *Berufsverbote*, as a sort of 'intellectual neutralization' of opponents, a way of incapacitating and isolating any form of even notional nonconformity. It is part of an ideological campaign conducted in order to establish the 'values' of this state firmly 'in the hearts and heads of the people', and 'give the whole people a positive lead'.[48]

The most far-reaching measure of 'moral rearmament' is to be the organization of *Berufsverbote* on a nationwide basis. The *Berufsverbot* is one of the most far-reaching forms of the state's political discipline. Under it West German citizens are denied entry into jobs in the public service because of their political views, because of membership of specific left-wing

organizations which are denounced as 'hostile to the constitution', or for taking part in demonstrations or meetings
organized by political groups which are similarly regarded as
'hostile to the state'. More recently there have been cases where
a *Berufsverbot* has been imposed because of contacts with
people who were themselves subject to a *Berufsverbot*. A *Berufsverbot* is a stigma, and a crucial part in this campaign of
denunciation and ideological snooping is played by the *Verfassungsschutz*, one of the West German secret services, and the
political police, who use dossiers and similar material to provide
employers and officials with information about people being
considered for jobs. Applicants must then submit to humili-
ating questions, interrogations about political views and activities reminiscent of the Inquisition. Ninety-nine per cent of the
victims are left-wingers; the West German state has notoriously
always been blind in the right eye. It should not be forgotten
that this is the state in which it was possible for old Nazis to
recover their grip on the levers of power immediately after
1949, in the important industries, the parliaments and governments, and in the judiciary. It is the very same people who are
today moving against the left, who hold their political views
against them and denounce them on the ground that socialists
and communists are intolerable as civil servants to a democratic
state. Most affected are teachers and lawyers who want to
become judges or prosecutors, but public service employees in
all grades have also suffered for a long time. The procedure,
which has all the marks of German thoroughness, has subsequently developed an independent momentum, a life of its
own. *Berufsverbote*, ideological checks and ideological persecution have begun to be carried out outside the public service
as well. Firms are dismissing politically undesirable employees
and disguising this when necessary with references to the economic crisis. Incredibly, the unions are playing along. They too
operate procedures comparable with *Berufsverbote*: the
members of particular communist groups are being expelled
from the unions, so losing any legal protection against the em-

ployer. The consequences of this are particularly serious since the only unions in West Germany are industrial unions: once a chemical worker is thrown out of the union for the chemical industry there is no other possibility of industrial organization. Again in the media, the churches and other social institutions and organizations, similar processes can be observed, initially prompted by the state practice of the *Berufsverbot*. This procedure, which 'exists nowhere else', as Interior Minister Maihofer proudly observed,[49] also has a long tradition – in the Federal Republic alone, quite apart from the practices of the Nazis.[50] The operation of bans once more, or, more exactly, since 1972, on the familiar scale, is the result of identifiable developments in society. After the purges of the fifties, there began to be signs at the beginning of the seventies that a new generation of civil servants was being appointed, whose political outlook has been influenced by the revolt against authority. The tactical slogan calling for a 'march through the institutions' put the administrators on their guard and made them act. The Social Democratic government of the state of Hamburg was the pioneer of the system subsequently established in 1972 by Chancellor Brandt and the chief ministers of the states. 'This was no improvised, spontaneous decision,' the leader of the Schleswig-Holstein state government, Stoltenberg, recalled. 'It was the result of thorough preparation carried out mainly by the Federal and state interior ministers, who, after lengthy discussions, produced a joint draft for the heads of government.'[51]

Naturally the main fear was not the appointment of a few hundred civil servants, since most of them could be expected to end their threatened march through the institutions comfortably within those very institutions. The fear was much more that the employment of people with a critical attitude, or merely with reservations towards the state, might speed up a political process which was inherent in the change in the state's own function. As capital tends towards a monopoly, the economic and political activities of the state spread, with the result that the state increasingly becomes part of the general crisis on which it is supposed to exercise a regulating influence. More and more, political disputes spill over and turn against the state. This can be seen in community protests, but also in struggles over wage-rates, as in the most recent printers' strike, when the police were used.

The *Berufsverbote* are an attempt by the state apparatus to secure its retreat, at least internally. 'The state,' explained the Constitutional Court,

requires, if it is not to call its own existence in question, a body of officials who will stand up for it and the prevailing constitutional system, and defend it in conflicts and crises of loyalty . . . If the civil service can no longer be relied on, society and its state are lost in critical situations . . . The proof of political loyalty is seen in times of crisis and serious conflicts,[52]

– in other words, in present conditions, which were the starting point for the thoughts on 'intellectual rearmament and mobilization'.

For the state to remain 'strong, healthy and intact',[53] moral rearmament must be accompanied by material rearmament. 'The state means repression, or it is not a state, that is, the suppressor of illegitimate and uncontrolled force,' commented the *Frankfurter Allgemeine*.[54] This preparedness is publicly demonstrated 'so that the state can resume the performance of its responsibilities for law and order with resolution in all the areas for which it is responsible, and recover lost authority through the way in which it presents itself'.[55]

Various carefully measured remedies and strategies either have proved their value or are being developed for this purpose. They range from psychological warfare techniques, through an ever more cunning arsenal of techniques for surveillance and control, to legal sanctions and the 'Major Security and Order Service' of the police.

In this book I describe this arsenal of modern state security in different sections for the different areas. This is simply for the sake of clarity. In practice, of course, the different measures merge, and are often combined and employed simultaneously;

the only criterion is the most effective implementation of the purpose common to them all. This purpose is the maintenance or restoration of the state monopoly of authority and force, or, as Willy Brandt put it, 'the calm and resolute assertion of normality'.[56]

2. Channelling Emotions

If this 'normality' is likely to be endangered by social crises and degenerate into instability, a well-tried remedy is to arouse the emotions of the population in order to anticipate and simulate what one wants to avert, i.e. unrest, insecurity and disorder. These are conjured up in order to get a grip on existing fears of crisis and channel them before they can develop in ways and to an extent where they become uncontrollable. In other words, making a virtue of necessity, the authorities conceal the real threat to the population under a simulated one. 'The threat to internal security', we are told, affects 'in the first place the working population': unemployment, inflation and social difficulties can in the long run be controlled; 'it is a much more serious situation when the Federal Republic has to face terrorism'.[1]

This insistent talk of 'threats to our security' is deliberately directed to feelings which affect everyone today – helplessness and weakness, impotence and vulnerability – though of course terrorists are the last thing which provokes these fears. The real worries are covered over with contrived problems and pushed out of sight. Fear is the instrument, and scare reports create a suitable atmosphere for justifying elaborate and costly 'security measures', while social and health policies, education and housing are cut to such an extent that very little is left of the programme with which the 'social-liberal' Government came into office.

' "The power of a mind is as great as that of its expression," in the words of Hegel,' said the Minister of the Interior in philosophical mood, as he bared his soul to Parliament on the subject.

If we look at the expressions of the spirit with which the social-liberal coalitions since 1969 have tackled matters of internal security, we find that there has been a greater expansion, qualitative as well as quantitative, of the Federal security services in these few years than in all the previous decades ... The firm determination to extend still further the Federal security services which inspires the present Government can be seen from its policy statement. The only point in it – deliberately – at which money is mentioned concerns internal security. We have acted accordingly.[2]

This total distortion of political priorities had to be put over to the public so as to create the impression that there had been no fundamental change in the political aims of the 'reforming government', that the improvement of social security provisions was still its priority. The suggestion was put about that the abstract threat to 'internal security' was connected with the real threats to the security of the lives of individuals. The reinforcement of 'our state', the suggestion ran, would remove one's own weakness at a stroke. 'The state,' the Minister of Justice explained, 'is in the last resort a protective association,' and not an end in itself,

and I would ask you to bear that in mind particularly in the present situation. The new [state security] measures are not designed to protect the state as an abstraction. What we are trying to protect essentially are the lives, the health and the freedom of the individual members of the association, which are endangered if the state is limited in its abilty to offer protection, or in its monopoly of force.[3]

The reforms announced with such a fanfare were thus not merely called off – 'Reforms have their time and their proper material basis. There are short periods of time in which there is no room for reforms'[4] – they were replaced by repressive measures which were then sold as reforms. Indeed, the 'internal security' programme was described as a reform the success of which was an essential preliminary to the 'postponed' proposals to 'raise the quality of life'. The reason? 'There will be no social progress without a system of internal order to protect it and make it possible in the first place.'[5] This roundabout approach had been made necessary, and the original reforms had to be 'deferred', solely because of the actions of those who were attacking this 'order' from within, in order 'to crush its potential for reform'.[6]

1. Public Enemies

The isolation and branding of such scapegoats as 'disruptive elements', who are held responsible for everything people feel to be wrong with society, is a classical instrument from the repertoire of psychological crisis management, used, in the words of Helmut Schmidt, 'to maintain the principal classical functions of the state in a proper state of readiness'.[7] Pointing to such 'disturbers of order' can work like a lightning conductor. Existing latent social discontents and tensions do not accumulate, but are transformed and diverted on to marked minorities, on whom they can work themselves out, and the people can release their anger. The mechanism is the smoother because political thought has a tendency to hold individuals responsible for situations which are socially determined.

The conservative constitutionalist Carl Schmitt has studied this concept in the transition from the Weimar Republic to fascism, and developed it into a theory of the 'proclamation of public enemies within the state'. Schmitt has written:

The function of a normal state consists primarily in inducing complete satisfaction within the state, creating 'calm, security and order', and so creating the normal situation. This is the necessary condition for legal norms to operate at all, since any norm presupposes a normal situation ... This need for satisfaction within the state leads in critical situations to the definition by the state of an 'internal enemy'. This commonly takes place by means of harsher or milder forms of proscription directed at racial, religious or political minorities. These may be automatic, or given legal form by special laws, public or concealed in general descriptions, and may consist of prohibition, proscription, or deprivation of legal protection.[8]

It might be a knitting pattern: once more the procedure is being put into practice, all the techniques for declaring 'public enemies' are being brought into action. Political opponents, their criticisms of existing conditions and their demands, are presented as criminal, to avoid the need for a political confrontation with them. They are presented as biological phenomena or evil forces and so denied the right to be treated as human beings. There is a revival and reinforcement of prejudices against all who are 'different' from 'us', whose ideas differ from 'normality', and who must be dealt with by means of different techniques. No insinuation or slander is too cheap or nasty to be used in the declaration of 'enemies' – we shouldn't be so fastidious, but at last 'describe things as the people feel them'.[9]

Ostensibly a 'struggle against terrorism' is being waged, but in reality there is a general onslaught on the whole of the left. They become the absolute enemy, and are placed in the centre of the target for defamation and vilification because in response to the lies of official government propaganda they call the capitalist causes of the current crisis and its symptoms by their true names. Socialists and Communists – and for the CDU for a long time now Liberals and Social Democrats too – are built up as 'the people behind the terrorists, the people who pull the strings', and stamped with a vague label which by now has serious legal consequences – 'sympathizers'. These are, according to Heinrich Böll, winner of the Nobel Prize for Literature and himself a victim of this charge, 'people who have committed the criminal sin of making distinctions'.

It is the left-wing intellectuals who 'keep getting out of step', the 'desk-bound activists' who 'put their poison in printers' ink', the 'intellectual stone-throwers', the 'criminals in the guise of left-wing reformers' whose 'theories placed on virgin paper with clean fingers drove the Baaders to murderous conclusions', this 'ideological swamp out of which bubbles of criminal intent are constantly rising'. Under the title 'Terrorists and Others', a leader-writer in the *Frankfurter Allgemeine* warned against ignoring or underestimating these 'men behind the scenes': 'A person who doesn't throw bombs or take hostages seems almost a supporter of the state, although he may, with greater subtlety, be planning something far more dangerous.' He may be trying 'to bring down the present system with the concealed weapons of the mind ... in nurseries, churches and cinemas. In schools, universities and ministries. In press, radio and television.' 'Talking about ... conflict, criticism and class conflict, questioning, mocking traditions, loosening ties, changing attitudes, creating envy, arousing expectations.'[10]

It is no longer the long hair and beards of the sixties at which anger is directed, the 'individuals' of whom Bürgermeister Schütz wrote in the Berlin Social Democratic newspaper that it needed only a 'good look' at their faces to tell 'that they are only interested in destroying the foundations of our democratic system'.[11] A quick look is no longer enough. The aim is the same, but 'the new disguise is perfect. Long hair and scruffy clothes are no longer the outward signs of the terrorist.' They appear 'nice and inconspicuous – the nice couple next door'.[12] The transformation was also described by the Federal Justice Minister: these were 'people who would be capable of combining their activities as terrorists with middle-class occupations'; they would not be 'desperadoes in damp basements, but established citizens in positions which command respect', as the *Frankfurter Allgemeine* explained. The leader was headed 'Enemies'.[13]

Jean-Paul Sartre, who had come to West Germany to protest against the prison conditions of the Baader–Meinhof prisoners, became a welcome victim of this campaign – as a foreigner, a left-winger and an intellectual. 'His heart', readers of *Bild* were told,

is deep red and his God is nothingness. His world: a wooden stool in a student quarter, Mao-leaflets, a little hash and a lot of cigarettes. When he's not actually handing out radical leaflets in the street, or popping off to Stuttgart to see his friend Baader, he's sitting on his wooden stool the whole day long, hunched over his untidy desk ... [He] said no to the Nobel Prize, adopted his secretary and often bends his dirty nails in his clenched fist to make the socialist greeting ... 'The nation's red cancer' is already a little hard of hearing, and is said to have had a stroke.[14]

Sartre was also sniped at by *Die Zeit*, which with the help of photos turned a trivial incident into a sensational story which was given the full treatment by news broadcasts: Hans-Joachim Klein, 'the Vienna kidnapper, took the philosopher to his meeting with Baader – The Terrorist Who Drove Sartre'[15] – understand: Sartre lets himself be driven by terrorists.

Bild's editorial, in the style of *Der Stürmer*, and *Die Zeit*'s discovery are a perfect example of the stereotype of public enemies. They are as revolting as their aims and methods: their behaviour, their activities or idleness and their interests, the disorder and the dirt which clings to them. They are not merely disgusting, but also dangerously mad. One can no longer talk to them because they are hard of hearing. They are unpredictable and treacherous. They are 'raving left-wing radicals who practically need a doctor more than a serious lawyer', a 'mixture of Communist agents, medical cases and criminals'.[16]

They are not simply ill, but themselves a disease, a 'plague', a 'moral epidemic', 'freaks', 'a cancerous sore . . . In every organism at any time there are innumerable germs of infection. Whether the organism can deal with them or not depends on whether it itself is healthy and possesses the capacity to resist or not.' Against Communism, this 'life-destroying pestilence of the twentieth century, which is fatal to mind and soul', only the strongest remedies are effective, and only if prescribed in time. 'Political delusions have always started with small groups. It is like an infection with bacilli.'[17]

Bacilli, bacteria, vermin – the left are not human beings at all. According to Helmut Schmidt, replying to hecklers at one of his pompous speeches, they should be 'sent back where they belong, to holes, with the mice and rats'.[18] They have no rights, since in the case of the insane and of animals 'the application of laws made for human beings is impossible because even with criminals these laws depend on reactions characteristic of the human creature'.[19]

Dung must be treated as dung, in other words, or 'Finish with the criminal pack once and for all', as television pundit Löwenthal translated his CSU friend Strauss. In his Sonthofen 'speech on strategy', Strauss had called for a final solution of the left-wing question ²... and when we get in, there'll be such a clean-up that for the rest of this century not one of these bandits will dare to open his mouth in Germany'.[20] Can there be any clearer indication which 'bandits' are really meant, in spite of all the talk about 'terrorists', of who will be put out of circulation, whose *voices* will be banned?

2. Permanent Horror

While the 'anarchist outrages' which appeared in the reports of the state security officials were first devised by left-wing theoreticians, and later, after the imprisonment of the 'hard core' of the RAF, directed from the Stammheim prison court – 'Terror Orders from the Cell, and the Gang Goes on Burning, Robbing and Shooting'[21] – the Federal Prosecutor and the Criminal Investigation Bureau have recently been offering a new account. Behind everything is an international conspiracy, an 'internationally organized threat to human society ... often probably held together by no more than hate and fanaticism'.[22] Interior Minister Maihofer has called it 'internationally organized criminal tourism', and Attorney-General Buback talked about 'German terrorists forming links with international groups'.[23] In the language of the annual report of an important business, secret service men inside and outside West Germany describe their latest invention, the ghostly 'Carlos', the independent 'operator who can be hired like a team of window-cleaners',[24] who has 'forty professional commandos waiting' for his orders,[25] the 'most sought after terrorist in the world', who 'never had to do any real work, rejects capitalism', regards Communism as 'too tame', and 'got together his own team on the Frankfurt anarchist scene'.[26] There is scarcely a left-wing group, bookshop or publishing house which has not been mentioned by name in the press in this context.

Like 'the people who pull the strings', the carefully planned attacks of 'the terrorists' are unpredictable and various – they are capable of anything. Whatever happens – even if only in the imagination of a few journalists on good terms with internal security officials – 'anarchist terrorists' and their 'intellectual accomplices' are denounced as the culprits. 'Attentive readers of the newspapers,' said the Attorney-General in a tribute to the easy contacts between his department and the editors of the West German press, 'will almost every day discover some activity which in some form or other can be traced back to anarchist terrorists.'[27] Such constructions always work 'in some form or other', and where the obligatory reference to 'clear', 'assumed', 'apparent' or 'possible' connections with 'the terrorists' is left out in the rush, the informed reader will draw his own conclusions. An egg-seller called by the prosecution as an eye-witness apparently recognized Gudrun Ensslin 'with absolute certainty' as the driver of a particular car, only to remember more clearly after questions from her counsel. The only thing he had actually seen and followed up were headlines – at the time he signed the record of his police interrogation 'we thought – everyone did – that it must have been the Baader–Meinhof gang who made this attack'.[28] Everyone thought so because it was drummed into people – one horror story on top of another. An apartment at the Berlin Hilton was burnt out: 'It is suspected in Berlin that terrorists of the Japanese Red Army Faction started the fire.' In Freiburg lights went out for several hours – 'Power Station Turned Off Current After Bomb Threat'. This was a particularly unfortunate headline in view of the subsequent revelation by a number of people who had recently left the CDU that at a party discussion on the direct action campaign against the building of a nuclear power station at Wyhl, it had been suggested that the electricity should be cut during an interstate football match; this was intended as a salutary shock for the opponents of the nuclear power station. The actual power cut lasted two hours, the same time as the interrupted transmission of the England v. West Germany football match the same evening.

The alleged theft of fifty-three canisters of the dangerous chemical weapon mustard gas from an army depot made headlines:

Has the gang got poison gas? After three bomb attacks by the terrorists, in Berlin, Mainz and Ludwigshafen, there is the possibility of a new danger. German security officials fear that the Baader–Meinhof gang is in possession of fifty-three steel canisters containing deadly mustard gas and plans to use them in attacks. A senior German secret service officer stated, 'The B–M gang made plans years ago to rob the depot.'

Not a word about the fact that the West German army has supplies of a gas that is proscribed by international conventions.

Alarm in the Bundestag. Terrorists are planning a poison attack. The Federal Criminal Investigation Bureau informed the speaker of the German Bundestag on Thursday that members of the Baader–Meinhof gang are planning a poison attack on the German parliament. According to the Bureau's reports, substantial quantities of poison gas which disappeared a few weeks ago from an army depot have fallen into the hands of members of the Baader–Meinhof gang ... Health departments and hospitals have been prepared for the possibility of a terrorist attack with the chemical weapon.

Three weeks later it was explained – naturally not in *Bild* – that possibly less than two litres had been stolen. The gas could be merely missing on paper, if there was a false count at some time. A few months later came the brief report: 'Missing Poison Gas Canisters Found'.

Other weapons have been 'disappearing' and suddenly turning up again. 'Explosives Theft by Baader–Meinhof Sympathizers?' Twenty-four hours later: 'Explosives Found in Garden – Thief Wanted to Trick Police'.

There was a 'mistake' on another occasion too.

Stabbing! Assassination attempt on Kohl. The dramatic incident took place on Monday evening. Kohl was to address students on 'Freedom in German Universities'. Thugs, armed with cudgels, knuckledusters and pieces of iron, were waiting for him. Most of the thugs were members of University Communist groups. A hundred police officers shepherded Kohl through the mob. His bodyguard – a tower of a man – shielded him with his body. Suddenly he screamed and collapsed. One of the group of thugs had stuck a knife twice between his ribs.

A day later it turned out that it was an over-excited CDU pensioner who had stabbed Kohl's bodyguard with a staghorn because he thought he was attacking his leader. Rumours start. Rolf Pohle, who was released in exchange for Peter Lorenz and flown to Southern Yemen, was said to have returned to West Germany. A judge claimed to have recognized Pohle, a former lawyer, in a subway under the Munich Stachus. *Der Spiegel* put two and two together: 'Is a terrorist attack likely? Between 18th and 30th December a plan of Munich's underground traffic centre under the Stachus disappeared from a telephone cabinet in the city.' Bavaria set off a full-scale nationwide manhunt. False alarm, as officials of the Bavarian Justice Ministry were later forced to admit: the judge who claimed to have seen Pohle was 'no longer quite sober' on the day in question.[29]

No one notices denials, if they appear at all. At best they produce boredom. The sensational creates excitement. The incredible makes an impression and sticks in the mind.

Like stories of bogeymen, new 'gangs' are started as required, and old ones withdrawn from circulation to provide success stories for the 'security services'. Attorney-General Buback would then mention various pieces of 'evidence' for the 're-founding of several anarchist terror gangs', whose activities 'are far more frequent than is commonly assumed'. This was confirmed by his boss, Justice Minister Vogel: 'The number of potential terrorists [is] greater than previously suspected.'[30]

The warning about such 'potential terrorists' had become necessary to keep the hue and cry at fever point after the imprisonment of those for whom warrants had been issued. It was true that the 'effectiveness of the terrorists' had been 'seriously damaged by the large number of arrests, but the threat continues to exist'; 'Deceptive Quiet in the Underworld', 'German Terrorists Regrouping.'[31] The 'experts', as usual, had an explanation: the groups put out of action were only a few of the many cogs in 'the anarchistic machinery active in the German underworld'.[32]

3. Call to a Witch-hunt

This sinister apparatus, operated by cold-blooded terrorists, was slowly but surely undermining 'everything', while the state, as though under a spell, contemplated its own destruction. 'Our country,' complained *Quick*, 'one of the strongest economic, industrial and military powers in the world, has been in a state of internal paralysis for years when it comes to an effective fight against the internal enemies of this country,'[33] a charge which the Government naturally rejected out of hand: 'We shall not let our state be destroyed, nor shall we let our state be taken away from us.'[34]

With phrases like this, and appeals to 'work together' and 'close ranks', attempts were made to establish new points of reference, to enable people to identify with the state now that the old 'values' had worn out. When the state is given a new look, as 'ours', the enemies of this state also take on a new look – they are 'our enemies', a threat to 'all of us', which 'we' must 'all' deal with. This 'we consciousness' can be used to cement up any dangerous cracks for the time being at least. 'Germans', the Chancellor knew, 'have a good deal of political common sense, which can be relied on in times of crisis',[35] and his Interior Minister needed no second telling:

In the hour of distress we all stand together.[36] [Some of you may object that] the state is being blackmailed. But who is the state? All of us! All of us who pay our taxes on time, stop at a red light and are always on time in the office and factory ... The reason we are all so unhappy these days [was simple]: citizens have been turned into important witnesses of successful blackmail ... They have been unable to do more than look on as their state fell, gravely wounded.[37]

Some of these witnesses might soon become wounded; no one was exempt in this 'war against our people'. 'That is how it is. It may strike you tomorrow, in your sitting-room or during the Sunday dinner.' 'Citizens see in the tragedy of Peter Lorenz a symbol of their own situation.' 'The day we all felt fear.' 'There is no special position here. We are all affected. We face a force which the New Testament calls demonic power. What is at stake here is not just the interests of a government or a party; our interests are involved.' 'To let terrorism win would mean, for every citizen, whether or not active in politics, the end of his security.' 'This is an attack on something which concerns us all ... whether attacks with explosives or bank raids.'[38] Since it can be anyone and all are threatened, all must join the hunt. 'The lukewarm must wake up,' insisted Benda, the President of the Constitutional Court, in Berlin,[39] whose population was held up as a model of action 'based on a sense of community':

Experience from the forties [had taught the Berliners] that the fight against a mortal danger could not be a matter for the authorities alone. A firm determination on the part of every individual is equally important, perhaps more important. There is very little difference between a blockade from outside and the obstruction of society's life from within.[40]

An atmosphere like that at a shoot begins to spread: 'activate the people, motivate them, bring them together ... Hunt the criminals. Hunt them all the time. Then they will get jumpy and make mistakes.'[41] But who to hunt when everyone must be suspected? The answer is simple: everyone who attracts attention in any way. If everyone 'looks closely at their immediate surroundings', advised the *Frankfurter Allgemeine*, 'at flats and cars with unusual occupants, at boat-sheds, abandoned factory premises and vaults, and reports anything unusual at once to the authorities, the police may get a fresh trail.'[42] Wouldn't it be easier to organize a supply of badges to make this week's 'troublemakers' easily recognizable, so that people would either keep out of their way or accost them?

Self-importance, sheriff's deputy posturing, an atmosphere of denunciation and do-it-yourself justice are encouraged – all those who otherwise have no parts to play now play their part; those without authority now have authority to deal with the 'internal enemy' – they are fair game.[43] If now and again someone gets killed or the wrong person is caught, this is the price of freedom which 'we all' have to pay. Loss of reputation, and all the problems this can bring for private life and career, is the least that can happen, but it is one of the 'risks of freedom of the press', as the chief editor of the *Darmstädter Echo* solemnly announced. 'The possibility of being talked about unjustly is not something one would wish on anyone, but it passes and there are no bones broken,'[44] but this makes it all the more useful as a technique for associating a person with a crime so as to get the now eager public to accept the equally dubious arrest warrant.

While this carefully staged spectacle is in progress, bills are steadily introduced and pushed through parliament (as part of the 'plan to crush the political gangs'[45]) whose real thrust has nothing to do with their ostensible purpose. 'To defend freedom against unusually dangerous enemies,' said a *Frankfurter Allgemeine* leader, 'unusual means are called for.'[46] In other words, it's a good time to put into action old plans for which plausible explanations could not previously be found or invented. Examples are the familiar calls for a tightening of the law on demonstrations and meetings, and for a more vigorous operation of the *Berufsverbot*. These discussions and proposals reappeared in connection with the Lorenz kidnapping, as though he had been kidnapped at a meeting after the plan had been rehearsed by a nursery teacher in a sandpit. There was also the new law 'for the preservation of communal peace', which made calls for the use of force or approval of it punishable. 'The crucial blow against the terrorists,' ran the argument, 'must be dealt before kidnappings and attacks take place.'[47]

It remains uncertain whether the scares and lies which precede and accompany all these measures as a justification will do the trick. Public opinion surveys have shown that the overwhelming majority of West German citizens do not regard 'the terrorists' as a threat to their personal security. The importance given to the issue of 'internal security' rose in each case after a specific incident (e.g. Drenkmann's murder) and in accordance with the publicity given by the media, only to fall again very sharply.[48] People have other problems, personal ones, and among these unemployment creates the most fear.[49] On the other hand, it would be rash to exaggerate the value of such data, and deny the lasting effect of the hysteria campaign. It may well be that the bulk of the population – apart from all the little Charles Bronsons – watch the whole show with indifference, but this is not a reliable guide to long-term reactions. Prejudices and slogans remain in the air, available to be exploited at any time by those who have the appropriate resources. Even more dangerous is the blunting of people's awareness, habituation to such reports, to the increasingly harsh security measures which accompany them and the surrounding political climate. A shake of the head or a shrug of the shoulders is then perhaps the only reaction.[50]

Some police experts nevertheless view the elaborate 'anti-terror' campaign with mixed feelings, on the ground that it could easily be its own undoing. 'Anyone who examines the background can see that the new laws are the product of developments stretching over several years, and that even the final versions were not produced in the last few weeks.' If some politicians and the media still insist that there is 'a connection between the Baader–Meinhof gang and measures designed to improve the security situation', this is 'false and dangerous. It implies that the security laws are hasty reactions to current events, which would justify a clamour later – when the situation is normal – for their repeal or relaxation.'[51]

3. The Perfecting of Surveillance

1. New Powers for the Security Service

For the infallible detection of any 'disruptions of order',
even if only potential, a police early warning and surveillance
system has been set up in the Federal Republic to which all
citizens – not just those declared 'enemies of the state' – are
exposed, either specifically or in random screening. The first
authorizations and instruments for this were provided as early
as the 1950s, when the Bundestag in quick succession in
Autumn 1950 and Spring 1951 passed the 'Law on Collaboration
between the Federal Government and the States in Matters
relating to the Protection of the Constitution' and the 'Law on
the Establishment of a Federal Criminal Investigation Bureau'
(BKA). The Government made Cologne the headquarters of
the 'Office for the Protection of the Constitution' (*Verfassungsschutz*), the headquarters of the Criminal Investigation
Bureau went to Wiesbaden, and a 'Bonn security group', orig-
inally entrusted with the duty of protecting politicians and state
visitors, but later made responsible for police action in defence
of state security, set up a branch in Bad Godesberg.[1]

In the beginning the powers of these bodies were very limited. Memories of the unlimited power and the methods of the
fascist Gestapo ('Secret State police') were still strong, and for
this reason the Allies had forbidden its revival in any similar
centralized and powerful state security service.[2] The law on the
Verfassungsschutz allowed merely the collection and evaluation
of 'information, reports and other material' about 'movements
hostile to the state'; the right to use secret service methods to
procure information was not mentioned in the law of 1950, and
police powers such as the right to confiscate and arrest were
expressly forbidden.

The powers of the Criminal Investigation Bureau were also limited at first to the collection and processing of information for the investigations of state police forces and the maintenance of record offices and scientific establishments. The Bureau could carry out its own investigations only at the request of a state or – 'for a serious reason' – at the explicit instruction of the Federal Interior Minister. Only twenty years later the hope was fulfilled which had been expressed during the reading of the 1951 Criminal Investigation Bureau bill. 'A feeling of resentment,' von Thadden had said, 'should not prevent us from reviving the good things [in the pre-1945 police organization]'.[3] After constant demands in the fifties and sixties from successive Ministers of the Interior for the extension of the powers of the Bureau and the security service, it was left to the 'social-liberal' government in 1972 to put these plans into effect by means of the appropriate laws and constitutional changes.[4] It was also SPD/FDP coalitions, by providing vast budgetary resources, which enabled these bodies to develop from unwieldy departments into efficient machines, to become 'the Mecca and Medina of detectives throughout the world',[5] with highly qualified staff and the necessary scientific equipment. The head of the Criminal Investigation Bureau was well aware of the value of this achievement. In a speech during the celebrations to mark the twenty-fifth anniversary of his organization Herold paid ample tribute to the SPD and FDP, and spoke of an 'era of rebirth and regeneration' which had dawned for his department on 28 October 1969, the day Willy Brandt presented his government's programme.[6]

By the new law of 1972 the Criminal Investigation Bureau obtained for the first time independent executive powers to investigate and prosecute offences involving arms, ammunition, explosives and narcotics, and 'crimes against the life and liberty' of politicians. The Bureau can now be called in on cases with which the Attorney-General is concerned (political offences), and has, through its own officials, authority to give instructions to state police forces as well as the right to inspect files and demand other information. On 11 April 1972, the Conference of Interior Ministers, an executive body not provided for in the constitution, described the Federal Criminal Investigation Bureau as having 'the central role in the collection and evaluation of information and in the scientific processing of evidence' in relation to political offences.[7]

The short-lived 'Terror Department' set up for this purpose became the coordination centre for a new type of search and surveillance operation carried out jointly by the Federal Government and the states, and the central evaluation point for all reports. The 'Terror Department' thus took over responsibility for police operations in defence of state security previously carried out by the 'Bonn security group' – 'work in plenty for the immediate and more distant future', as Werner Maihofer declared,

work which no one will do for the Criminal Investigation Bureau, but which it must carry out and develop on its own, as in the past, with the flair for detection and political judgment which has distinguished its staff in the first twenty-five years and guided them safely in new fields.[8]

This 'flair for detection' and officers acting 'on their own as in the past' were and are the basis of the Bureau's methods:

From the beginning the Bureau had to work outside the BKA law to cater for the work and the needs of criminal investigation in Germany and the common problems of the fight against crime, and had recourse to agreements with the Criminal Investigation Bureaux of the individual states.

Herold ended these frank words with a tribute to his staff:

The twenty-fifth anniversary of the Federal Criminal Investigation Bureau is therefore at the same time a celebration of those voluntary contacts through which almost all the fundamental decisions about the internal operation of collaboration in criminal investigation were taken – without doubt an impressive example of how intelligence and rationality can make their own rules.[9]

A new law also gave the security service the official right to operate in a way which it had already been doing all along 'on its own initiative', namely to use 'intelligence methods' to 'observe' 'movements hostile to the constitution'. According to the service's unofficial commentary on this law this includes 'movements' whose aim is 'to carry out deliberate long-term propaganda to undermine the existence or security of the state, or to weaken it to such an extent that in the event of crisis the civil order and its organs would collapse like a house of cards'.[10]

Finally, the law legalized the secret surveillance of foreigners when required by 'foreign interests of the Federal Republic'. This supplemented the legal controls on foreigners which affect particularly the 'guest'-workers from abroad.[11] The new state security law did not remove the prohibition on the use of police procedures by the secret service (§ 3, para. 3, Law on the *Verfassungsschutz*). This was not and is not necessary, since the departments did this outside the law, by simply ignoring it. This is what an official of the ordinary rural police in Darmstadt said in confidence: 'In these things we work hand in hand. Officially, we are supposed only to assist if invited, but in practice we work closely together,'[12] and it was further illustrated by an important security officer, the former Federal Attorney-General Martin, with examples from normal practice. Martin referred to the 'Guidelines for Criminal Procedure', in force throughout the Federal Republic, which in cases involving state security call for the involvement of security experts for interrogations, the examination of the scene of crimes, searches and seizure of evidence. The state's senior prosecutor described his experiences of security men in the following terms:

Their suggestions and guidance can materially increase the success of legal measures ... For example, their expert advice can help investigating officers to discover important clues and safeguard them against the loss of evidence as a result of unskilled handling. Their wide background knowledge can help to refute untrue statements by accused persons and check the truth of witnesses' statements.

After making clear who really investigates and interrogates in

security cases, that is, who is engaged in police work in spite of
the legal ban, the ex-Attorney-General summed up:

with mutual understanding and good will on the part of all the
agencies involved, it is almost always possible to find a legally de-
fensible way of reconciling the operating interests of the security
service and the need for a smooth and efficient investigation of
offences.[13]

2. Target Surveillance

The Federal Post Office is always available when called upon
by the secret services or other security authorities. It is the Post
Office which organizes the 'simple' or ' "technical" monitoring
of the non-publicly spoken word', and the 'supervision of the
post and telephone', as telephone tapping and the breaching of
the confidentiality of the mails are called in bureaucratese.[14]

'Simple monitoring' is when an official listens in direct, on the
line, as it were. 'Technical' surveillance is carried out with the
help of a tape-recorder connected at the exchange to selected
telephone lines; when these numbers are dialled the tape starts
to run, often announcing itself by a 'click' on the line. When
recently the people who normally have others kept under observation were themselves the object of these 'services', it was a
real delight to witness the resulting indignation – this was the
publication of the boring telephone conversation between two
leaders of the parliamentary opposition. It was then a 'Phone-
Tapping Scandal' and an 'Attack on a Basic Right'. Kohl talked
about 'gangster methods', and the Chancellor pretended
'amazement'. His main party paper called for 'a stop to be put
to political spying by telephone'[15] – crocodile tears from the
people who had successfully led the 'attack on a basic right' and
are now permitting further refinements in the technique of the
'gangster methods'.

This tried and tested 'intelligence method' was given legal
backing by an amendment passed as part of the Emergency
Powers Act to Article 10 of the Basic Law. Until 1968 this ran:
'The secrecy of the mails and of the posts and telephones is

inviolable. Restrictions may only be ordered by virtue of a law.' Today there is a new paragraph 2: 'If the restriction is designed to protect the basic democratic order or the existence or security of the Federal Republic or of a state the law may provide that those affected are not informed, and that in place of legal process complaints may be dealt with by services and auxiliary services appointed by Parliament.'[16]

In addition provisions were introduced into the code of criminal procedure which allow telephone surveillance particularly in the case of people suspected by the security service of any offences or 'preparatory acts' in the field of political crime, including especially the 'formation or support of a criminal organization' in terms of Section 129 of the Penal Code.[17] The watchers' suspicions do not need to be particularly strong; all that has to be taken into account are 'the findings of professional investigators'.[18]

Other 'intelligence methods' employed by the security service are observation, the taking of secret photographs and the recruitment of 'secret assistants', also known as 'V-men' or 'informants'. This does not exhaust the catalogue of informers' tricks. According to the commentary on the *Verfassungsschutz* law, the term 'intelligence methods' is an 'undefined legal term'; 'a detailed enumeration of the methods concerned' in the law is not possible, we are told, 'in view of the constant development in techniques and equipment'.[19]

Observation is carried out by specially trained and equipped officers, from what are known as 'tracking' and 'active depots'. Security men distinguish between 'target' and 'random', 'covert' and 'overt' observation. Overt observation is the exception, and plays no role in information gathering; its purpose is to intimidate the people affected, who are obviously and persistently shadowed.

Covert observation usually takes place over a longer period and is intended to provide information about habits, behaviour and contacts. The informers travel in disguised vehicles and match their appearance to that of the environment they are penetrating.

'Modern equipment, and the training carried out in recent years', according to a commentary on Police Service Regulation 100, 'make operations possible today which go far beyond the popular idea of classical "shadowing". The obligation of secrecy restricts comment at this point.'[20]

Similarly obscure and impossible to check is the use of the so-called informants or 'V-men'. They are as shadowy as their work and their controllers.

This category does not include people in permanent contact with the police, such as the 'security officers' of larger firms. Nor does it include the numerous editors of local papers who haunt local CID offices to exchange information, or similar 'informants' who 'occasionally, on their own initiative, provide the police with relevant information', obtained 'from sources not normally accessible to the police'.[21]

More important in this connection are the famous 'secret assistants' of the security service, who are attached to political groups, specifically and with precise instructions. Their role is not limited to passive observation. They do not work just as look-outs but as *agents provocateurs*.

Their first task is to create in their surroundings the confidence necessary for them to be able to suggest or take control of activities, influence and encourage them, activities which give the authorities the desired pretext for pursuits, house searches, arrests, and so on. According to security man Schwagerl, in his 'Handbook of Theory and Practice',

The use of V-men is not just based on the principle of obtaining knowledge from an object in the normal way, but can at times lead to an active role, when the voice or views of the V-man influence the decisions of a politically suspect group in a direction desired by his superiors[22]

– in the direction, that is, which helps to justify the most spectacular intervention by his superiors. An expert summed up the results of his investigation of the security service as follows: 'An intelligence agency which succeeds in planting a number of V-men on an opponent to a certain extent controls that opponent's actions.'[23]

These 'secret assistants' do not generally come to the notice of the law, since they can only be prosecuted if the act they instigate is in fact carried out. That can be prevented in time by the prompt intervention of the police whom they inform, and this then presented as a successful piece of detective work. And if nothing has gone beyond the preparatory state, there is no intention to incite and so no offence – for the informer, that is; the others may have had his help into the cells, but now they must stand on their own.[24]

Even if the V-man does not content himself with inciting others, but takes a hand himself – for example, in order not to endanger the position of confidence he has won – he still goes unpunished if he has acted 'according to instructions', if 'his mission' constituted 'the justification for his action'.[25] The present minister of justice for North-Rhine-Westphalia argued in court in 1957 that this 'is a point about which we can no longer keep silent', and explained:

> In numerous political prosecutions we find agents appearing. In a case against a minor official of a Communist Group in North-Rhine-Westphalia it turned out that at the time of the 1953 parliamentary elections the majority of senior officials were agents. These agents had encouraged the defendant in this case to perform the act which had brought him a charge of endangering the state. In acting in this way the officials who later revealed themselves as agents went beyond the rule of *agents provocateurs*. These agents were active forces in the organization, and led on other, sincere colleagues.[26]

How far do such 'secret assistants' go? What actions do their superiors authorize them to engage in? This is the crucial question. The head of the Hamburg security service, Horchem ('I can only say that our methods are not based on moral categories'), dealt with this problem in a discussion. 'Are you, as the executive manager, prepared to take the risk that this source [the 'secret assistants'] may become involved in criminal actions? Would you tolerate their committing a robbery? Or does tolerance go no further than the printing of pamphlets?' To the additional question, 'Where does it stop?', the secret service man's answer was evasive: 'It depends on the individual case.'[27]

3. Preventive Surveillance

Symptomatic of the extension of systematic surveillance of all citizens is the practice recently reported from West Berlin. At traffic blocks details of all the occupants of vehicles are taken down on prepared forms which are then sorted and stored by computers. Significantly, this action is justified by an appeal to a provision of the code of criminal procedure (§ 163) which is called 'The First Intervention of the Police' and comes in the section of this law entitled 'preparation of the Official Charge'.[28] Before the police can intervene under section 163 the law has previously required that 'sufficient factual evidence should exist to justify the suspicion that a criminal offence has been committed which requires investigation',[29] a presumption which may now evidently be applied to any driver and his passengers.

Against this background, the deputy head of the *Verfassungsschutz* commented on the widespread but false belief that the secret service

kept harmless citizens under surveillance indiscriminately. Information is collected only about known opponents of our liberal constitutional state and about people whom there are grounds to suspect of involvement in activities hostile to the constitution or threatening security.[30]

It follows that his officers must have seen 'disruptive elements' and 'apparent disruptive elements', and 'reasonable grounds to suspect activity likely to endanger security' in the town of Biblis, where citizens are beginning to organize in opposition to the putting into service of the nuclear power station built there. The citizens whom the RWE Company had 'warmly invited' to take part in a 'citizens' dialogue' about the atomic reactor were photographed by the political police, and their questions and contributions to the discussion secretly recorded. The security service's snooping was made known while the meeting was still going on, and resulted in most of the visitors leaving the hall in protest.

The interior minister of Hesse, Bielefeld, justified the action on the ground that 'the stability and effectiveness of our democratic state' had their price, which was laid down by 'the resources of the law'. This implied that 'in particular cases, in and around potentially controversial meetings, a gathering of peaceful citizens must accept the presence of police officers for their own protection'.[31]

The police were here appealing to those 'resources of the law' made available to them only a short time before by the Federal High Court, in an appeal judgment which overturned a liberal decision by the Tübingen provincial court. The Stuttgart students' union had called a demonstration in Spring 1973 against the educational policies of the state government. Along with the students came security men, who photographed the demonstration, agents with the graphic official title of 'burrs', but not so easy to shake off as their namesakes. Observers of this sort usually stroll around in the area of demonstrations or other 'potentially controversial' meetings, and in Frankfurt they have for a long time been undisguised and carried a large array of equipment. What is less usual is for demonstrators not simply to accept such company, but defend themselves. This was what happened in Tübingen. Some students noticed that one café customer was a policeman carefully following events with a camera and telephoto lens. He was abruptly dislodged, interrogated and 'disarmed'. As a result, one of the students, who was recognized, was charged by the Tübingen public prosecutor, and this led to the case in question.

As well as the camera, the policeman had a briefcase containing microphones, binoculars, a note-pad with notes about the demonstration and the development of the strike at the university and details of the Baader–Meinhof hunt. Other contents of the briefcase included a pistol, a replacement magazine with six cartridges, and two fairly old descriptions of bodies found.[32]

In the subsequent hearing the policeman said, explaining at least the presence of the camera, that his task had been the identification of 'ringleaders' and as many participants in the demonstration as possible. The photographs were to be used as a help in checking names and drawing up lists.[33]

The Tübingen Provincial Court condemned this action of the security division of the police as a serious interference with the basic right of the freedom to demonstrate, an essential part of which was protection 'against official recording of the exercise of this right'. There was nothing to stop card indexes of demonstrators being compiled from such photographs and then passed on to the state security service. According to the law, however, (§ 81b StPO), the keeping of records was allowed only in the case of convicted persons, not indiscriminately, and certainly not as a precautionary measure. In the opinion of the court, therefore, the accused was under no obligation to allow himself to be photographed. 'At a later time the accused would no longer have been able to defend himself effectively against injury resulting from the use of the photographs.' The taking by the accused of the case, camera and film 'was necessary to his self-defence because the police officer had refused to surrender the film. There was no less direct defensive action which could have been effective.'[34]

The public prosecutor appealed to the Federal High Court against this judgment, and was completely successful. Photographing the demonstration for reasons of police tactics was justified by 'overriding public interests'. The officers, said the High Court, had started from the premise that 'the photographs would help them to identify' from among the demonstrators 'the unknown authors of wall-sprayings and disruptions of lectures, since they were presumed to be taking part in the demonstration'.

At the very beginning of police inquiries the investigation must often be wide-ranging and include people who are immediately ruled out as suspects. When people on whom no suspicion lies are present at a public meeting with suspects, it is in general inevitable that they should also be photographed.

The fear that the photographs 'might be made into files of demonstrators and in certain cases passed on to the state security service' was, said the High Court, groundless; after all, anyone affected could always 'defend himself in the administrative courts'[35] – presuming, of course, that he knows he has been photographed.

The Federal High Court had made things clear again. The *Hessische Polizeirundschau* triumphantly published the key sentences of the judgment a few pages after interior minister Bielefeld's comments on the events in Biblis which were quoted above.[36]

The 'duties of the security service in the front line of the police's preventive operations and their pursuit of crime', as they are described in the official description of the Federal Criminal Investigation Bureau and the secret services,[37] is not undertaken only by these official institutions. Alongside and within them semi-official procedures have been developed for 'preventive and repressive defence against threats to internal security'. These are described as 'possible anywhere at any time',[38] and are liable to be seen on the same scale. For the individual the increase of discretion in detecting 'disturbances', which officials assume as required, means a decrease in the accountability of state activity. Distrust, suspicion and denunciation increase, and with them willingness to toe the line and behave, reticence and self-censorship on the part of those who are afraid of falling into the sphere of political surveillance. Today this can affect anyone who has ever caught the attention of a security man, or even suspects that they may have.

It would be a false interpretation of the Federal Constitutional Court's judgment of May 1975 on the *Berufsverbot* to call it 'liberal' simply because it advised that 'political wild oats' should not be held against applicants for posts in the civil service.[39] This is not liberal; it is effective. The absolution acts as a signal; for example, it makes new graduates begin to calculate carefully, and keep a low profile.

And not just graduates. Anyone who wants to become a civil servant – or who, because of his training, must become one – anyone who applies for a job, at whatever level, in the public service, is checked for 'political acceptability'.

In the period from the beginning of 1973 to the middle of 1975 the security services, according to official figures, made investigations in 1,500,000 cases, to see if anything was known against the applicants. The result was positive in the case of about 3,000 candidates for the public service; in the case of the other 1,497,000 the only step taken was to open a file.[40]

A few thousand out of 1,500,000 – what does that matter? So ran the public arithmetic. But this figure only has meaning when looked at the other way round. Almost 1·5 million checks, or, as they have recently begun to be called in official language, 'inquiry procedures',[41] were carried out.

Since 'enemies of the constitution who try to infiltrate our constitutional system silently [are] worse than those who use violent methods',[42] the 'inquiries' do not remain within the secret service. In the case of certain people, friends, neighbours and relatives will be asked questions, either during an 'inquiry procedure' or during a short visit from an interested, ordinary-looking gentleman.[43] In either case you are advised 'in your own interest' to tell and to answer, without compulsion, of course – it's quite voluntary. H. J. Schwagerl, the official of the Wiesbaden interior ministry whose duties include keeping an eye on the teachers of Hesse, and who, to save time, has been given 'teaching duties' at Darmstadt University, makes this clear with typical delicacy:

The person interviewed is not obliged to answer. Nevertheless in the normal case the citizen will be anxious to clear up the points in question with the representative of the security service if he, the citizen, identifies with the liberal democratic system.[44]

Many people have already had to discover that they no longer counted as 'normal cases', but had entered the ranks of the 'enemies of the state or of the constitution'. After inquisitorial interrogations and snooping into their views they were rejected as 'unsuitable'. So arbitrary is the procedure that it must be called terrorism. No one apart from the inquisitors who make it knows what is 'relevant' to the decision, a situation which puts applicants – metaphorically – on the rack.

Since then representatives of every possible profession have been unmasked as 'enemies of the state', even cemetery gardeners and engine-drivers. This does not just show, as *Der Spiegel* thinks, the 'grotesque spread of the Radicals Decree';[45] there is system to it, it is carefully calculated. The incalculability for future applicants is increased, and with it prudent political abstinence and isolation.

Deterrence and discipline, i.e. the guarantee that a 'body of loyal civil servants' will be recruited, is the declared aim of the procedure. This was emphasized on another occasion by the Darmstadt administrative court: on the application of a member of the Christian Democrat Student Organization from Giessen, the court was asked to rule on whether the Giessen University students' union had 'illegitimately made political statements'. The plaintiff cited three instances, a declaration of solidarity on Portugal, criticism of the West German health service and criticism of the use of the *Berufsverbot* against former Giessen student representatives.

The Darmstadt judges ruled in precisely the same way as all other administrative courts before, against the 'political mandate', in this case against Portugal and for the existing system of health care. This is not surprising and not very relevant to our subject.

The only remarkable part of the judgment is the court's comments on the *Berufsverbot* or, as it was called in the judgment to avoid the use of 'political slogans and provocative terms', 'difficulties in the pursuit of a career'. In dealing with this the court made explicit reference to the right, and even duty, of a students' union to issue clear declarations – on grounds of well-understood civic instruction:

The leaflet [complained of] – 'Berufsverbot Threatens Former Giessen Students' [a campaign based on the experiences of the former Giessen student R.] – is, contrary to the view of the plaintiff [the CDU students' organization], related to the university since former Giessen students and therefore former members of the defendant organization are its main concern. It is certainly among the responsibilities of the students' union to take an interest in the further professional careers of former members in so far as this may have an effect on present students.

This applies to both cases taken up by the defendant, that of the applicant for a teaching post and that of the applicant for teaching duties. Both were deeply involved in the organization of the defendant body while they were students and are now encountering special difficulties in pursuing their careers precisely because of their involvement.

This development makes it appear justified for the defendant organization to use the cases cited to make general statements about the so-called Radicals Decree, since this is of direct relevance to all students and, even while studying, they have to regulate their behaviour with it in mind.[46]

Already a disturbing number of people have regulated or moderated their behaviour in this way. An open letter to President Scheel from Amnesty International, the organization founded to help political prisoners throughout the world, gives an idea of the situation. To an increasing extent, the organization wrote, citizens were becoming reluctant to support signature campaigns, even in support of such demands as the abolition of torture. 'The reason given to us is that the person approached worked in the public service, or intended to apply for a position in the public service and was afraid that signing a petition would work to their disadvantage.'[47]

We know now that this fear is not unfounded. Amnesty, still praised in 1972 during the Bundestag debate on the new state security law as a group by which 'the whole German people should be guided',[48] has since attracted the attentions of the secret services. Through an indiscretion it became known that, as for some time with other organizations, records were being kept of who organized or led campaigns or demonstrations for Amnesty, when, with whom and where. 'Prejudicial to the state', an old Gestapo coinage unearthed again, was the label attached to a woman who had 'come to attention several times now as applicant for permission for activities on behalf of the organization'.[49] The criminal content of 'applying for permission' or 'coming to notice' was something security law, hitherto at least, had been unfamiliar with.

The officials of the Lower Saxony interior ministry, which had responsibility for the case, and which was still at the time controlled by an SPD/FDP coalition, tried to cover up the affair so clumsily that with each new denial even more came out. At first it was said that the 'mistaken views' of an over-zealous low-ranking policeman were the cause of it all, and that the security service report had long since ended up in the waste paper basket. Evidently this is the bureaucrats' code for 'file', because the Amnesty dossiers are still in the filing cabinets of the security service, as was confirmed by the new CDU interior minister, correcting his predecessor. Nor was that the only place: a copy had been sent to the state Criminal Investigation Bureau, and one to the minister-president, whose responsibilities include the appointment of teachers.

This, according to police security men, is the rule rather than the exception. And not just for the activities of Amnesty. 'Routine reports on a standard form' are prepared on all the activities of youth centres and community action and women's groups, etc., 'with details of the nature, place and subject of the activity, the names of the organizers, the number of participants, the titles of publications distributed', any 'unusual occurrences' and criminal proceedings opened.[50] These forms lie in officials' drawers to be filled in at need, filed in the appropriate places and brought out again at the right time – as, for example, the 'basis for the judgment' in *Berufsverbot* cases, among which the Constitutional Court specifically lists 'statements, participation in demonstrations, political activities'.[51]

Strikes are also observed by security snoopers, who report how long they last, who the 'ringleaders' are, and where further strikes are likely.[52] This surveillance of labour disputes as one of the main elements of police action against strikers is to be given a legal basis. In June 1973 the conference of interior ministers published the draft of a uniform law to govern the security services of the states. This included regulations for the 'transmission of information to other official bodies', in other words, legalized cooperation between industrial and security police.[53]

'Information obtained' by the political police about individual employees could be passed on to managements, a process which has worked beautifully for a long time in the opposite direction. After Bremen, Bavaria, Rhineland-Palatinate, Schleswig-Holstein, and Saarland, and after West Berlin, Lower Saxony has also now passed a similar secret service law on the model of one introduced by the previous SPD/FDP government in Hanover.[54] This goes even further. It also stipulates that, 'in addition to purely technical assistance', 'state authorities,' municipalities, districts, all other legal persons, the state courts and the officials of the security service' are to keep each other informed, and not to wait for specific inquiries.[55] The 'other legal persons' include schools and universities, chambers of trade, industry and commerce, tax offices and doctors employed by public authorities. 'Not even the Gestapo,' said a member of the council of the Federal Chamber of Notaries, 'could call on such a range of collaboration; it only had the right to information from police authorities.'[56]

A quite special form of 'technical assistance' has been developed by the West Berlin police, and they have been followed by Frankfurt, Ludwigshafen, Mainz, Trier and Darmstadt. This is the 'area contact officer' (KOB), the 'accessible policeman' on the corner. On foot, 'familiar, accepted, confidence-inspiring, easy-going' and as far as possible coming from his area, this 'is just the type of officer that gets on well with the people' because he knows his district and its people and 'has a feel for where danger threatens'.[57]

No one wants to have reason for dealing with the police. Indifference, suspicion and aggression are the usual reactions to which officers on duty are exposed. Because of this, an attempt is now being made to improve the image of the force through the introduction of a new type of uniformed section leader, to whom anyone can turn with worries, however small, who is at everyone's service. 'I am your area contact officer. To help us keep in touch, in the last few days I have taken up my duties in your immediate neighbourhood.' So read a brochure which West Berlin citizens found in their letterboxes in October 1974, and a little later they could see 'their KOB', coming round the corner with a smile and a friendly word.

This is one result of the reform of the Berlin police. For you it means greater security through the regular and accessible presence of the police, through a concentration of police work, through more carefully organized patrols and raids . . . As I say, I am 'your police-man on the corner'. What does this mean for you? Among other things, that I shall not just keep an eye on the danger spots of interest to the police and if necessary take initial action. I also welcome your advice, requests and complaints, and give infor-mation. On the enclosed visiting card you will find my name and the address of my station . . . In addition, through more carefully organ-ized patrolling by uniformed and plain-clothes officers our city's security net will be drawn ever tighter . . . From now on a mobile police force, suited to our modern technical age, will be available to you at any time where you live. But the security which you rightly expect from the police and which we want to ensure is only possible through a relationship of trust and cooperation with you. Your con-tact officer is counting on your cooperation.[58]

The KOB hopes to get this cooperation from the many people he will talk to in his section, caretakers, customers and shopkeepers in the corner shop, pensioners and children at play, and – as an exceptional concession – will buy them a beer in the local bar and have a little chat. 'The state,' according to Herold of the BKA, 'is not an organism, but it must behave like an organism in order to survive . . . One means of keeping in con-stant touch with reality is this osmotic filter of the police.'[59]

In the 'citizen body' the KOB will not only see a lot, but also hear a lot, interesting and trivial, pieces of a mosaic which day by day will gradually build up a clearer picture of his section and its inhabitants, a picture which the crew of a patrol car or a desk-bound official could never obtain, friendships and enmities and their causes, and what will or might happen tomorrow.

The hope is that this sort of policeman will win confidence because he is visible and people know he's around. 'When he notices something wrong, the "contact officer" tells his colleagues',[60] who then see that the police make contact in the old way: first the KOB, then the MEK (Mobile Intervention Unit). In Berlin the new surveillance system is said to have produced a doubling in the rate of charges brought and of information about the areas concerned.[61]

'The police', in the words of the optimistic blueprint,

must have their eyes, ears, hearts and hands as far forward as possible. Correct judgments of situations and the resulting correct police intervention, appropriate surveillance of areas of interest to the police and the useful clues this produces are fed ultimately by knowledge about the people, by their life and ideas, in other words learning and feeling in a local area.[62]

In Munich, Frankfurt and Berlin this procedure has been further refined. At the same time that public spending on youth work, and especially for work with unemployed young people, is being reduced, and social workers' jobs are being cut, there is talk about the introduction of 'youth policemen'. These would be police officers who would go around youth centres and bars in plain clothes to reveal themselves subsequently as uniquely qualified 'social workers': i.e. trained to investigate offences whenever they hear of them.

What informers – in uniform or in plain clothes – report, what V-men have arranged or set up, what has been recorded on tape or film, all this 'information' on its own is worthless. It must be collected, assessed, sorted and combined and be available again at any moment. The days are gone when a police state could be run on mountains of dusty files and unusable card indexes. To deal with this, electronic filing was introduced. Individuals and 'movements' on whom information has been collected and files opened are – as secret service official Schwagerl calls it – 'carded'.[63] Individual facts and links between people are classified on punched cards and magnetic tapes by person, crime and area, and can be summoned up in the space of a few seconds at the touch of a button. These installations are available to the secret services, the Federal Criminal Investigation Bureau and the detective forces of the states; frontier crossings are also connected, and more recently individual radio cars. 'In my previous district of Nürnberg,' boasted BKA chief Herold, 'we trained our computer to print out for us in the form of town maps details of where and when concentrations of crime existed or were expected. Maps of this sort were orders to the duty police to intervene, telling them to go with appropriate forces to the scene at the time the events were due to take place'[64] – so that someone is on the spot even if, contrary to the calculation, 'it' doesn't happen.

Whose details and history are in the government computers – the security service alone has records of more than two million citizens[65] – a person affected has no means of discovering, any more than they can check the combinations possible with this information and that from other computers. Someone who is sought by the police, as former interior minister Genscher put it bluntly, 'has no right to keep his details private'.[66] But naturally many fewer people are sought in comparison with the numbers who have been 'carded' over the years and those who are constantly added to them as a matter of routine. Instead the police regard any name in their electronic bank as a clue to a potential 'trouble-maker'.

To produce a complete 'inventory' of the population there is at present being developed in the Federal Republic an information system and registration law which recalls the frightening visions of Orwell's *Nineteen Eighty-Four*: there is a plan for what are known as personal numbers. These would make it possible to combine all the information about a person stored in both private and public sources – information from finance and employment offices, from health and other insurance organizations and educational institutions, information about work records, political interests, political activities, etc., in short about the whole personal development of each and every citizen. It can easily be imagined what power will be possessed by the people and institutions who at any time are in possession of such details and able to pass them on.

4. Criminal Law as a Weapon

To talk about political criminal law is really a tautology, for what criminal law, what penal enactment is not political, is not the expression of the current social definition of crime? In this chapter, however, the term 'political criminal law' will be used, to indicate the area relevant to our subject, the use of the criminal law to maintain state security. This means the state's confrontation with its political opponents through the forms of justice, their suppression and neutralization by means of a specially created and uniquely applied body of law.

The fact that the 'Particular Section' of the Penal Code in the Federal Republic, in other words its list of crimes, begins with political criminal law, and that this again begins with provisions dealing with 'treason', and in particular with 'high treason', must be a sign of the importance attached to the state, its security and the allegiance to the state which is required. On the other hand, the frequently expressed view that a different arrangement of the Penal Code would produce 'in the minds of the people a reduced sense of the seriousness of these offences', and so of the majesty of the state,[1] is heavily idealistic. It nevertheless corresponds to the norm-fixated juristic attitude which underlies the provisions on 'internal security', the attempt to establish and impose obligatory substitutes for the claims to legitimacy and 'values' of the state's monopoly of force which are becoming ever harder to derive and foster in the life of society itself. This attempt to bolster the authority of the state is impressively illustrated by the development of political criminal law and its administration.

1. 'Defence Lines against the Cold Revolution'

When the Federal Republic was founded in 1949 the old Penal Code of the Reich remained in force, though the state security provisions, which derived from the Nazi period, had been suspended by the Allies.[2] In order to fill this 'legal vacuum' and 'close at least provisionally these gaps in the law', new 'provisions essential to the security of the state' were passed in Summer 1951[3] – this, significantly, was the first reform of the criminal law – which, however, did not subsequently lapse, even provisionally.

The Government's bill, and even more forthrightly the SPD's proposal for a 'Law against the enemies of democracy', referred to the attacks which had still be be faced 'from the camp of the incorrigible criminal supporters of National Socialist ideology',[4] but it was made clear by the Government at a very early stage of the discussions whom the proposals were directed against. The 'villains', 'enemies of the state', 'mortal enemies of human society', 'subversive organizations', 'voles' and 'rats gnawing beneath the surface at the supports of our state' who figured in the debates and who were to be met with 'implacable' and 'unyielding firmness' and 'forceful measures' were none other than socialists and communists.[5]

In particular, the Korean war (which began on 25 June 1950) provided the Government with the ammunition it needed to shoot down objections to its law raised during the discussions in committee, among others by the Bundesrat. The minister of justice made an emotional appeal to the Bundestag during the first reading; since they were all in the same boat they should throw overboard objections to the new state security laws:

The Bundesrat feels the problem needs more specialist study. Well, on the day of the Bundesrat vote – that was the 23 July – there was still time to talk about things like that. But two days later, ladies and gentlemen, came Korea! Surely, if anyone was hesitant that must have opened their eyes. And we don't need to go as far as Korea. The evil is so close. We have what is happening in the Eastern Zone. Over there every instrument of propaganda and subversion is being used to bring about the disintegration and collapse of the Federal Republic. In my view we cannot look on passively. The battle-cry is not 'Hannibal at the gates!', but 'The Trojan horse is in our midst.'[6]

With all speed, on 11 July 1951 the Bundestag duly passed the new state security measures. The minister of justice described the core of these as being the sections dealing with the 'actions which precede high treason',[7] designed to combat 'ideological high treason', 'ideological subversion' and 'intellectual sabotage'.[8] This law places radical criticism of the prevailing system on the same level as acts of violence, explicitly connecting them in the section quoted, and this is the specific function of state security in the Federal Republic: it advances the area of punishable behaviour into that of ideas, intentions and statements of opinion.

During the discussion of the bill the purpose of the state security measures was described as being to protect the state from 'attempts at subversion' carried out not by force but 'with the resources of propaganda of an ideology prejudicial to the state'. It was necessary to meet 'new revolutionary movements which do not use violent methods, or at least do not let their violence be seen'.[9] The modern state, it was said, faced opponents who no longer tried to win power at the barricades or by armed force, but increasingly used the 'silent and insidious technique of internal subversion', the 'press, radio' and 'publications of all sorts'. This 'cold revolution' was dangerous because it consisted of

a system of individual acts, each on its own apparently fairly harmless, which, however, all together, acting at the most disparate points to further the same end, could create a situation in which the overthrow of the state was inevitable and left it to be plucked like a ripe fruit.[10]

The people were being played off against the Government by 'a planned campaign to mislead the masses'[11]:

When the sense of the legitimacy of the state's authority is successfully weakened in the minds of the people, and instead a belief implanted in the validity of the revolutionary idea, so that in the event of conflict they follow the authority of the revolutionary and refuse obedience to the state, the revolution has reached its goal.[12]

To prevent this, to maintain the authority of the state and allow it to exercise unchallenged its monopoly of force, 'new security provisions' were established to protect the state, to 'bring forward its line of defence into the area in which the enemies of the state try to work their way into power under the mask of non-violence'.[13]

This forward state security is far from being 'new wine' in the Penal Code's 'old bottles', as Dehler maintained,[14] but a touch of 1935. With its 'front line security', the state security provisions of the Federal Republic's criminal law are in continuity with the Nazi laws against undesirable opinions, one of the 'inventors' of which was Roland Freisler. Freisler's slogan, 'The criminal law moves the battle-line forward',[15] denoted a strategy developed at length in an article of 1935 mentioned by Freisler which acquired fundamental importance for fascist criminal law. Its arguments have striking similarities with the arguments quoted in support of the Federal Republic's political criminal law:

The discussion on the concept of an act of violence deals with much more than a technical matter; it touches on a question fundamental to the life of the state and the people, namely the question whether the state should make use of the weapon of the criminal law only in extreme cases (in war or in the face of open revolt) or at a previous stage. Or in practical terms, must the state passively accept the undermining of the intellectual foundations on which it rests, and wait until it is openly attacked?[16]

The question was rhetorical, and was answered in the negative:

The National Socialist state will bring forward its defence line; it will not wait until the criminal has carried out his purpose.[17]

Fifteen years later the Federal minister of justice took up the idea again: 'enemies of the state' had to be 'met and rendered harmless before they [could] go into action'.[18]

It is clear that this goal can only be achieved by a limitation on the freedom of opinion, by a criminalization of certain political views. For this purpose the Federal Constitutional Court has coined the term 'views which endanger the state', which must be opposed for the sake of the 'common good': 'Freedom of opinion as such is essential to the liberal system. If such a basic right is to be limited, such action must be justified by special needs of the system itself.'[19]

Simply out of consideration for the efficient running of the courts, not every political remark involving criticism of existing conditions will be punished. It is not that there are what the Federal minister of justice called 'duty-free ideas'; it depends on 'the external effect which comes from the internal centre [of a person]'.[20] It is a matter of words or documents which could have practical consequences, which are not just expressed but also implemented because they are addressed to obvious problems in a particular situation, with reference to a specific context, and imply action. Their danger is that they indicate and strengthen the potential for action. 'Opinion as such must be free in a democracy, but not every form of action on these opinions can be allowed.'[21]

The political opinions which may be expressed and 'acted on', and the forms this may take, are defined by political criminal law in five sections: 'High Treason', 'Dangers to the State' (since 1968 under the slightly pleasanter title 'Dangers to the Democratic Constitutional State'), 'Offences against Constitutional Organs', 'Resistance to the Authority of the State', and 'Offences against Public Order'.

As well as actions themselves, the provisions of these sections also turn 'expressions of opinion', the 'advance guard' of actions, into crimes. In the section headed 'High Treason', this classical 'crime against the state', there also occurs 'the planning of an action constituting high treason' (§ 83 StGB) by means of 'the exercise of intellectual or moral influence on the population'.[22] The section 'Dangers to the State' includes 'the propagation of a party declared unconstitutional' (§ 84 StGB), 'anti-constitutional sabotage', (§ 88 StGB), 'the dissemination of propaganda material from unconstitutional organizations' (§ 86 StGB), the exercise of 'anti-constitutional influence on the army and other organs of public security' (§ 89 StGB), 'defamation of the Federal President' (§ 90 StGB), 'defamation of the state and its symbols' (§ 90a StGB), 'anti-constitutional defamation of constitutional organs' (§ 90b StGB), and since 1976 – inserted by the 'communal peace' law – 'anti-constitutional encouragement of offences' (§ 88 StGB). The section 'Offences against Constitutional Organs' includes 'the exercise of compulsion' on parliaments, governments and courts by force or by 'threats of force' (§ 105 StGB). In the section 'Resistance to the Authority of the State' 'resistance to executive officers' (§ 113 StGB) appears alongside 'public invitation to commit offences' (§ 111 StGB).

The section 'Offences against Public Order' includes 'breach of domestic peace' (§ 123 § 124 StGB), 'breach of public peace' (§ 125, 125a StGB), the 'formation of armed bands' (§ 127 StGB), but also 'the disturbance of public peace by threats of offences' (§ 126 StGB, considerably strengthened by the 'community peace' law of 1976), 'incitement of the population' (§ 130 StGB), the 'glorification of violence' (§ 131 StGB), 'failure to report planned offences' (§ 138 StGB), the 'rewarding and approval of offences' (§ 140 StGB, also considerably strengthened by the 'communal peace' law of 1976), 'concealment of an offence from an official body' (§ 145d StGB), and 'encouragement to commit offences' (§ 130a StGB, a product of the 'communal peace' law).

The 'formation of a criminal organization (§ 129 StGB) occupies an ambiguous position between criminal actions and criminal utterances. The relevant clause penalizes not only the setting up of such an 'organization', but also 'support' for it and 'advertisement' of it, crimes which the judiciary has advanced well into the area of 'ideological support'.

All five sections share certain characteristics, which will be examined in detail below.

Force is identified not just with the exercise of direct physical compulsion, but even with the announcement and use of passive resistance; in either case the purpose sought, the goal of the action or behaviour decides its criminality. The monopoly of defining legitimate and illegitimate force lies in the hands of the security service; it decides what words or actions are 'supportive of the state' or 'hostile to the state'. Not all force or every violent act is automatically illegal, and this fact is naturally of particular significance to the treatment of crimes under the state security laws, both political appeals and political action.

Secondly, contrary to what their headings lead one to suppose, the offences are not concerned with actual dangers, 'disturbances to public order' and their origins. They are rather what are known as crimes involving abstract danger, which, unlike crimes concerned with an action, do not depend on the actual occurrence of a determinable danger for something like 'national security'. It is sufficient for prosecutors and courts to see this possibility or to deduce it from the 'personality of the accused'. This is another piece of 'advanced state security', ensured by means of a technical legal trick, by the use of general terms such as 'influence', 'defamation', 'encouragement' and so on, which require and invite interpretation from case to case. These terms enable utterances to be classified under actions if the 'anti-constitutional intent' to which they refer can be 'discovered' in the accused – or it may simply be assumed that particular words or publications are 'likely in the circumstances' to 'disturb public peace'.

The third and final feature is the campaign, not against any individual and isolated statement, nor against an action which remains isolated, but against 'organized opinion', the 'idea in organized form',[23] and the attack on people who act collectively, in solidarity.

In these features, which will constantly reappear in the course of this study, there recurs something described at the start in connection with the political background to the debates and measures dealing with 'internal security'. This red thread, which runs through the whole of the political criminal law and binds it together, is fear of the formation of alternative power and an alternative public, even of what BKA president Herold called alternative power symbols, in other words models of autonomous political action.

According to Reinhart Maurach, a notable criminal lawyer before and after 1945, the 'threatening actions' to be guarded against

can be divided into three groups: acts constituting criminal incitement, the act of making criminal threats, and the acts constituting criminal association ... State power needs not only protection against attacks on its actual functioning, not only protection against injuries to its dignity, but also special protection against the unleashing of forces which represent no more than a potential threat to the machinery and operation of government, but give rise to the danger of destructive anarchy.[24]

2. 'Reprehensible' Violence

In order to ensure a smooth restoration of the capitalist system of control in the Federal Republic, any sign of effective socialist opposition was, from the very beginning, consistently neutralized. The new 1951 state security legislation had hardly been three months on the statute book when the Federal Government applied to the Constitutional Court for the proscription of the KPD, which was duly granted in 1956. In the subsequent period, the High Court, in its role as one of 'the communal institutions which have responsibility for maintaining internal security',[25] developed, often against the judgments of lower courts, a judicial practice which has to the present remained normative for the administration of the political criminal law. A book published to celebrate the twenty-fifth anniversary of the setting-up of the High Court rightly noted that it was the court's panel with responsibility for political cases which had 'given the judicial side of state security its essential features'.[26]

Numerous judgments on the permissibility of expressing and campaigning for political views and demands other than at elections, i.e. directly, defined the area within which force could be a criminal offence. The direction was set by a series of trials in the fifties in which socialist and communist organizations were charged with every possible offence constituting 'treason' or 'high treason' for acts which included calling demonstrations, meetings, referenda and strikes against the plans for rearmament, and against the entry of the Federal Republic into the Western alliance.

'This method of agitation,' said the High Court, 'seeks' the appearance of democratic legitimation by 'appealing to "the decision of the people". In fact it represents an attempt to undermine the governmental system by attacking and weakening the essential foundations of representative democracy and their acceptance by the people.'[27]

What the expression and defence of political interests by appeal to the people really means to the High Court, and whose authority it regards as threatened by extra-parliamentary activity, can hardly be better described than by one source-reference to this decision in the official record of High Court decisions. There, under 'Referendum', we find 'see "High Treason" and "Dangers to the State" '.[28]

The organization and promotion of these demonstrations, meetings and strikes – 'weapons', according to the High Court, 'not excluding large-scale or general strikes' – was regarded by the court as an attempt to exploit 'disturbances and disruptions of public order',[29] to make the continued activity of the 'constitutional organs' impossible and paralyse government and parliament. It made no difference whether or not this action involved plans for 'the use of physical force in any form' against members of the Government or parliament.

> The crucial factor can only be the exercise of compulsion ... If this is accepted, demonstrations and strikes can in no sense be regarded as 'typical methods of non-violent protest' ... Whether an effect comparable to that of the use of physical force is sought, will depend on the nature and extent of the strike, and on who is intended to be influenced by it.[30]

Thus whether a strike, demonstration or other activity is to be banned and stopped as violent does not depend simply on whether it results in violence or damage; what decides the question is on whom it wants to exert influence, on what scale and for what purpose or advantage. The crucial factor is the effect it seeks to produce, the actual 'social relation' in which the event stands, but not the event 'on its own – in the abstract'.[31] The provisions on compulsion (§ 240 StGB) explicitly require the 'illegality' and so the criminality of actions to be deduced from their aim and purpose:

Anyone who by force or threat of physical injury illegally compels another to perform, tolerate or refrain from performing an act will be liable to ... The act is illegal if the use of force or the threat of injury for the purpose sought can be regarded as reprehensible [§ 240 sections 1 and 2 StGB]

– and what is 'reprehensible' is decided by the courts.

This elastic label 'reprehensible' has not been part of the law on compulsion for very long – and here again the Nazis led the way, with an even more flexible formulation. By a 'Criminal Law Standardization Regulation' of 1943, Section 240 for the first time acquired a second paragraph 'defining' the criterion of illegality. It ran: 'The act [of compulsion] shall be illegal if the use of force or the inflicting of the threatened injury for the purpose sought conflicts with sound national sentiment.'[32]

This refinement of such an important provision of the criminal code as that on 'compulsion' clearly pleased the legislators after 1949 so much that they left it until 1953 to change the wording, and then without doing anything to its vagueness. By an 'emending law' they simply replaced 'conflicts with sound national sentiment' by 'reprehensibility'.[33]

Otto Schwarz, Reich Court judge and commentator on criminal law under the Nazis, mentioned the emendment in his 1954 commentary on the criminal law with the curt note that the new term was a clearer criterion than the old one.[34]

'Reprehensible,' added Eduard Dreher, the present editor of the Criminal Code,

means a higher degree of moral disapproval ... The determining factor is objective reprehensibility, which has to be judged by normal legal criteria. The means of compulsion and its purpose are placed in relation to each other.[35]

How does it work? In 1969 the High Court had to decide whether it was 'morally acceptable' or alternatively 'reprehensible' for citizens to organize a sit-down strike on a city's tram lines in protest against a planned fare increase. The demonstrators, mostly school and university students, and therefore particularly affected by the fare increase, had demanded that they should be heard by the city council before it took a final decision. This, said the High Court, was a 'reprehensible' use of force, 'street pressure', which could not be accepted:

A constitutional right of the citizen or any organization to be heard by official agencies or representatives in general before the adoption of any measure affecting the individual or affecting an organization protecting his interests in those interests does not exist, nor can it be desirable, since thereby the activity of the legislative and executive organs would be impeded . . . to the detriment of the common good.

The relevant decisions, in this case the fare increases, 'must be left, without forcible interference, in the hands of those bodies authorized for that purpose by the constitution and the law'. Any other attitude 'would result in the legalization of terrorism practised by militant minorities'.[36]

In plain terms, protection is always available for force 'from above'. Protest and resistance by those affected is made an offence, as 'a breach of the peace' or 'compulsion', etc., not accidentally but essentially, as the High Court made clear in a judgment against anti-Springer demonstrators. Lower courts had

expressed the view that the right to demonstrate guaranteed by Article 5 and Article 8 of the Basic Law was sufficient to justify the use of force under certain conditions. On examining the details of individual cases, some courts have also deemed a limited use of force to emphasize the objects of a demonstration to be not an offence. However, the decisions of the higher courts have consistently deemed the use of force – even in the form of passive resistance [sit-down strikes] – to be illegal. These decisions must be followed.[37]

On the occasion of the nationwide campaign of mass obstruction against distributors of the *Bild* newspaper in protest against the paper's continual pillorying of minorities and rabble-rousing calls to 'decent' citizens, the High Court casually dismissed the reasons for the campaign with a reference to the 'free market economy'. The obstruction of the editorial offices and presses, it said,

was intended to protest against the concentration of press ownership in the hands of the publisher Axel Springer and against the reporting of newspapers belonging to this concern, which was felt to be tendentious, and to make the public aware of the dangers of this situation ... This action was illegal.

It 'constituted a use of force' which could not appeal to the right of self-defence 'since it has not been shown that the newspapers whose distribution the demonstration sought to prevent contained any attacks on the legal rights of third parties'.[38]

How could this be shown in court when all the charges against the Springer Company for 'incitement' had been dropped almost as soon as they were brought?

'Not even considerations of "equality of opportunity",' continued the court,

justify a different assessment. The Basic Law guarantees the opportunity to have one's opinion heard by eliminating force and compulsion as weapons in the battle of opinions ... It may be that distinctions exist in the real possibility of exercise of the basic right of freedom of expression by individuals because not all possess the same technical or organizational resources for dissemination, but this is accepted by the Basic Law as a consequence of freedom of action.

The demonstrators' behaviour 'is incompatible with the principle of press freedom since in practice it amounts to an impermissible censorship by people of different views'.[39]

The judicial attitude to the lawfulness of strikes – not just

83

general strikes or political strikes – is similar. This too depends on the effect and aims of the struggle, as former Federal prosecutor Wagner clearly explained:

A strike in itself has as little to do with criminal law as, say, the use of a walking stick. But the person who uses a walking-stick to inflict injury renders himself liable to action for assault.[40]

A strike, its preparation and discussion remain without legal consequences for as long as the action itself remains inconsequential, as long as the employer to be affected is not affected or does not feel any effect. But if the strikers link arms in front of the gates, and are called on or 'encouraged' to do so, so that the strike becomes solid and the struggle begins to have an effect, then the strike is illegal. It is enough to give clear indications to strike-breakers of what isn't on – 'the obstruction of exits is generally a use of force as defined in the concept of "breach of the peace" '. Pickets are supposed to behave as though they were not on a picket line – they must leave

a completely safe, sufficiently wide and easily recognizable entrance to the workplace, the use of which must not necessitate any running of a gauntlet; further, anyone wishing to work who fails to notice the free passage must be directed to it ... The united presence of the pickets becomes a disorderly assembly immediately they unduly restrict the usual access to work by forming a closed line.[41]

Since, as the superior provincial court at Hamm declared, 'from riotous assembly to insurrection is only a short step', and since 'the presence of a crowd at any time' may create 'a danger for public security and order',[42] sentences for 'breach of the peace' and 'compulsion' are generally quite heavy on so-called mass crimes: 'Such disorders, which undermine the liberal system of a constitutional state and have been shown by experience to provoke imitation, cannot be treated lightly.'[43]

Demonstrators against fare increases were consequently punished by the provincial court at Frankfurt with 'periods of imprisonment which will hurt,' to prevent their 'anti-social behaviour from infecting other citizens'.[44] According to a court

in Munich in a demonstration case, only exemplary punishments 'would be adequate to counteract an increase in mass
crimes'.[45]

After the disturbances at the nuclear power station in Wyhl,
the minister-president of Baden-Württemberg agreed: 'If it
becomes normal for any large-scale project to be faced with
opposition from people with ideological or other interests who
will use force directly or indirectly, this country will become
ungovernable.'[46]

3. 'Anti-State Intentions and Movements'

Alongside the general principle of prevention, what governs the
use of the laws against mass actions is the assessment of the aim
pursued by means of such actions, and this also characterizes
the so-called crimes of expression. What determines whether
words, texts, pictures, films and the like are tolerated or not is
the political effect they produce. Since normally this is only
produced when it is already too late for intervention – in the
audience reaction – the authorities impute to the authors and
distributors of undesirable political arguments an 'anti-constitutional intention', which turns appeals, declarations and descriptions into criminal attempts at 'defamation of the state',
'subversion of its security organs' or expressions of 'approval of
criminal acts'.

This is incorporated in the law by means of phrases which say
everything and nothing. Examples are: 'thereby knowingly give
support to movements' which 'work for' the 'prejudice' of the
'external or internal security' or 'stability' of the state, or the
'elimination, invalidation or subversion of principles of the constitution'.[47]

The term 'movement', which appears in all these laws, and
which, moreover, derives from the anti-socialist law of 1878, is
no less vague than 'give support to' and 'work for'. They are
empty legal formulae which can be given content as required.
Most notably, it is irrelevant whether the 'movements' concerned already exist or have yet to be formed:

Anti-constitutional movements do not need to have reached the stage of planned attacks on a security agency; it is sufficient for there to be a probability of attacks on the constitution as a result of their political effects.[48]

The prosecution of such an 'effect' has nothing to do with a law which punishes guilt; it has been replaced by arbitrariness. The 'anti-constitutional intention' for which, for example, a speaker may be prosecuted has nothing to do with a foreseeable criminal action referred to by the speaker and planned by him; it derives from a 'disturbance', nowhere more precisely defined, which might be caused – if at all – sometime, by someone, by imaginary 'movements', as a result of the speech.

This procedure is taken to an extreme in the most recent crime involving 'danger to the state', the 'anti-constitutional encouragement of criminal acts' (§ 88 StGB), under which penalties are provided not only for the use by a person of words, pictures or publication 'likely' to 'give support to' a 'movement' working for 'anti-constitutional ends', but also for any 'encouragement of others', i.e. third parties, to 'engage in support . . . for movements against . . .'

The prosecutors and judges who will be the users of this new law can now attribute to the authors and distributors of leaflets the same 'far-sightedness' in assessing the intentions and reactions of others that they normally claim when drawing up and justifying indictments.

Anyone who seeks to produce an anti-constitutional effect . . . acts with anti-constitutional intent . . . It is not, however, legally required that the effect of injury to the constitution should be the sole, the chief or the final end of such action. This end may also be a subordinate or incidental aim of the action, provided that the agent intended it.[49]

In the 1950s the Federal High Court ruled against socialists and communists in numerous condemnations of 'inflammatory propaganda endangering the constitutional system'[50] or 'systematic but covert subversion of the structure of the state'.[51]

The use of these sections of the political criminal law then declined during the preparations for the 'new *Ostpolitik*'. The proposed trade with the East was so important to the Social Democrats that in 1968 they even made a call, which today sounds more like a bad joke, for the 'freeing' of the criminal code 'from provisions which impede intellectual confrontation with the communists'.[52]

It was well known that this was merely a tactical move. The opening to the East was accompanied by an all the more severe campaign against the domestic political left. Once *Berufsverbote* began to be practised again in an organized way after 1972 and other areas of state security were extended, the courts dropped their temporary toleration of 'utterances with anti-state intent' or 'opinions constituting a danger to the state'. Since then the number and severity of sentences under section 90a of the Penal Code – 'defamation of the state' – alone has increased as the activity of the state has provoked radical criticism.

But to avoid sentences for calling the Federal Republic a 'repainted Coca-Cola stall' – this too is one of the High Court's judgments[53] – the court in a recent decision has re-defined the criteria for intervention. Since the aim was to protect the state, the first step should be to examine 'whether and to what extent the state' was affected by utterances, 'in what forms and in what outside context the defamation takes place and whether it produces a precise general effect'.[54]

The boundary between criticism which is tolerated and criticism which is condemned can be seen by the sensitive reactions of politicians and political justice to publicly conducted challenges to the forms and effects of the exercise of state authority. The 'security organs' have been declared untouchable, and any attempt to bring light into the twilight in which they operate must be silenced. Official charges of criminal actions against legal officials or the police must be suppressed. These charges are normally relegated to leaflets, improvised newspapers and public meetings, since the press and television usually ignore them, with the connivance of prosecuting authorities, who close any investigation before it gets under way and then frequently reply with an action of their own for 'slander' or the like.

It is risky to publicize and protest against, for example, the fact that in West German prisons – in other words, under the protection of the state – the health and personality of prisoners on remand or under sentence is destroyed, that political prisoners are kept in particularly strict isolation which breaks them physically and mentally, or that breaches of the law by police officers are coming to be accepted practice, and already anyone runs the risk of being a victim of such attacks. Anyone who says this, and offers evidence of it, makes himself liable to a prosecution which those responsible for the situations need have no fear of.

The reversal of the roles of attacker and victim is complete. Anyone who uses the word 'murder' in connection with a policeman can expect a charge of 'defamation' – unless the policeman was the victim. Those who use hard and accurate words are punished; the crimes they describe and denounce are excused or approved: 'anyone who does not regard the servants of the state – judges, soldiers and police officers – as representatives of the community, damages internal security.'[55]

Anyone who makes direct contact with these 'servants of the community' also acts 'with an anti-state intention' and 'in such a way as to endanger security'. This covers anyone who incites police officers not to let themselves be the tools of interests which are not their own and the aims of which they do not know, but which, in the absence of any machinery for political mediation, they must assert by force.

Leaflets and discussions explaining the reasons for and aims of campaigns of resistance such as squatting or Wyhl have had an effect on many police officers, particularly when they connected with their own uncertainties and with existing conflicts within the force. This has been shown not only by reports from Wyhl, but also by a survey conducted by the chiefs of the Frankfurt police in connection with the housing struggle.[56]

A recent judgment of the security chamber of the state court in Berlin must be interpreted in this context. Berlin squatters were found guilty of an 'anti-constitutional attempt to influence public security agencies' (§ 89 StGB). They had distributed leaflets outside an emergency police barracks, calling on the men not to take part in the eviction planned by the Senate, to refuse to work or to report sick. The penalty was a year's imprisonment; 'the defence of law and order requires implementation,' said the court, and a suspension of the sentences was said to be out of the question because of the 'persistently hostile attitude of those convicted towards the state'.[57]

This slippery term 'anti-state intention' was introduced as a 'technical legal device for separating the enemies of the state from the constitutional opposition',[58] which is nothing less than a classical justification of laws against freedom of opinion, the legal exclusion of minorities from citizenship because of their political aims.

Objections on these grounds were rejected by former justice minister von Merkatz with references to the 'existing knowledge acquired by the theory and practice of criminal law':

The claim that the framers of criminal law should treat the same behaviour by two people in the same way without regard to their associated motives and aims is simply incorrect. There are many actions where it is only a particular intention of the agent that brings some morally neutral behaviour within the scope of the criminal law and so makes it criminal. It depends in these cases on an internal action, a subjective attitude of the agent's will sealed within his breast.[59]

To make it possible for the political views and aims of defendants in trials involving 'danger to the state' to be used as a means of 'convicting' them, the Federal High Court has developed a series of techniques for determining the 'anti-constitutional intent' which gives rise to an offence. In the case of 'politicals' no investigation is necessary; 'proof' only becomes difficult 'in the case of a defendant without political affiliations'. In such a case the most important consideration is 'the role [previously] played by the anti-constitutional side in his outward actions, the extent to which he has come into contact with anti-constitutional movements' and so on.[60] 'The details of the defendant's character' should also be examined, 'since these can lead to motives and motives can become aims'.[61] Finally, 'striking coincidence' in time and content with slogans used by anti-constitutional organizations, an 'identity in language', is an indication of an attitude of 'hostility to the state'.[62]

In cases where these inquisitions fail to produce, and the 'inside' remains concealed, the High Court simply uses arguments about a defendant's 'real intention', his 'true and real desires', his 'real' or 'true aims', 'underlying aims' or the 'single dominating basic idea' which every left-winger is known to have in his head and which he only conceals 'to keep the organs of the state in uncertainty for as long as possible'.[63]

This way of 'unmasking enemies of the state' – a practice subsquently made familiar by *Berufsverbot* hearings – was already being recommended in the thirties by the strategist of the campaign against internal enemies, Carl Schmitt. 'The proscription' of political opponents, wrote Schmitt, 'can be carried out in the same way that an absence of peaceable or legal attitudes is presumed in the case of adherents of particular religions or parties'.[64] In other words: you are answerable, not just for what you think, but also for what state security officials 'presume' you may have thought.[65]

This, indeed, is the only way the law can function. If it were necessary 'to demonstrate in every case', complained government spokesman Schafheutle in the legal committee, that an accused 'had the intention of contravening a [principle of the constitution]', the 'practical application of the law would suffer from the impossibility in many cases of proving this'.[66]

But what is meant by 'legal views', and, on the other hand, what is meant by 'taking up a position' against the 'existence', 'security' or the 'principles of the constitution' of the Federal Republic, 'prejudicing' it or 'undermining' it?

It should first be noted that these 'objects of protection' involved in offences causing 'danger to the state' are listed as alternatives, that it is therefore enough to accuse someone of a 'verbal attack' on one of them. 'Prejudice to the existence' of the Federal Republic, i.e. to its sovereignty in international law, is relatively unimportant here; it is the other two 'objects of protection' which are important:

The frequently invoked concept of 'security', which only has to be 'prejudiced', is a formal legal concept, a shell to be filled to suit political requirements.

'What is involved', says the commentary on 'internal emergency', is 'the concept of danger in police law'. 'A danger threatens [security] when there exists a serious danger of its being violated ... This formula derives from police law, and can only be interpreted in terms of police law.'[67]

This remark comes from Theodor Maunz, one of the Federal Republic's leading constitutional lawyers. He knows what he's talking about. In 1943, while still a loyal servant of the Nazis, Maunz wrote enthusiastically of the malleability and flexibility of police law:

The concepts of security, order and danger [have proved] themselves so elastic that they can be used to justify more or less any behaviour of the police which strengthens the community, protects national values and supports social order. This gives them a tactical superiority over their attackers. Hardly a new case appears but the previous rulings [on these concepts] are abandoned and the defence against danger is extended to include the new case.[68]

As regards the 'principles of the constitution', the *Berufsverbote* practised for a long time now between and against SPD members should be enough to show what opinions state security officials regard as conflicting with the 'liberal democratic system'. Specifically, the 'principles of the constitution' in the sense of the offences causing 'danger to the state' are listed in § 92, para. 2 StGB, which explicitly includes the provision for the 'right to exercise parliamentary opposition'. The legal definition of the 'principles of the constitution' as contained in the Penal Code is thus restrictive, in the sense of being tied to the current parliamentary constitution, as the High Court openly declares: the object of protection is 'the liberal democratic form of government'.[69] It follows that the elaboration and propagation of ideas of direct communal, non-parliamentary democracy can infringe the 'principles of the constitution' – 'purposes and activities' are 'directed against the constitutional order' even if they do no more than 'adhere to attitudes' which 'give support to a view of the state opposed to liberal democracy'.[70]

'Subversion' of the 'order' is also involved when such attitudes are encouraged in an attempt to 'turn the people against the organs established by the constitution', 'undermine the recognition of the order by the people and their willingness to come to its defence'. Other examples are 'purely negative' attempts to 'reduce the significance and status of the liberal system and its inviolable validity', to engage in 'propaganda denigrating the Federal Republic' or 'shake the confidence of the people in its political leaders and gradually transform it into hatred and contempt'. 'The intention to create a situation of disorder' is sufficient.[71]

4. The 'Law for the Protection of Communal Peace'

The function of the political criminal law is summed up with exemplary clarity in its most recent product to date, the 'Law for the Protection of Communal Peace'. This law, which was passed unanimously by the Bundestag in January 1976 and came into force on 1 May, puts all previously known or operated measures of advanced state security in the shade.[72] Its purpose, according to the official preamble, is to punish the 'giving of support and approval to violence' by means of words, publications and films 'likely in the circumstances to disturb the public peace'. The aim, according to the Federal minister of justice, is 'to curb violence and its verbal preliminaries'; on 'careful examination a penal vacuum' had been revealed in this area.[73]

Penalties may be incurred by anyone who in the manner specified 'displays, suggests, presents or otherwise makes accessible, produces, procures, supplies, stocks, offers, announces or recommends, seeks to introduce into the area covered by this law or to export from it . . . matter likely to disrupt the peace' in order 'to use it or enable another to use it' with an intention hostile to the state. This is the new Section 88a StGB.

German lawyers had been at work – the jargon and the thoroughness are unmistakable. The measure is unprecedented in Europe, apart from two significant exceptions, the press law imposed on Greece by the military junta in 1969 and Article 1b of the Spanish emergency law of August 1975.[74]

Although the new law consists of several sections, newspaper readers learned only of this one, the 'violence section'. In addition to the introduction of Section 88, four other sections were substantially modified: 'Threatening a crime dangerous to the community', now 'Disturbing the public peace by threats of criminal acts' (126), 'The rewarding or approval of criminal acts' (40), 'Concealing a criminal act from an official' (145d), and 'Threatening another person with a criminal act' (241).[75] One day after the third reading in the Bundestag, the *Frankfurter Rundschau* reproduced in full this provision, and only this one,[76] no doubt to strengthen the impression that things were not that bad – we're not 'violent enemies of the state', and that's all it's about. Maybe, but what counts as 'violent'? Who even today is under suspicion, denounced, prosecuted, as an 'enemy of the state', and who will be tomorrow?

Other legends about the targets of the law were put into circulation: it was necessary in order finally to have a way of punishing people who publicly welcomed deaths such as that of the judge von Drenkmann or distributed publications containing instructions for the manufacture and use of explosives. And – a particular favourite this – fears of legal censorship of literary or historical works were completely unfounded; the law explicitly privileged academic works, art, and historical narrative[77] – but what is 'art', what is 'academic', and who decides in case of doubt?

An inventory of the law in force before these changes in the Penal Code and an analysis of the provisions of the new law show that none of these claims are tenable. It has always been punishable to welcome publicly a death such as that of Judge von Drenkmann (§ 140 StGB, old version, together with § 138, para. 1, No. 6). Encouragement of the production of Molotov cocktails was made an offence by the recently modified weapons law (§ § 37, 53 Weapons Law of 1974).[78] The claim that works dealing with violence in academic, artistic or historical contexts enjoy 'privileges' under the criminal law is an invention of government and opposition propaganda.

This section will not only document this; it will also show how this new law differs from the previously existing provisions, where and in respect of whom a 'prosecution gap' really existed for legal reasons. In other words, it will show who – in spite of all assertions to the contrary – are the people who are regarded as potential 'disturbers of communal peace' and to be punished when political circumstances require.

Political writings and discussions have been made punishable offences not because of the so often invoked 'threat' from 'the terrorists'. It is simply a popular cry which is being used and passed off as the purpose of a measure which would otherwise be very hard to justify.[79]

What is common practice in industry, the threat of punishment for 'disturbing industrial peace', what happens in 'situations where a particular authority prevails' such as prisons and now also universities, the maintenance of the 'prescribed functioning of the institution' by means of administrative laws which make use of *Berufsverbote*, the separation of 'having political views', which is allowed, and 'expressing' them when this is done in a 'hostile way'[80] – this is now to apply to all areas of social life. Seen in this way, genuinely existing gaps are being closed.

Historically, too, the laws for the 'protection of communal peace' have their models, in the anti-socialist law of the last century, the various 'Decrees of the Reich President for the Protection of the German People' of the Weimar period, and in the measures of the Nazis. The purpose of these last was 'to force political life in Germany to return to the forms which correspond to good German custom'[81] – who was prepared to oppose that?

At first sight it looks beautifully idealistic, the fear that mere words could stimulate political activities. On a second look, however, and from the point of view of those who have made these laws, the usefulness of the measures becomes clear. The contradictions of social development are so blatant that it has come to be seen as dangerous for them to be openly expressed.

Maihofer's programmatic slogan for state security, 'Expect the worst; use every weapon against it',[82] was taken up by CDU deputy Eyrich in the legal committee in the discussion of the 'communal peace' law:

We cannot know what the future will bring ... In the present situation particularly we must take care not to give the impression that crimes against communal peace are being taken less seriously ... The legislator must take movements of opinion and tendencies into his considerations.[83]

During a 'security' debate Alfred Dregger made clear the movements to be watched. They were not the hysterically denounced activities of individual militant political groups, but the frightening increase in extra-parliamentary, even anti-parliamentary activities by citizens no longer prepared to let their interests be trampled on by their alleged representatives, whose words and promises no one any longer believes. 'Eventually,' said Dregger,

the political fate of this country will not be decided in parliaments formed by elections, but in the schools, in the colleges of education, in the universities, in the mass media – wherever political opinions are created and shaped.

Precautions had to be taken in good time against these 'dangers to the existence of our liberal democracy'.[84]

The forms of law have been used to give prosecutors an improved capacity for retaliation, and the very title of the law speaks clearly. The 'protection of communal peace', a term applied to the cornerstone of the Nazi legal system – outside the 'community' there was no law – taken in conjunction with 'the protection of the national community' (*Volksgemeinschaft*) reproduces the fascist model of state and society, the denial of social class contradictions and the punishment of even references to them.[85]

The tabooing of the class character, the violent character of social relations, also became crucial to the Federal Republic and the working out of its political conflicts after 1949. This is clear from the history of this state, first and foremost a history of permanent class war directed from above, and from the political programmes which have buttressed it, the framing and application of law whether it took shape under the CDU label of the 'Disciplined Society' or amidst the appeals of the SPD and the unions for 'social partnership' and 'concerted action'.

Even the position of the provisions in the Penal Code indicates their purpose. They are part of political criminal law, and within that in company with well-known sections: 88a ('giving approval to criminal acts out of opposition to the constitution'), between 'anti-constitutional sabotage' (§ 88 StGB) and 'attempting to influence the army and organs of public security against the constitution' (§ 89 StGB); section 130a ('encouragement to commit criminal acts'), in immediate proximity to section 129 ('criminal association') and just beside section 130, which is today called 'Agitation', but until 1960 bluntly 'incitement to class war', a concept described by the standard commentary on the Penal Code as 'sociologically outdated'.[86] The term 'class war' may have been abolished, but what it describes is far from 'outdated' as these laws show their inventors to be well aware. So great is their evident concern about 'internal peace' in the 'community' that they want to use their new law not just to punish 'acts of disruption' but even utterances 'preceding the actual crime of commission'[87] – this is the core of the measure. 'Advocating' means expressing and discussing ideas, verbally sympathizing with a particular course of action, but not the action itself, not practical 'support', which has been a punishable offence for a long time.

The Federal Government had objected to the term 'advocate' in the Bundesrat's draft as 'relatively imprecise',[88] only to introduce it itself four weeks later.[89] All the things it wishes to regard and punish as criminal advocacy of violence were explained by the government spokesman in the legal committee. He went through a revealing catalogue of forms of advocacy which is well worth a second reading, especially by those who mistakenly regard the law as an 'anti-terrorist law':

'First,' said a government spokesman who is now a judge in the Supreme Court for Political Trials,

there is advocacy in the form of an indirect appeal, second advocacy in the form of an apparent distancing of oneself, thirdly the description of criminal actions which invite imitation, fourthly advocacy in the form of giving approval to a historical event with the intention of presenting it as a model to be imitated, fifthly advocacy in the form of an announcement or prediction of acts of violence which invite imitation, and sixthly advocacy of violence in the form of reproduction of the opinions of others in which the author identifies himself with that opinion in order to produce a particular impression.[90]

Action must be taken against the advocacy of violence when the violence is 'presented as something to be welcomed or simply necessary or unavoidable',[91] since 'the dissemination of such statements makes young people in particular more inclined to regard the use of force as a permissible political instrument',[92] a result which is 'socially harmful and dangerous to the community'.[93]

Obviously there will be no action, nor is any intended, if a police chief or interior minister explains why it was 'necessary and unavoidable' for his officers to move against pickets to clear the way into a factory for strike-breakers.

Obviously there should be no action when the Federal Chancellor 'welcomes in the name of the free world' the US army's 'defence' of 'our freedom' in Vietnam or elsewhere with genocide.

Obviously no case will be brought if a mayor tries to explain to his fellow citizens why a speculator has a right to have his house cleared by the police, the tenants put out on the street, and the house then demolished under police protection to make way for a lavish office block.

In other words it is clear that the government will not use these laws to block its own plans. 'We are not concerned here with the general policy on violence,' as justice minister Vogel told party comrades. 'What we are trying to protect is the internal security of our country; we want to keep our discussion free from the germ of violence which is unfortunately spreading even in our midst.'[94]

The violence the advocacy of which is to be 'curbed' by law is – to take only the examples mentioned – the attempts of workers to secure their demands by striking, the struggle of people against centuries of oppression, the resistance of occupants of a house whose home is being destroyed to make a property owner even richer.

There are penalties for anyone who, by means of statements or publications, 'plots' or shows solidarity with such acts of resistance – for what else is 'advocacy'? All that is needed to constitute a crime is the 'likelihood', to be judged 'according to the circumstances', of an utterance to 'disturb' the 'public peace'. In future, it is not just appeals to violence or discussions of violence whose content 'disturbs the public peace' which will be punishable. This causality of statement and effect was still a requirement of the previous formulation of § § 126 and 140 StGB. The law

differs from the current form of the law in not requiring that a disturbance of the public peace should already have taken place. It allows the likelihood to cause a disturbance to suffice ... This means among other things that – in contrast to the current legal position – it is [no longer] required that there should be an appeal addressed at least to a potential audience. A quite general appeal – similar in form to modern radical premises – to commit a criminal offence or to engage in violence will now also be punishable. The aim is to include the advocacy of violence or the committing of criminal acts which is frequently cloaked in the form of theoretical discussion ... In all cases the determining factor will be the general tendency of the material or utterance.[95]

The question whose laws are being sharpened for use against whose violence thus answers itself. It still has to be explained, however, why the Penal Code was given these new sections when a whole range of legal provisions – quite apart from the laws on the 'protection of minors' and assembly – was already available with the declared aim of combating any appeal to or approval of violence. As late as 1973, Section 131 was added to the Penal Code to provide penalties for 'attempts to glamorize or trivialize violence'. In addition, even before the 'communal peace' law, powers were available to call in 'publications with a content such that anyone deliberately distributing them with knowledge of their content would commit a criminal offence' (§ 74d StGB). There was also the prohibition of public incitement to commit criminal actions by means of meetings or publications (§ 111 StGB), irrespective of whether the 'incitement' was successful or unsuccessful, deliberate or accidental. The prohibition of 'threats of a crime which would endanger the community' (§ 126 StGB, old version) included particularly, as well as offences involving arson and explosives, so-called disruptive actions directed against important economic and transport enterprises. The list also includes penalties for 'agitation' (§ 130 StGB); 'attempts to influence a group of people for the purpose of encouraging them to commit acts of violence' (§ 125, para. 1, No. 2 StGB); penalties for failing to report specified crimes (§ 138 StGB), which is treated as equivalent to acceptance, toleration or 'passive advocacy'; penalties for 'giving approval to and rewarding criminal acts' committed by others (§ 140 StGB, old version); 'the illegal threat of physical injury' (§ 240 StGB); and finally 'threatening another with a criminal act' (§ 241 StGB). In addition, the offices of the chief public prosecutors of the states have had attached to them 'centres for combating works which glamorize violence, pornography, and other works likely to endanger young people'.

Public prosecutors needed no instruction in the use of this well-stocked arsenal, but these clauses were invoked against everything but the glorification and trivialization of violence in periodicals, provocative speeches by politicians, or films like *Death Wish*. Numerous complaints were made about this film

99

– a typical example – because it shows in the most repulsive form a poor white American taking the law into his own hands when he feels 'the police no longer guarantee his security. The murder of 'asocial elements' and 'trouble-makers' is given a moderate, sympathetic and very impressive presentation, and the proceedings against the film just mentioned were abandoned for that very reason. According to the public prosecutor's offices in Aachen and Münster, 'the hero acts neither out of crude, merciless feelings nor out of a lust to kill; his motives are rather revenge for the injustice done him and in particular the desire to fight crime'.[96]

The sort of 'crime' the public prosecutors evidently want to see fought, if need be with the help of such spirited citizens, can be seen from the cases brought under these sections, which often ended, and are still ending, with heavy penalties. They are directed at socialist writers and artists, publishers, printers, booksellers, against the 'ringleaders' and 'people behind' demonstrations and strikes, and allege and condemn 'defamation' and 'provocations' arising out of crimes such as 'resistance to state authority', 'breach of domestic peace', 'breach of the peace', 'the formation of a criminal organization', and so on.[97] The searches and confiscations carried out at the premises of the Munich Trikont-Verlag because of their 'Bommi Baumann biography' under laws including § 140 StGB are perhaps the best known of such actions in the recent past.[98] Nevertheless the hitherto existing law was felt by Government and Opposition not to be sufficiently flexible. Because of 'difficulties in its practical application', the use of § 111 StGB ('public invitation to commit criminal acts') has resulted in many investigations, but few convictions. The reason is that Section 111 requires not just general appeals, but specific invitation and the occurrence of a 'disturbance', 'a specific statement of intent to commit specific criminal acts described in legal form'. For the area of the advocacy of criminal acts, 'the Federal Government has suggested the new offence to deal with certain cases which ought to be offences but which are not incitement in the sense of Section 111'. It frequently happened, said the Government, that 'propaganda in favour of violence can be dangerous but nevertheless not fall under § 111 StGB because it [only] creates a general climate in which specific criminal acts could spread. Because of this there must be a seamless interweaving of the present and the proposed law.'

What was proposed was a 'harmonization of mutually supplementary provisions', to provide penalties for an 'advocacy and encouragement of violence at an earlier stage than under [the present] § 111 StGB', that is, for words which are not – as previously required for a prosecution – incitement in the strict legal sense.[99]

In many fields a call to commit criminal acts addressed to an indefinite and indeterminable number of people has a higher degree of danger than an invitation to a single person to commit a criminal act ... In a certain atmosphere a mass can be mobilized by mass media and by skilled people in a more dangerous way than when individuals are induced to commit a particular criminal act ... Appropriate propaganda and appropriate appeals can release and encourage an underlying hatred, [especially in] a group which has been worked up so that its members have lost all control over themselves.[100]

One could hardly have a clearer demonstration that, in contrast to all the assurances, the purpose of this law was not the prosecution of a few 'terrorists', but the prevention of so-called mass crimes and mass activities, the prevention of 'outbreaks of disorder' as a 'blatant case of a disturbance of the peace', as the Government spokesman put it.[101]

These frank words about the real purpose of the legislation were spoken in the legal committee and so remained unknown to the general public. Confusion was not long in coming. Since the ostensible aims of the law which continued to be publicized outside the committees were taken as true, liberal voices were raised, expressing fears of possible restrictions on critical literature: 'Böll for Prison?' was the vogue question. The answer, of course, was 'no', not at least for his *Katharina Blum*. This made the FDP try to smooth the waves by making the purpose of the law clear in an addendum:

Violence as a means of political argument is to be penalized. Individual misbehaviour will not be covered by the law. Collective groups must be regarded as a dangerous source of the use of force in political arguments. This means that the advocacy of violence is dangerous when either a collective group takes this as its aim or when at the beginning an individual calls for violence and as a result a group adopts such a goal.[102]

In having the collective activities on which the FDP statement lays such stress as its central object, the law 'for the protection of communal peace' is in line with the other provisions of the political criminal law. As the Federal High Court observed, 'the measures on danger to the state are concerned with organized forces.'[103]

What is shown by the explanations in the legal committee, and what the FDP emphasized once again, can also be seen in the measures included in the Penal Code to extend and supplement existing law. The most important of these penalizes the approval or advocacy of actions which may take place in the course of mass activities such as demonstrations and strikes and are regarded as 'grave' by current law, first and foremost 'breaches of the peace'. This must be borne in mind when the Government hypocritically states that advocacy of strikes would not be punished under the community peace law if this 'seems unjustified in terms of strike law'.[104]

What this 'strike law' looks like, that is, how strikers can make themselves guilty of offences, and the fact that a 'breach of the peace' has been judged to be 'a typical strike offence',[105] has already been described. Logically, 'breaches of the peace' are now also among the criminal acts listed in the expanded and renamed § 126 StGB, advocacy of which is forbidden by the similarly expanded § 140 StGB ('the approval and rewarding of criminal acts').[106]

The principal aim is thus not to punish 'encouragement' to commit certain actions; the main target is much more commentaries and assessments, the spreading of information about acts of resistance already in progress, which cannot be kept going without public support. A main aim is to punish 'the approval and rewarding' of actions declared to be crimes in so far as such commentaries are likely to 'disturb the public peace' (§ 140 StGB in the new version) by possibly inviting imitation.[107] Every slogan, every placard, leaflet or banner can – but does not have to be – regarded as 'socially harmful' according as the situation offers an opportunity to public prosecutors.

The concentration so far of the debate on the 'communal peace' law on the 'encouragement of violence' has in a way become stranded both on the 'ringleader' fantasies of the opposition and on 'avant-garde' dreams among protesters. What needs to be realized instead is that what the legislators are interested in is depriving supporters of resistance and alternative power of an important weapon, the exchange, discussion and assimilation of experiences, the publicity and public preparation of decisions which is the only basis for effective political work. The creation of alternative media makes it possible to indicate political connections, overcome local limitations, use actions as a means of education and so create a basis for further activities. Bomb attacks, which were much talked about during the discussion of the law, certainly do not come into this category. They are not violent activities whose performance requires a prior wide public discussion; on the contrary, this would make them as impossible to carry out as the announcement of a kidnapping.

There are, on the other hand, activities which depend for their success or failure on public discussion and preparation and supporting commentaries and campaigns. These include strikes to some extent, demonstrations, squatting campaigns or protests such as that in Wyhl. Only the tactics of employers in labour disputes depend on conspiracy and surprise, but a strike not supported by an informed work-force has as little chance of success as a demonstration which is not publicly announced.

The 'encouragement to commit criminal acts' punishable under § 130a StGB has equally little to do with any 'tips on TNT' – why otherwise does the second paragraph of the section refer to 'public gatherings'? It would take a complete fool or an *agent provocateur* to announce public training in bomb-making on the lines of a first-aid course. The real aim is to be able to act against any hints on how empty houses or factories or building sites can be occupied and held, how to organize a strike properly and so on. All the decisions on such cases in recent individual prosecutions and verdicts are now to be made binding on every court.[108]

As regards positions on events abroad, such as declarations of solidarity with liberation movements, here again the decisions of the High Court on the old version of § 140 StGB (the 'approval and rewarding of criminal acts') is clearer than the waffle of many politicians. 'It would be wrong', said the court, 'to dismiss the argument that even giving approval to crimes committed abroad by foreigners which show no evidence of connection with this country can be an [abstract] threat to the German public peace and must therefore be covered by penal sanctions', if giving approval to such 'crimes committed abroad' contributes to the growth of 'general readiness for criminal activity' at home.[109]

The new law also extends the range of forms which count as approving comment on violence and so become liable to prosecution: in addition to the 'public approval' already mentioned in the old § 140 StGB, the new § 140 covers meetings and publications. 'This extension of sanctions seems required', it was claimed, because publications were often formulated 'as though they were theoretical treatises'; it was also necessary to be able to deal with such 'ostensibly academic treatises on the necessity, in order to achieve certain goals, to engage even in criminal actions'.[110]

The alleged privileges enjoyed by works of an academic, artistic or historical character which are constantly cited in this context (see the references to § 86 para. 3 StGB in § § 88a and 130a) are a deception practised on the public which is hardly accidental, a pure piece of sleight of hand.

First, the relevant provision of § 86 para. 3 StGB is a 'social utility' clause; there is no mention of any privileges.[111] And in judicial decisions and legal writing on this problem there are even clearer statements of the sort of writing, the sort of academic work, the sort of art and the sort of history which is 'required' and so deserves protection. The CDU thinks there already exist 'forms of socially harmful teaching and research',[112] and the Federal Administrative Court distinguishes 'art' from 'non-art', as it does 'science' from 'unscientific activity'. Whether an individual case is a 'serious work of art' or a piece of academic work which enjoys the protection of the constitution is a decision for the courts.[113] If we wonder what sort of judicial decisions may be expected as a result of the new law, we should remember the references in the preamble to the bill to 'ostensibly academic treatises', 'theoretical camouflage' and historical events given approval 'with an intention of imitation'. During his exposition of the 'community peace' law, public prosecutor and SPD deputy Müller-Emmert gave a demonstration of the detective flair and inventive genius of his legal colleagues. He spoke of the need to prosecute the 'numerous theoretical treatises which' – note well – 'judged from the outward content', merely described 'the course of revolutions in the past, but at a deeper level call for revolutions to be carried out here with comparable methods'. Such 'covert advocacy of the use of force', he said, made very clever use of 'complicated and cunningly devised mechanisms'.[114]

Secondly, a book may be confiscated even if, in the opinion of the public prosecutor, 'elements derived from it' might be 'likely' to move 'others' to undertake 'anti-constitutional' activity. The investigation of the possibility in suspicious cases will certainly be assisted by a good many house searches.

Thirdly, press freedom to report current events has long been guaranteed by the constitution – not, however, without limit, but under the express provision that 'general laws' may withdraw this basic right (Art. 5, para. 2, GG), one of these 'general laws' now being the 'communal peace' law. This is another mark of the West German constitution, its additional cover – the original meaning of basic rights, that they should limit all other rights, is turned into the opposite in the Basic Law:

According to the constant view of the Federal Constitutional Court, general laws are all those which do not prohibit an opinion as such, are not directed against the expression of the opinion as such, but rather serve to protect a legal right which needs protection without reference to a particular opinion, to protect a communal value which takes priority over the exercise of freedom of opinion.[115]

Fourthly, the Federal Constitutional Court long ago gave a final decision on 'communal values which need protection' and the extent of 'academic freedom' – in its 1956 judgment on the KPD ban:

The clearly definable boundary between academic theory, which is protected by Article 5 paragraph 3 of the Basic Law, and the political aims of a party, which are subject to evaluation under Article 21, Paragraph 2 of the Basic Law [unconstitutionality], falls where the knowledge a party derives from study is taken into its will and is turned into motivation for its political action.[116]

So that is where 'academic work' stops being 'value-free study' and where 'subversion' begins. It is an idea which has been generously and inventively developed in the most recent decisions of the administrative court, an exercise in which the courts are trying to outdo each other as though there had never been – even in bourgeois history and philosophy of science – clear statements of the social determination of the development and use of theory. The courts will make good use of these decisions.

And fifthly and finally, even if these facts are firmly ignored, and it is still claimed that art, science and history are privileged, even if significance continues to be allowed to the 'social utility clause' in Sections 88a and 130a – there is nothing about this in the revised section 140 ('approval of criminal acts already committed'). In case of doubt, reports, approving, informative, sympathetic, about Wyhl, Lip (in France), the Frankfurt housing struggle, Erwitte, strikes or other resistance campaigns, and leaflets or meetings about them are always 'socially harmful' and 'dangerous to the community', but never 'socially useful'. In all the talk about Section 88a this should not be forgotten.

The Federal Republic has previously had provision for prosecuting the authors, distributors and readers of unpopular political writings, § 93 StGB (old version), which was repealed in 1968. Its text was as follows:

§ 93 – Writings which Constitute a Danger to the State
Anyone who produces, copies or distributes writings, sound recordings, diagrams or pictures the content of which might create or encourage movements with the aim of prejudicing the existence of the Federal Republic of Germany or of eliminating or nullifying a principle of the constitution in order to suppress democratic freedom...

This provision, introduced into the Penal Code in 1951, was faced from the very beginning with wholesale criticism, in particular from the Social Democrats. In 1968 they moved in the Bundestag that § 93 should be dropped:

It makes possible infringements of the freedom of information which is rooted in the Basic Law, since a clear line between dangerous writings in the sense of § 93 and the permissible exercise of freedom of opinion by means of critical utterances can be drawn only with difficulty, and may be judged differently as political attitudes change. The task of evaluating such writings in terms of the criminal law may lead the judiciary to go outside its province. It ought not to be the function of the courts to take the initiative in political matters and to take far-reaching political decisions.[117]

Well, well. Today, as the governing party and themselves the target of radical criticism, the Social Democrats take a very different view. They have not just restored the old position, but toughened it up.

Apart from its title the wording of the old § 93 StGB resembles the new § 88a. The two laws differ considerably, however, in one important point: the new § 88a goes further. Whereas the former § 93 explicitly required that the content of the writings itself must be 'a danger to the state' – it 'is not sufficient', commented the High Court on this point, 'that the work should be merely likely to encourage anti-constitutional movements'[118] – precisely this does now suffice for action to be taken against authors, distributors, sellers, readers, etc., of such works, or against speakers. It was the SPD and FDP deputies who brought about this significant extension of the scope of the law in the legal committee by loosening the definition of the offence.[119]

A look back at the ominous decisions of the High Court under the comparatively harmless Section 93 in the old version gives an idea of what public prosecutors and courts 'according to the varying circumstances' may think up as a 'suitable' way of dealing with the left. As an illustration, here are some examples of the High Court's decisions under the Section 93 dropped in 1968:

The definition of the offence does not presuppose that the producer, distributor, etc., approves of the content of the work as such, that is, fundamentally agrees with it ... It is sufficient that he should think it possible that the content is anti-constitutional and nevertheless distribute, propagate etc., the work, in other words, give approval to the performance of the act (as defined in § 93) by putting up with it or tolerating it.[120]

Putting up posters constitutes distribution in the sense of § 93 StGB when it is done in generally accessible places.[121]

The reproduction or dissemination of 'the ideas of others in the form of speeches, political programmes, etc.' constitutes a danger to the state when

the intelligent reader can tell, from all the circumstances relevant to the effect of the work, that the reproduction of another's text is combined with the adoption of its anti-constitutional aims. Therefore, in the case of a work which reproduces the ideas of another it will depend, in addition to the text, on the external presentation, emphases in the type, on titles, but above all on the significance the ideas reproduced could have for a reader in the Federal Republic.[122]

In the assessment of the content of a work permitted and required under § 93 StGB account must therefore be taken also of ideas which the intelligent reader can recognize even if they are only present between the lines.[123]

Whether the new law will bring a wave of convictions in its train remains to be seen. The Damoclean sword of the possibility of investigations and confiscations by public prosecutor's offices at any time is often a much more effective means of intimidation. It is certain that because of this the prosecuting authorities will make ample use of this new instrument. Herr Schmude, secretary of state in the Federal Ministry of the Interior, has already announced it: one of 'the main areas of police work in the future', he said, would be that of the protection of the 'communal peace'.[124]

5. 'Organizations Which Threaten the State'

A state security law designed to oppose politically effective slogans and campaigns – that is, those which can be repeated or invite imitation – must necessarily be directed at organized, collective attempts to create an alternative public and alternative power.

'The individual', explains the Constitutional Court, will

not be affected by political criminal law when he himself seeks and supports certain political goals ... His action becomes dangerous as a result of the effect produced by an organization ... Defensive measures are [therefore] not directed at the action of the individual as such but at the organizational support connected with it.[125]

The commentary on the state security law of 1951 puts it bluntly: 'The dangers which threaten the civil order stem from people as members of a collective, or organizations.'[126]

One of the main criminal provisions for the repression of organized action is § 129 StGB, 'formation of criminal organizations', known in the 1950s as 'underground organizations', by the Nazis as 'anti-state combinations', and at a still earlier period, 'combinations contrary to the civil order' or 'prejudicial to the state'.[127]

§ 129 StGB provides penalties for 'anyone who forms an organization the purposes or activity of which are directed to the committing of criminal acts, or anyone who takes part in such an association as a member, publicizes it or supports it'. Particularly severe penalties threaten 'ringleaders' and 'organ-

109

izers',[128] though police 'V-men' enjoy an informer's privilege.[129]

Whether a case under § 129 is brought, and in which court, lies in the political discretion of the state's supreme prosecutor: in 'cases of particular importance' the Federal Attorney-General may take over the case or suspend it 'if the prosecution is against public interests'.[130] In other words, considerations of political opportunism decide the use of § 129 StGB, and judicial decisions follow suit. The courts have always been against collective left-wing activities, in the Weimar period to such an extent that it was remarked sarcastically that it could only be a question of time before the Supreme Court declared the whole labour movement a criminal organization.[131]

In the practice of the Federal High Court too during the first peak of anti-communist persecution in the 1950s, there was no socialist or communist organization with any political influence which did not face charges of being an 'underground organization' which had repeatedly spread 'opinions constituting a danger to the state'. The official collections of High Court decisions reveals only one judgment against a right-wing group under § 129 StGB.

Even today the picture is still the same – dog won't eat dog. Even militant fascists have nothing to fear – at most they are dismissed patronizingly as 'political hot-heads' and handled by the law with kid gloves.[132]

In the second leftist hunt currently in progress § 129 is again being increasingly used. One factor making trials easier is that the law does not presuppose an 'organization', with a structure fixed by rules. The external organizational form is completely insignificant. The Federal High Court has consistently ruled that even 'a loose association with no vertical structure' satisfies the definition.[133] The only requirement is a recognizable desire jointly to pursue joint political aims and interests, a 'sense of organization', as the High Court puts it, since this is what gives the 'mere "individual fighter"' the increased potential for danger which comes from organized enemies of the constitution'.[134]

In the High Court's conspiracy theory such a flexible mode

of application is necessary to deal with the 'division of labour' adopted by the 'enemies of the constitution':

One participant practises an activity whose anti-constitutional character is immediately obvious, while another carries on agitation disguised in general political aims and a third engages in tasks of a purely technical nature.[135]

The concept of 'support' is also given an indefinitely broad sense by the High Court, which, following a proposed Nazi reform,[136] equates it with participation in a 'criminal organization': 'Support is assistance from a non-member of the organization which by developing its own autonomy has become guilt.' It is sufficient

if the organization is aided, and especially strengthened, in its aims and activity, or if its work is made easier. On the other hand, the concept of organization does not entail that the organization should demonstrably have received measurable benefit for its political aim as a result of the defendant's action. The defendant gives support if his help is effective in itself and in any way beneficial to the organization.[137]

This 'definition' immediately makes it possible to keep watch on and take action against an indeterminate range of people, 'suspects', in the words of the security officials, 'who might themselves commit offences'.[138] This is the famous ring of 'sympathizers', who are pursued, not just for some political reflections they have engaged in, but because of feelings they are 'presumed' to have.

To 'observe this scene', following on the Lorenz hunt, the police developed their own computer programme, which also takes in the 'environment' – 'in the broadest sense of this word', as West Berlin police commissioner Hübner explained.[139]

The charge of belonging to 'a criminal organization', 'publicizing' it or 'supporting' it 'in any way' is quickly constructed, and justifies telephone surveillance, observation, house searches, confiscations, interrogation and imprisonment, guilt by association, collective liability – in short, arbitrariness is the unwritten rule in the application of § 129 StGB. 'Organizations' in whose existence only public prosecutors believe are made the basis of criminal actions or provide the necessary pretext for keeping people out of the way on remand for unlimited periods. The statutory maximum remand period of six months is vastly exceeded, and this is then turned against the victims when they complain: why do they refuse to be helpful in their investigations, to produce the evidence which the authorities are clumsily trying to find? Why do they persist in denying the charges against them instead of giving up and admitting? Why do they keep quiet if they have nothing to keep quiet about? These and similar methods of 'incrimination' simply transfer the burden of proof: people who have been put in prison now have to justify their being there.

In case of doubt, judges who want to imprison can fall back on the danger of 'collusion' or escape to justify detention on remand, and references to obscure 'organizations' and people 'behind the scenes' keep things going as long as public prosecutors' political calculations demand. A more recent pretext is suspicion of membership of 'a group of a terrorist nature'.[140]

In interpreting § 129 prosecutors and courts have for some time been going back to the idea of 'ideological assistance', an idea which the 1968 criminal law reform sought to exclude, in view of the practice of the fifties and sixties. In the minutes of the Legal Committee of 1968 we find that in future 'simply promoting ideas by ideological utterances' would no longer constitute 'the formal act of "supporting" ',[141] while the same committee today regards as 'significant evidence' of support 'attendance at meetings and activities' of various organizations, participation in 'votes and resolutions', 'subscription to periodicals, the keeping of publications or of material for producing publications, the composition and distribution of publications'. It is totally immaterial 'whether the defendant received instructions from the organization for his act of support or whether he acted on his own initiative'.[142]

In doing this the Legal Committee had only brought together all the refinements made by court decisions since § 129 StGB to the notions of 'setting up', 'supporting' and 'publicizing'. The

Provincial court in Berlin, for example, imposed a suspended sentence of nine months on the publisher Klaus Wagenbach for 'unsuccessful incitement for the formation of a criminal association'. The instrument of the 'crime' was a book, *Uber den bewaffneten Kampf in Westeuropa* ('On the Armed Struggle in Western Europe'), by the RAF collective. The Berlin public prosecutor's office had claimed that the book, whose arguments had been praised by reviewers, was an 'unsuccessful invitation to commit acts of high treason', which was going too far even for the court, which found the feature of precision absent from the 'revolutionary plan'. Arguments under § 129 StGB, however, were easily found. The book was not only said to lay 'the theoretical foundations for a revolutionary theory', but also engaged in 'political agitation with immediate aims in the Federal Republic', and was also on sale in the bookshops.[143]

The lawyer Klaus Croissant was excluded from the rest of the defence at the Stammheim trial because he was accused of 'supporting a criminal organization'. The association in question was his clients, who had themselves not yet been convicted of being a 'criminal organization'. The Stuttgart court's accusation against the lawyer claimed that even before their arrest his attitude 'to this criminal group and its revolutionary aims' had been 'at least not negative'. He was said to have 'imitated, in the form and content of his statements, the language of the criminal organization,' and to have addressed his clients familiarly, and used their first names. Another charge was that he had arranged an interview with the defendants in *Der Speigel*, 'aimed at the sympathizer scene and intended to reach and influence those of like mind among them and outside the Federal Republic'. *Der Spiegel*, the 'vehicle' of this 'publicity for an act of subversion', was not prosecuted. These 'incidents' had removed 'the panel's doubts whether the agreement and support was merely linguistic or also practical'; Croissant's further appearance at Stammheim was said to contravene the new defence counsel exclusion ruling of § 138a StPO, which had finally been passed in 1974 and was meant to be used.[144] The Federal Attorney-General's office struck again a few weeks later, and succeeded with the same arguments in obtaining a warrant for Croissant's arrest. By means of 'numerous public demonstrations, press statements and similar campaigns inside and outside the Federal Republic', he was said to have tried 'to arouse international interest in the members of the criminal association and their ostensible political aims'.[145] These demonstrations were an attempt by defence counsel to inform at least the foreign public of the conditions in which his clients were being kept in prison, in order to break through the wall of silence with which the judicial authorities had tried to surround the matter.

The security division of the Provincial Court in Karlsruhe used similar arguments to convict a woman student and a doctor for 'conspiring to publicize a criminal organization'. They had distributed leaflets describing the RAF's solitary confinement and putting forward the group's political reaction to it. In the view of the authorities this was 'calculated to turn others towards the aims of the "RAF" ', and was indeed 'a particularly subtle approach'. The severity of the punishments – six and nine months' imprisonment – was determined by 'the particularly dangerous character – known to both defendants – of this criminal organization and by the need to deter the accused and influence other people prepared to engage in similar actions'.

The sentence was suspended

in order to give the defendants, who had no previous convictions, an opportunity to earn a pardon by law-abiding conduct. There was nothing to show how ready the accused are to re-engage in activities of this kind. Indeed, the court ventures to express the expectation that the accused will not let themselves be involved in further offences. They have been made clearly aware of the consequences of such actions.[146]

The High Court took a completely different view. It was unwilling to take the risk, and overruled the lower court after the public prosecutor had appealed, arguing that there were no grounds for suspension:

The Provincial Court gave both defendants a favourable social prognosis. It also took the view that the defence of the rule of law does not require the carrying out of the sentences. Even in regard to the first assumption, the Provincial Court's arguments are open to many serious objections ... The defendants are not criminals who realize their offence and who can be expected to respect and follow the words of a court. No, they are what has been called convinced criminals, who regard the court as the representative of the state whose overthrow is their goal and who by and large cannot be expected to be influenced by a conviction towards observing the laws in future.

The view 'that the distribution of the leaflets was a less danger-ous form of publicity' was also false, the prosecutor argued. The Provincial Court

should firstly have recognized that the activity of the criminal organization which the accused publicized is directed precisely towards undermining the people's regard for the law ... Publicity for these aims [was created] in a dangerous form. The accused did not limit themselves to speaking to individuals in private, but by means of the leaflets sought to make contact with large numbers of people, and principally with young people, who are easily influenced in this way. The action was also of a kind particularly likely to endanger public peace ... The Provin-cial Court should have taken account of these points in its con-siderations and should have asked itself whether, in view of the dangerous increase in terrorism in recent years, a suspension of the sentence may not give rise to misinterpretation and also contribute to a decline in public confidence in the effectiveness of the admin-istration of justice. Nor should the possibility of imitation by poten-tial criminals be ignored. Whether the sentence on the accused will remain largely unknown is not important; what is important is the effect it will inevitably have on people who do know of it.[147]

Two events show the direction in which the use of § 129 StGB has since been extended. The public prosecutor's office opened an investigation into the Frankfurt women's centre's organization of transport to Dutch abortion clinics (*prima facie* 'formation of a criminal organization' to commit offences under § 218 StGB), and the High Court has ruled against squatting. The effect is to stigmatize as 'gang behaviour' any campaigns of resistance or self-help which are collectively organized and make an impact on the public, together with preparatory work on them or solidarity with them.

The state security court in Hamburg had convicted six workers, five school pupils, a student and an industrial salesman who had taken part in a squat of 'breach of domestic peace', 'breach of the civil peace' and 'resistance to state authority', but not of being a 'criminal organization', as the prosecution had asked. The prosecution appealed to the High Court and was successful: 'The squatters,' said the court's judgment, 'constituted a criminal organization in the sense of § 129 StGB.' A 'loose combination' was sufficient to constitute an offence, and there was clear evidence of this

at least in the case of the organizing group. It is shown notably in the formation of a house council or 'Eckhofstrasse 39 Committee', the production of leaflets, the setting up of an information centre and the measures taken for the defence of the house ... The setting up of a system of lookouts and of a radio centre completes the picture of resolute mobilization. [All] those who took part in the occupation had a common aim, to bring the house under their control as a way of demonstrating against failures in house-building, the level of rents and the housing shortage, and also against the lack of community facilities in new developments and the isolation resulting from this. In all this they regarded themselves as a single organization ... The fact that committing offences was not the ultimate purpose of the organization is immaterial. It is sufficient for the activity of an organization to be directed towards the performance of criminal actions as a means to some end. The criminal nature of a grouping formed for the purpose of committing offences in the future follows from the disregard for the law shown by its members and supporters in misusing the right of freedom of association. They collectively flout the principles of order laid down by the criminal law.

The measures adopted by the squatters

were intended by them as means to the end of attracting the attention of the public. Consequently they are not of minor importance in comparison with the breach of domestic peace; indeed they fulfilled the function of a demonstration. Without them interest in the squat would soon have died ... The occupation lasted almost five weeks ... As far as the squatters were concerned, it would have lasted longer, had not the police put an end to the illegal situation.

The judgment appealed against, said the court, completely misunderstood this situation. 'The Provincial Court's condemnation of the squatters' actions fails to appreciate its significance as a massive infringement of internal security.'

The defendants discovered during the clearing of the house by the police – they were arrested and remanded in custody – should, said the High Court, be convicted of 'support for a criminal organization' in a new trial because 'since a criminal organization existed, the defendants supported this organization by their actions. They stayed in the house on many occasions and by their presence encouraged those who had decided to defend the house in their will to resist.'[148]

Severe penalties for squatters were also recommended by a court in Bielefeld, 'to make an impression on the defendants, but especially to preserve the sense of law and order of those of the population who are still [!] law-abiding'.[149]

In summer 1976 the Bundestag passed a supplement to § 129 StGB. This was § 129a, which prescribed penalties for the 'formation and support' of a 'particularly dangerous criminal' or 'seriously criminal' organization,[150] so as to improve measures for dealing with 'crimes which are particularly dangerous to internal security'.[151]

Since the High Court had already done its bit, it was now 'the particular responsibility of the legislature to make its contribution to supporting the Government and the organs of justice in the performance of their tasks'.[152] The most important instance of this was the radical alteration of the rules of criminal procedure made at the same time as the passing of the new § 129a. Section 112 of the Code of Criminal Procedure was widened to make the suspicion that a person belonged to a 'particularly criminal organization', 'supported' it or 'publicized' it mandatory grounds for imprisonment. The purpose of

117

this equation of § 129a with crimes such as murder, manslaughter or genocide was, according to the terse explanation given by the SPD and FDP, to ensure 'that the judge will be able to issue a warrant in all cases in which a temporary period of custody seems appropriate'. This 'has hitherto not always been possible, particularly when grounds such as the danger of flight or collusion could not be demonstrated with sufficient force.'[153] The new measure was at long last recognizing the lesson of 'recent experience', 'that the resources for combating the activities of these criminal gangs must be further refined and extended'.[154]

5. Political Trials

1. 'Selected' and 'Reliable' Judges

A feature of political criminal law is its rag-bag of unspecific legal terms and vague phrases: 'support', 'advocate', 'induce', 'give approval to', 'movement', 'promote a willingness in others', 'subvert', 'reprehensible', 'undermine', 'likely in the circumstances', 'security', 'public peace', 'deliberately', 'work for', 'disturb', etc. These schemas of offences were plausibly justified by former Federal Attorney-General Wagner. He claimed that state security law had to deal with 'events and phenomena which by their nature cannot have a constant shape or structure, but are like viruses. For this reason it is very hard to reduce them to the normal, clearly defined formulas of legal language.'[1]

Liberals have constantly criticized this situation – most recently in the case of the 'communal peace' law – and have invoked the requirement of precision of Article 103 of the Basic Law in support of their demand for 'great legal safeguards' and more predictability. For all their correctness, however, these criticisms fail to touch the real point of political criminal law. Its *raison d'être* is to have definitions flexible enough to allow every new set of 'enemies of the state' to be labelled and fought at any time, or, more accurately, as the occasion demands.[2]

Both the Constitutional Court and the Federal High Court have also decreed this to be a necessary means for the performance of the political task of state security legislation: 'Not even criminal law can avoid using general terms which need additional interpretation by a judge. They are indispensable ... If such fluid terms were not used, the legislators would be unable to control the complexity of life'[3] – or, in plain English, to control the way the masses organize their lives. Federal prosecutor Träger, the prosecutor in the Stammheim trial, agreed:

We cannot rely solely on the formal definitions of the penal provisions of the state security legislation to ensure successful defence
against the numerous attacks on our constitution. These are only the
raw materials, inherently liable to provoke controversy as a result
of the constantly shifting conflicts of interest on the political stage,
and have to be applied as effective, living law.[4]

Not every court is called upon to do this, to interpret the
'fluid concepts' or draw out the 'values underlying the rules'.
The 'weighty and finally conclusive details' are not left to any
common or garden judge to determine.[5] As 'part of a healthy
legal system', they are left 'in the hands of a conscientious,
aware and select body of judges who are willing to accept responsibility', as one of the authors of the political criminal law
assured parliament during the debate.[6]

'Why', asked a ministry spokesman, later to become president
of the state security panel in the High Court,

Why cannot a German judge share in a certain measure in the
general political responsibility? Why, when a norm is not completely formulated, can he not use his creative intuition to elaborate
it into the decisions and principles which, flexibly applied to the
changing needs of the times, ensure the necessary minimum of legal
security?[7]

The judges meant here are those of the special courts responsible for political cases, the '74a courts' which exist in some
states, named after the relevant section of the law on judicial
organization (§ 74a GVG). This section provides for certain
cases to be heard in special courts, before 'suitably experienced
judges' who possess a 'special competence to take decisions in
this field' which 'not every judge can be expected to possess'.
The cases concerned include those against 'unconstitutional
organizations', charges of 'distributing unconstitutional propaganda', 'anti-constitutional sabotage', 'anti-constitutional advocacy of offences', 'undermining the loyalty of the armed
forces to the constitution', 'defamation of the state and its
symbols', 'forming and supporting a criminal organization'. It is

the task of these state security courts – 'a task not within the competence of everyone' – to ensure that the law 'in this special field' is 'reliably' applied, that 'standards are set' and 'experience collected' in order to avoid 'the fragmentation of the law which might otherwise occur'.[8]

2. Lawyers and Prosecutors

The principles of state security legislation are implemented with the help of procedural regulations which determine not only the outcome but also the conduct of political trials, generally automatically to the detriment of the defendants. Defendants, their lawyers and the public prosecutors are given very unequal roles, and they may be compelled to keep to them if it proves necessary. Already the conduct of political trials, the Bundestag was told, is 'part of the general task of crime prevention',[9] i.e. of deterrence and intimidation.

'The complex problems with which state security is now confronted on an increasing scale,' said Federal Prosecutor Träger, discussing these show trials, 'show how necessary it is to demonstrate the effectiveness of our state security laws against attacks from within and to show their power by the public condemnation of apprehended criminals'[10] – not, for example, to prove their guilt.

In the last three years a number of major changes in trial procedure have considerably extended the powers of the prosecuting authorities at the expense of the accused. They have been granted rights which previously only judges enjoyed. Since the beginning of 1975, for example, defendants, witnesses and experts have been obliged to obey summonses from the prosecution; they can be compelled to make statements to the prosecutor, and there is no right, as there is with questioning by a judge, to have a lawyer present.[11] Prosecutors may examine all documents they pick up in searches, they can confiscate and open letters.[12] 'It seems right,' explained a statement on the change by the Federal Government, 'to give public prosecutors, who are judicial officers with an obligation to objectivity and justice, the powers they need to perform their legal task more effectively than in the past.'[13]

The withholding of such wide-ranging powers from prosecutors for so long was said to be the result of a prejudice which could be explained historically, 'the suspicion of the legislators of 1877 of what was then the new office of public prosecutor' ... After a hundred years of history this had now 'proved to be unfounded': 'The public prosecutor service, as a judicial organ attached to the third power, is itself a guarantee that it will make fair and correct use of the rights granted to it.'[14]

With this blinkered historical argument the prosecuting authorities have now been given the formal control of the judicial process which – in security cases at least – they have always possessed in practice. If proof is needed, there are the 'reasons of security' they advance, which decide whether, in what conditions and for how long political offenders shall be detained in custody, and have in practice nullified legal regulations and powers. There are the well-oiled institutionalized links with the police and secret services which enable the prosecutors to guide any investigation in the desired direction, break it off, suspend it and reopen it. There is the refusal to produce important documents and the production of selected witnesses with coordinated and limited statements, which enable the state security officials to control the range and effect of the evidence given at the trial itself.[15] And finally there is the complicated game of arguing that 'x' is 'common knowledge'. The prosecution can imply anything it likes as proved of the defendants without having to fear the production of contrary evidence if it claims that its assertions are 'common knowledge' or 'known to the court'. Under Section 244 of the Code of Criminal Procedure, an application by the defence to call evidence in rebuttal can be rejected 'if the fact to be proved is irrelevant to the verdict or already proved', or if the application is made 'for the purpose of delaying the proceedings'. In the determination of historical data or physical quantities such an approach is, of course, straightforward. In state security trials, however, which involve political estimates and judgments, it is quite different.

'I frequently saw the evidence begin,' reported Posser from his time as a lawyer in political trials, 'with the reading of a huge list: "It is known to the court that such and such an organization is an anti-constitutional organization. It is known to the court that such and such an organization is a criminal organization with such and such aims," and so on.'[16] The presentation of further detailed evidence on these matters is then declared superfluous. A defendant 'incriminated' in this way by association with this assortment of 'well-known facts' is as good as convicted – how could he or she not have known what is common knowledge to every state security court?

This simplification of evidence and hearing is also used today, for example in the case mentioned above brought against the distributors of leaflets on solitary confinement. The judgment read: 'All members of the court are aware ... and it also follows from the binding judgment of the Düsseldorf Provincial Court (IV 12/71 of 15.3.72) against a previous member of this group that the "Red Army Faction" (previously the Baader-Mahler-Meinhof group) is a criminal organization,'[17] and concluded that the leaflets were therefore criminal 'publicity' for it.

'Common knowledge' under § 244 StPO was first introduced in 1935, when the Nazis gave it as a handy tool to their state security service. When it was taken into the West German criminal procedure in 1950, it was also declared admissible in political cases.[18]

State security trials have been turned into a complete farce by the extension of the prosecuting authorities' powers which came into force on 1 January 1975. Under this, counsel who do not limit their activity to a plea for clemency and defendants who invoke the Federal Republic's official title of 'constitutional state' may be removed from the proceedings on the ground that they are obstructing the 'orderly administration of justice', and practising 'procedural sabotage'. Their further presence – despite the 'legal hearing' occasionally guaranteed in the constitution (Art. 103 GG) – is declared unnecessary, and then, to preserve the façade, the trial is allowed to run to the con-

clusion dictated by public prejudice with the dummy figures of
the lawyers appointed by the court. 'Justice must look like justice' was the *Frankfurter Allgemeine's* comment.[19]

The much praised 'freedom of the legal profession' and the
right to an unrestricted choice of confidential defenders have
been as good as abolished. The joint defence of a number of
accused is forbidden even when they are accused, as a group, of
'criminal association', that is to say, the prosecution uses a
block charge. Correspondence between lawyers and their clients
in custody can be held up and inspected. The right to issue
statements not in direct connection with an application to the
court has been quashed, depriving accused and defenders of the
chance to issue or repeat statements about the political motivation of particular actions or about the background of the trial at
the stages they choose and without hindrance from the prosecution.[20]

These measures were pulled across the parliamentary stage in
a few days, after the public had been rehearsed by propaganda
to perfection. Lawyers who tried to defend the few rights left to
their clients were summarily labelled with the terms of the
indictment, and had to endure such descriptions as 'criminal
lawyers who are nothing but criminals themselves'.[21] Federal
Attorney-General Buback declared 'accepting such briefs' to be
'unprofessional',[22] and an official of the Hesse Criminal Investigation Bureau took the choice of defender of some recently
arrested suspects as an admission of guilt: 'Now that these
lawyers are involved, we know we have got the right people.'[23]
Defence lawyers who refuse to become accomplices or puppets
of the security authorities face criminal proceedings or charges of
professional misconduct. The authorities' aim is to get a *Berufsverbot* issued against them, which will get awkward lawyers
off their backs, not just for the length of a trial but for ever.[24]

3. Political Offenders

One of the achievements of the bourgeois revolution was to
give political offenders a privileged position in criminal pro-

ceedings and penalties, not to treat them as people who had acted for personal reasons, but as defeated enemies, who had fought in an unequal struggle for a political conviction. In this attitude the bourgeoisie showed a certain respect for one of the means of political conflict through which they themselves had come to power, force.

This privileged status accorded to political opponents was gradually withdrawn and turned into the opposite as the former allies of the bourgeoisie took them at their word and refused to be content with the results of the bourgeois revolution. In Germany the privileged position of political offenders was institutionalized in the 'fortress confinement' of section 17 of the Imperial Criminal Code, which was nevertheless retained to the end of the Weimar Republic. It was the Nazis, whose Führer, as is well known, was able to commit his programme to paper during such a period of confinement in Landsberg, who in effect abolished it. 'It was', they said,

little more than considerations of pure expediency on the part of a political system marked by cowardice which gave privileges to political criminals: 'Victory is never sure; the wheel may turn.' These ideas dominated our criminal law and judicial decisions until the National Socialist Revolution of 1933 . . . The purpose of our criminal laws is to protect the national community. Every act is punished in proportion to the degree of injury or threat to the national community and to the degree of atrocity. The most serious attack on the national community consists in committing one of the so-called political offences. For this reason the penalty of fortress confinement must be removed from the current Penal Code.[25]

Here too, federal state security law, designed to protect 'communal peace', left things as they were. First, in a borrowing from Nazi sentencing practice, political offenders were legally disadvantaged by the introduction, for particular offences ranging from 'resistance to state authority', 'violation of privacy', 'breach of the peace' to 'crimes involving danger to the community', of an optional increase in the penalty if, in the view of the court, the action had been performed 'with deliberate hostility towards the state'. This was contained in

§ 94 StGB, which was repealed in 1968 and not replaced.[26] There remained the 'negative privileges' of the accused. They are described as political offenders, because they commit a two-fold offence. Not only do they despise the laws in force; they also despise the rules under which they are called to account. In the words of the High Court decision on 'convinced offenders', they replace 'the community's order of values' with one of their own, 'behaviour which is regarded by the community as contemptible', if 'the underlying conviction is not in accord with the moral law'.[27] Particularly dangerous are the accused who 'hold passionately to their belief and are ready at any moment to resume the struggle'; these are 'convinced offenders who are not resocializable in the normal sense'.[28] Since they cannot be made to conform by normal penalties, attempts are made to break them by special treatment. In the view of the state security courts, their 'unreasonableness' and 'stubbornness', their 'hostility to the law', their 'court behaviour', and finally the nature of the acts with which they are charged, justify special restrictions during pre-trial custody, an increase in the penalty at sentence and immediate implementation of the sentence. The High Court decision on the leaflet distributors already mentioned and the judgment on the Berliners for 'undermining the morale of the forces' are examples from a wealth of such decisions in security cases.[29] Nevertheless, the following case exceeds the hitherto known bounds of justice based on opinions.

Peter-Paul Zahl was put on trial in 1974 for trying to escape during a police 'identity check'. Two policemen followed him and fired twelve shots. Zahl was wounded in both arms. While running he fired back and wounded a policeman.

The prosecution brought a charge of 'attempted murder' and asked for a prison sentence of twelve years. The court did not agree. It found Zahl guilty of 'prolonged resistance to officers carrying out their duty in a particularly serious case, combined with grievous bodily harm', and sentenced him to four years. The court found that Zahl had shot at the officers pursuing him without any intention of killing, and that there were no grounds for a murder charge. The judgment went on to say that

quite apart from his avowed political aims he cannot be classed as a confirmed violent criminal, to whom for the achievement of his purposes all means – even the destruction of the lives of policemen in their exercise of their official duties – are acceptable. The taking of human life is incompatible with Zahl's personality. No contrary conclusion can be drawn from his proclaimed political convictions or from his advocacy of the use of force to bring about the overthrow of the present civil and social order. Zahl's statement that he does not regard an ordinary policeman as an enemy to be pursued with any weapon cannot be refuted. Indeed the decisive factor here was that the statement made by Zahl does seem honest; he shows all the characteristics of a man who applies an exaggerated standard of moral seriousness – even to himself.[30]

The prosecution appealed to the High Court against this judgment and was successful. The High Court quashed the verdict, ordered a new trial before a different court, and agreed with the prosecution that Zahl should be convicted not just of 'resisting arrest' but of 'attempted murder'.[31]

The case was retried in March 1976. This time – for 'attempted murder in two cases combined with a particularly serious case of resistance to officers in the course of their duty' – Zahl received a sentence of fifteen years' imprisonment. The details of the incident could naturally not have changed in the intervening period; what had changed was the court's attitude to Zahl's political views. The judgment is a condemnation of opinion *par excellence*. The legally required 'base motives', which have to be demonstrated for an attack on a person to count as murder or attempted murder (§ 211 StGB), were constructed from the same 'personality of the defendant' from which the first court's analysis had drawn the exoneration quoted above. The new judgment simply turned the arguments round:

There are weighty arguments against Zahl. He is possessed by a deep hatred of our constitution and intolerantly disregards social and

127

political cooperation ... Moreover, even today he refuses to acknowledge his offence. Not even a period of custody lasting more than three years has so far made any impression on the accused ... The seriousness of the offence and the personality of the accused both therefore call for the imposition of a long period of imprisonment. The most important considerations in imposing such a sentence are the particular need to deter the accused and the need to protect the public from him.[32]

Quite openly, a remand in custody is here described as a means of repression, punishment in advance of trial, and Zahl's intention to commit murder constructed from an 'attitude of hostility towards the state'. The minimum sentence for attempted murder is three years. With the fifteen-year sentence – a 400 per cent addition for opinions, as Zahl described it – the court stretched the penal code to its furthest limit – and then regretted that the law did not provide an even harsher sentence.[33]

The use of special punishments to destroy the identity of political offenders was suggested as early as 1951 during the debate on the state security law:

For offences which are committed only by a particular group of people we can think in terms of special penalties detrimental to an interest particular to this group. We are dealing here with political offences. Political criminals have political interests through which they can be affected ... The true revolutionary is affected [only by measures which] fundamentally limit his political activity. It is this activity we must get at. It is quite possible, and attempts are already being made. Bans on speaking and writing, a ban on publication [are measures] which come to mind as genuine punishments with the addition of a strong preventive effect.[34]

The stage of 'attempts' is long over; since then there have been renewed demands for 'the preservation of security' and the death penalty for political prisoners. All these are a reply to the question put by CDU deputy Vogel: 'What is to happen when the prisoners have finished their sentences and continue to be convinced of their ideology? There will then be a problem of

128

internal security which we must definitely think about in good time.'[35]

As to the form of imprisonment, here there has not just been thought but also action: political prisoners are strictly isolated, hermetically separated from the other prisoners, who do not even see them. Visits and correspondence are restricted. 'Isolation is taken so far,' reports the psychiatrist Rasch of the prison conditions of the RAF,

that even the prison officers have been told, 'if you have anything to do with that lot, you'll come under suspicion.' You have to imagine the situation in Stammheim as like under a bell-jar. It's as though there is suction somewhere, and everything is being sealed off until you suffocate.[36]

This isolation within isolation seems to be the state's revenge on its most radical opponents, brought forward even into pre-trial custody, and to be an elaborate experiment in scientific police methods which gives information about the physical capacity of prisoners who put up resistance to their imprisonment, who do not conform, do not let themselves be broken. Previously the effects of such isolation could only be studied under specially constructed laboratory conditions, with volunteer subjects and only over short periods.

Access to radio and television – the repeatedly cited 'privileges' of the RAF prisoners – comes nowhere near compensating for the restriction of opportunities for physical contact and perception, 'sensory deprivation', as it is called in social psychology. It only accentuates the separation, loneliness and confinement and strengthens the unquenchable desire for tenderness and communication. The effect of strict isolation on the person exposed to it in the core of his personality is automatic and impersonal; it is torture, not by action but by withdrawal. Quite often, without leaving traces of outside interference, it drives its victims to death, which is then cynically announced as 'suicide'.[37]

For years solitary confinement was fiercely attacked, and anyone who publicly attacked it and called for its abolition was brought to court. Only after the Stuttgart prison doctor Henck, under cross-examination by lawyers, admitted the extreme social isolation of the accused and agreed that he had never before, in his twenty years' practice as a prison doctor, seen harsher prison conditions,[38] did the court finally agree to have the prisoners examined by specialists. Experts appointed by the court came independently to the hardly surprising conclusion that the severe physical and mental disabilities they found in the accused were principally due to their prison conditions. Continuation of this imprisonment, they said, was not compatible with the rehabilitation of the prisoners and could not be countenanced medically, and they called for the strict isolation to be ended immediately: Expert Professor W. Rasch found the accused, Andreas Baader, Gudrun Ensslin, Ulrike Meinhof and Jan-Carl Raspe, to be in a 'reduced general physical condition' and suffering from

disturbances to coordination and orientation, lack of concentration, dizziness, limited perception, forgetfulness, increased tiredness, reduced energy, exhaustion, articulatory disturbances, fits of depression, reduced spontaneity, and emotional withdrawal ... Each of the subjects show a marked state of psycho-physical reduction with vegetative dysregulation and a reduction in physical and mental capacity ... A worsening of the state of health of each of the accused may occur, though at what point it is not now possible to predict. The damage noted requires treatment, though this is probably not possible during the course of the hearing and under the present prison conditions.

The question of treating these disturbances cannot be discussed in isolation from that of their causes. In the discussion of these matters so far two possible causes were suggested, under-nourishment as a result of the accused's repeated hunger strikes, and the prison conditions. The examinations just completed suggest that both possibilities must be considered ... The extensive international penological and psychological literature devoted to this topic shows that isolation in itself is likely to cause serious damage to a person's mental and physical constitution. Among the symptoms described are chronic apathy, loss of initiative, memory disturbances, tiredness, a reduced emotional level, disturbances in concentration, reduced intellectual capacity and neuro-vegetative complaints ... As far as I know, there is no study in existence dealing with comparable conditions to those in which the accused have been kept in the last few years. From the psychiatric and psychological point of view it must be stated that the conditions in which the accused are being kept are an obstacle to the start of appropriate treatment, and may also lead to a deterioration in their state of health ... The 'privileges' granted to the prisoners (cell furnishings, etc.) and the opportunity of contact (with each other) make no basic difference to the previous conditions, which are wholly exceptional in modern prison practice. The particular situation which now exists is comparable with that of a small group under extreme conditions. The relationships of the accused are also forced into rigid channels. They are screened fron normal or quasi-normal interaction, living outside the informal infrastructure of the prison, which normally provides prisoners with an emotional prop.[39]

Here again the Federal High court had the final say. 'Naturally', came the word from Karlsruhe,

any term of imprisonment, but especially an unusually long one such as the accused are having to undergo, entails detrimental effects on the health and mental and psychological state of these affected ... Normally penal institutions counteract this by a form of imprisonment which allows opportunities for contact with other prisoners and for physical activity ... The complainants live under different prison conditions. They are obliged to accept restrictions which, in Professor Rasch's opinion, are not balanced by the 'privileges' granted to them ... The danger constituted by the complainants left the authorities responsible for deciding the form of pre-trial custody no other choice than to take account of this by a corresponding increase in the severity of the prison conditions. The accused and their lawyers describe the resulting form of imprisonment as destructive torture by isolation. This cannot be treated as any more than a propagandistic slander, particularly since the extent and length of the conditions of confinement were only forced on the authorities by the behaviour of the accused. [However, the description] 'destructive torture by isolation' shows that [the accused] realize the detrimental effect of the prison conditions. There can be no serious doubt that in view of their above average intelligence they have recognized the effects of imprisonment in solitary confinement for a long time. If nevertheless they have continued for years the behaviour which has forced the organs of the state to introduce these conditions of imprisonment, they have thereby accepted their resulting unfitness to take part in the trial.[40]

In other words the Federal High Court makes no attempt to deny the fact of solitary confinement and its destructive effect – quite the reverse. What it does do is deny the validity of the basic right of prisoners to enjoy freedom from physical injury even when they do not fit the 'rule', 'refuse all acknowledgment of the organs of the state', do not 'show that they are willing to participate in their trial in their role of accused', and 'offer resistance' to their condemnation[41] – to their condemnation! No other judgment would be tenable –

Incalculable damage would otherwise be done to the sense of justice of the law-abiding population who daily see wrong-doers punished for far less serious offences than those alleged against the complainants.[42]

– condemnation in advance by 'healthy national sentiment' demands its price.

6. Military State Security

In addition to the 'front-line security' of the secret services and the criminal law, a comprehensive system of military state security is ready as a repressive instrument of crisis management. For this purpose in recent years work has been carried on, on a previously unknown scale, to enlarge and re-equip the police. The development of the legislation on the state police forces and the Federal Border Guard, and the measures taken to train and arm them, also show that the organization of more effective defence against the threat of mass activities is being concentrated in this area.

'There is no doubt in my mind,' writes a state security expert,

that we face even more critical times. To some extent, in certain areas and at particular stages, we have quite limited indications of a pre-revolutionary period. But there is no reason at all for timid resignation; we can keep things well in hand. On the other hand there is every reason to prepare ourselves in time for the new and increased demands. There can also be no doubt that this will mean particularly heavy calls on the police in the next few years. Indeed, the very existence of the state may depend on whether its police stand firm or not.[1]

The following measures have been taken or introduced for this purpose. The strength of the ordinary police is to be increased in stages from its already high level of 120,000 men to around 140,000, to reach a ratio of one officer to 400 inhabitants, and their operational resources and powers are being considerably increased.[2] Among the state police forces and the Federal Border Guard a special force is being set up, the so-called Mobile Operational Units, MEK and GSG9, 'men who receive a tough and unconventional training and are motivated

133

for the job', who develop an 'élite consciousness' and operate with the most modern weapons and special unwritten rules; they 'fight with a desire to destroy the enemy – shooting to disable is rubbish'.[3] The emergency police force, who are housed in barracks and were set up in 1950 under an agreement between the Federal Government and the states, are being increased under new agreements by 2,000 men to around 24,000 by 1977;[4] in the opinion of the Constitutional Court this force is an 'important and essential instrument for dealing with sudden crises such as natural catastrophes, emergencies or political crises'. Finally, the Federal Border Guard (BGS) has since 1972 been available as a Federal police force of 21,000 men (16,000 in 1969) to help the states on request. Two lines of development can be seen, first an increasing militarization of the police, and, second, a simultaneous transfer to police duties of military organizations, particularly the Federal Border Guard.

1. The Federal Border Guard Acquires a Police Role

The Federal Border Guard (BGS) was founded in 1951 as an armed body with military training and operating from barracks. Its strength was fixed first at 10,000 soldiers and its activity restricted exclusively to the border area 'to a depth of thirty kilometres', as even the first BGS law stipulated.[5] It was only the emergency legislation of 1968 and the new BGS law of 1972 which legalized the use of these troops in the interior of the Federal Republic as well,[6] though this had occurred previously, in other words, without the necessary authority: 'I would finally like to stress,' said SPD deputy Konrad in the Bundestag, 'that the new BGS law does no more than make legal provision for much that has been going on in practice for a long time, largely to the satisfaction of the Federal Government and the states.'[7]

On the basis of the new law the BGS may now legally 'help in the last resort',[8] and for this purpose has been given general authority 'for the maintenance or restoration of public safety or order in cases of particular gravity' to take 'whatever measures

seem necessary in their professional judgment'.[9] The rights
mentioned in the law – to check identity, to detain, to gather
information, to search buildings, to confiscate – are an indica-
tive rather than a comprehensive list.[10] It is the duty of the
Federal Border Guard 'quite generally to clear up disturbances
or threats to public safety or order' – lengthy deliberations in
every case would only reduce their operational value.[11]

In spite of this acquisition of police powers, the BGS, unlike
the state police forces and the emergency police, continue to
possess military combatant status. 'The Federal Government is
acting on the principle, "Assimilation to the state police as far
as possible, special regulations as far as necessary".'[12] As a unit
for dealing with civil war, the Federal Border Guard fills the
gap between ordinary police and the army, allowing the unpopular use of regular troops within the country to be kept for
situations of extreme political tension without making it necessary to do without militarily trained and equipped forces in the
front line of an 'emergency'. As a professional force, the BGS is
also politically more reliable than the conscript Bundeswehr, in
which every other man regards his period of service as point-
less.[13]

Since the coming into force of a new law on manpower structure, the BGS no longer accepts applicants who will only
commit themselves for a short term. This is the result in terms
of service, salaries and career of the development of the BGS
into a police force. There has also been an agreement between
the Federal Government and the states that in future the state
police forces will take 20 per cent of their annual quota of
recruits from applicants who have previously had a number of
years' service with the BGS and want to transfer to the regular
police. The military permeation of the police is thus complete –
the state police can call on a core of specially trained men, and
the BGS avoids becoming an ageing force.[14]

The equipment and training of the Federal Border Guard
have also been modified for its new function as an 'internal
security service' and 'permanently available intervention reserve'.[15] Its arsenal of military weapons has been supplemented

with water-cannon, batons, handy troop-carriers and battle-dress. The uniforms of the state and Federal police are to become identical.[16] The border guards' operations and manoeuvres have been permanently modified with an eye to domestic conflicts: 'The border guard of the future,' urged former interior minister Benda several years ago, 'must be able to cope with all police duties, not just in field and forest, but also on the asphalt of our cities.' The BGS would have to be prepared for clashes with 'trouble-makers armed not with guns but with paving stones or tomatoes. We must expect, for example, that a state may call for the support of the BGS when its own police are overstretched by mass demonstrations which are unarmed but get out of hand, and perhaps appear in several places simultaneously.'[17]

One problem, however, has still not been finally solved, the remoteness from the centre of BGS units, which results from its original purpose and is a drawback in the fight against 'internal enemies'. For years there have been calls for a 'displacement' of the BGS, its movement into the heart of the country:

The organization of the BGS must match the new and largely different tasks. We must set up new camps in the western part of the Federal Republic. The camps ought as far as possible be set up in large conurbations where the weight of any domestic operation will fall, not just to ensure an immediate presence in an operational situation, but also to accustom the units to the atmosphere and psychology of the city.[18]

2. The Militarization of the Police

Particularly in recent times, the methods and equipment employed in police operations have begun to blur the line between police and military operations and finally to reduce to absurdity the division of powers – by now anyway no more than formal – between the executive and the judiciary. Conflicts to which political solutions are no longer possible are 'settled' by the police with paramilitary methods, and the police are increasingly often taking over in their own way the work of the politicians. 'In particular circumstances' the citizen's legal guarantees against the state, from the inviolability of his home to the safety of life and limb, exist for the police only on paper. As their commander in Hamburg put it picturesquely, 'the police regard themselves as a part of our national body. They are the red [he means white, of course] corpuscles with the task of preventing disease and keeping harmful substances away from this national body.'[19] The police show what they mean by this 'body culture' in the use of firearms, the increase in the number of armed police, and in carrying out aggressive large-scale operations.

Although the police regulations still in force in the states permit the use of a firearm by a policeman only as the ultimate means of defence, and to render a person 'incapable of escape or attack',[20] i.e. in distinction from military practice explicitly forbid shooting to kill, the police are increasingly acting on the principle that the only harmless 'trouble-maker' is a dead one.

The senator responsible for the interior ministry in Hamburg certainly implied that the life and health of citizens is left to the discretion of the police when he sent newly sworn-in officers on their way with these words: 'Weapons are always available to you to enable you to enforce the requirements of the law. But when you use them do not leave your sound common sense behind. This is the principle of the proportionality of means.'[21]

Some of the courses of action this common sense leads policemen into can be seen from the number of their victims. The very reluctantly published statistics of fatal shootings by police officers make it clear that in the majority of cases the police did not shoot to prevent crimes or ward off attacks, but in order to prevent an escape or to make an arrest, to assert 'the state's right to punish', as German legal jargon puts it.[22] The bloody results of this sort of implementation of punishment by the police make the conclusion unavoidable that the death penalty has in practice been re-introduced through the back door in the face of the constitution and the law, decided now individually and on the spot, and carried out by police officers. The figures show even more; they do away with the legend that being a policeman is a particularly dangerous job. They show that since 1945 incomparably fewer policemen were shot on duty than citizens by the police. In the years of 1973-5 alone there were thirty-eight,[23] and since 1976 another nineteen. Such disguised executions are not unfortunate accidents, but the expression of a training reduced to a concentration on a sense of order, a mania for order, on physical control and the mobilization of prejudices against minorities. This was confirmed by the police psychologist Suttinger from his examination of a policeman who killed a car thief he had arrested by shooting him through the neck. His reason was that he wanted 'a bit of peace'. Officers like this are typical cases of people who need orders, who can only get through their everyday duties satisfactorily by matching 'their rigid ideas of right and duty with equally schematic views about wrong and bad people'.[24] This training and the routine of duty produce a blindness to the nature of the social conflicts with which the police are faced, and lead directly and dangerously to a blind rage when they have to settle such conflicts. As Frankfurt police chief Müller laconically remarked of this situation: 'Maybe we have overstepped the mark now and then. We don't deny it. It can happen. It's part of us.'[25]

The readiness to use firearms is further increased by the certainty of getting off, if charges are ever brought. The self-defence provisions of civil and criminal law are invoked, usually in the fiction of 'putative self-defence', to remove all responsibility from the police and transfer it to their victims. The practice of judicial decisions was surpassed by a decision of principle by the Federal High Court which gave the police *carte blanche* in the use of firearms. In the spring of 1975 the High Court quashed the conviction of a policeman who had shot in the back a seventeen-year-old youth who was in local authority care. According to the court, the 'use of firearms for the purpose of recapturing a criminal in flight' was justified if the criminal constituted 'a not inconsiderable danger to the public'. This condition had been satisfied: the youth who was shot had repeatedly stolen groceries and delicacies, portable radios, record-players and cash. In four cases he also stole bicycles. When caught in the act, he had broken away violently and escaped ... Public safety therefore required his immediate recapture ... in view of the danger to the community presented by this young criminal ... The fact that a risk of killing was present did not make the firing of a careful shot at the fugitive's leg wrong,

for, as the High Court said in explanation of this curious logic, 'any use of a firearm, particularly a hand-held weapon, involves such a risk'. The accused policeman 'therefore acted legally. He is to be acquitted and awarded costs.'[26]

With arguments of this sort the High Court was also contributing to the 'moral rearmament' of policemen for which their leaders so insistently called to accompany the issue of better weapons: 'an external renewal of weapons and other equipment' alone, it was argued, was

incomparably easier to carry out than a change in the basic inner attitudes of our officers. To put it bluntly, after inwardly disarming the police for years, you cannot from one day to the next make them ready for anything. You can take away an officer's 7·65mm pistol and put a 9mm weapon in his hand instead, but you can't from one day to the next put a totally new attitude to his job inside him.[27]

If the High Court had taken an important step in this direction, the 'German Judges' Association' now set out to remove the last scruples. The association intervened in the debate on whether the police should in future be allowed to shoot to kill, and gave supporting fire to the advocates of the change. In the judges' opinion, a 'final shot' was justified when a policeman considered it the 'appropriate course'; even a 'criminal' did have the right to have his life respected, but if it came to a choice the life of a 'law-abiding citizen' was more important.[28] The *Hesse Police Review* spelt it out even more clearly for its readers; it quoted a well-known jurist's view that a distinction had to be made 'between individuals worthy of basic rights and those unworthy of them'.[29]

A new draft police law for the states was unanimously approved by the conference of interior ministers on 11 June 1976. In addition to dealing with the right of the police to shoot to kill when facing individual 'trouble-makers', it also regulates the use of weapons against groups, and here standardizes the relevant provisions already contained in the laws of a number of states. Under § 43 of the draft, weapons may be used against a group 'if acts of violence are being committed or are about to be committed by it or from within it, and action against individuals seems unlikely to be successful'. In implementing this most flexible regulation – what are 'acts of violence' and how do the police know that they are 'about to be committed'? – the police can use military weapons, i.e. weapons whose function is to destroy an opponent: automatic weapons, machine pistols, machine guns and hand grenades (§ 36 of the draft). This is justified by a reference to 'conceivable control situations in which the use of these weapons may be necessary', for example, as the Rhineland-Palatinate interior minister, Schwarz, explained, 'in a pre-revolutionary situation'.[80] When the Berlin House of Deputies some years ago passed a similar measure, the so-called hand grenade law of 1970, CDU deputy Schmitz gave an assurance that the police would 'never' use these weapons 'against citizens, but – if at all – only against criminals and anti-democrats'.[31] Who all these people are who have been legally deprived of citizenship, and who such weapons will be directed at when the state monopoly of violence has to be defended, if need be by military force, was made clear by an official of the interior ministry:

No one wants an internal crisis. On the other hand, it is unrealistic to rule out completely such extraordinary situations ... When we talk about arming the police, we must ask first of all what situations the police are likely to face in the future. Remember that radical groups openly declare their intention of destroying the existing order of the Federal Republic by force. Think of the forms this conflict has already taken. If we think that a situation of economic crisis with unemployment and the consequent dissatisfaction and tensions is not a total impossibility for the future, and if we remember the growth of the wave of demonstrations in the Federal Republic in 1967 and the events of 1968 in France, who can then say that armed attacks within the Federal Republic are impossible?[32]

Simultaneously with the introduction of a single nationwide procedure for the military repression of mass activities by the police, a new regulation for police training was drafted, 'PD 201'. Under the regulation, which was produced by the Federal Border Guard, every policeman, in addition to his basic training with the Emergency Police, will have to be trained in the use of weapons in civil war.[33] The police are in addition being equipped with 'riot-control' agents. Among those already known are the chemical sprays 'Chemical Mace' and 'pepper fog', and chemical, electrical and acoustic paralysing devices, such as are already in use in America, are being tested.[34]

This re-equipping is not being carried out with any sort of secrecy, but in full view – 'Citizens must get as used to the sight of policemen with machine pistols as they are to paying tax',[35] and they will have to see what 'it's all about,' what they can look forward to, when the police treat them as 'trouble-makers'.

Police operations such as the eviction of squatters from houses and building sites, and terroristic large-scale manhunts like the one after the kidnapping of Lorenz,[36] also provide training in the use of equipment and in police coordination. The martial spectacle with which such operations are carried out is meant to obscure the police's open breaches of the law. 'No smoke without fire' is what the terrified people are supposed to say, and no one will remember to ask who lit the fire.

These operations also provide an opportunity to search homes and arrest people whom the security services have had their eye on for a long time, but without any legal ground for action. So the night-time police manoeuvre 'Winter Journey' in November 1974 in Frankfurt, which was described as a search, 'included general problem houses, where the occupants were organizing rent strikes or stirring up other sorts of trouble', as the Frankfurt police put it in their explanation of the numerous arrests and the trail of damage they left behind them.[37]

The new police law will make such operations easier to authorize and give them a sounder legal basis. What is already possible in Baden-Württemburg will be legal throughout West Germany: it will be possible at any time to search districts and houses in which 'in the experience of the police people plan crimes'.[38] Without any specific suspicion, anyone may be held, searched and made the object of 'information-gathering procedures'. The 'inviolability of the home' guaranteed in the Basic Law (Art. 13) and the protection of individual freedom against excesses of state authority (Art. 104) are being finally suspended.

Conclusion

Even though the extension and use of the state security apparatus described in this book reveals elements of a fascist potential, it would nevertheless be totally inappropriate to describe the political situation in West Germany as fascism. This would lead to a trivialization of the open terror of the Nazis, and to an underestimate of its differences from the present more differentiated and more subtle forms in which the state exercises its power and consolidates its rule. It would also lead to a premature abandonment of what remains the crucial means of political action and organization, the open and offensive development of an alternative public and alternative power.

West Germany is on the way to becoming a Big Brother police state. If one considers all the measures and plans described in this book, one finds a gradual removal of the constitutional limits on the exercise of power by the state which distinguish a constitutional state from a police state. 'The constitutional state is being tuned to the actual situation', was the Justice Minister's solemn description of the process by which civil rights are gradually being abolished.[1] The classical idea of the constitutional state is being turned into its opposite; from being a protection for the citizen against arbitrary acts by the state it is now giving the state wider and wider powers to intervene in the lives of its citizens. In accordance with German tradition the process follows legal procedures, and these legal forms give any set of measures the appearance of legitimacy which makes the introduction and application more acceptable to the public. People may now be legally put outside the law.

In part the process is assisted by the courts; breaches of the law by the authorities are declared to be authentic interpretations of the current statute. The courts, led by the Federal High Court and now including the Constitutional Court, have thereby become organs of justification rather than justice. As for the legislature, it retrospectively legalizes illegal state action which has long been established practice – breaches of previous law themselves become law. This makes the new provisions – see the forthcoming police law, the most recent changes in the political criminal law (§ § 88a, 129a, 130a, 142 StGB) and the 'contact ban law' – ultimately nothing other than free licence for state action, the limits of which can no longer be guessed in the absence of definitions of offences.

If all else fails, the government falls back on a 'supra-legal state of emergency' which gives it limitless freedom of action, a grey area where actions do not have to be accounted for. Former Federal Attorney-General Buback made no secret of this practice. Asked whether he felt that further legal measures to increase the powers of his department were useful or necessary, he said no:

> If you have a legal provision and only have to stretch it, it usually doesn't work. State security survives because it is run by people who are committed to it. And people who are committed like Herold [the head of the detective force] and me will always find a way.[2]

This process was impressively demonstrated in the emergence of the 'contact ban law', which would be better named the solitary confinement law.[3] After the kidnapping of employers' president Schleyer, the Federal Minister of Justice and the justice ministers of the states ordered the total isolation of about a hundred prisoners accused of 'supporting' or 'membership of a terrorist organization'. Not only was contact with other prisoners forbidden; newspapers were stopped, prisoners were not allowed to listen to the radio, send or receive letters, or even to talk to or correspond with their lawyers.

With this change these prison conditions far exceeded the previous degree of isolation, with its physical and psychological effects on those subject to it. The ministers responsible realized that this order by the executive was a clear breach of the law and therefore invoked a 'supra-legal state of emergency'. The exceptional measure, they said, would have to be retained 'until the end of the kidnapping' since there was 'a fear that without such a measure forbidden messages will pass between the kidnappers and the prisoners'.[4]

There followed judgments by courts after appeals from lawyers for the prisoners concerned declaring this manoeuvre by the government illegal – decisions which the authorities ignored. The 'state security panel' of the High Court then certified to the government that its 'emergency measure' was permissible, and a number of lawyers appealed to the Constitutional Court.[5] At this point the 'large crisis committee' decided that attack was the best form of defence, and presented the so-called 'contact ban law' to the Bundestag for approval.[6] It is now known that the law had been prepared in its essentials long before Schleyer's kidnapping,[7] but before that event there had seemed no chance of getting the Bundestag to pass such a law.

Without any chance for public control or influence – the text of the bill was not even available to outsiders before the vote, and the news blackout was a further obstacle – the 'large crisis committee' secured the approval of Bundestag and Bundesrat for its law under a cloak of Nazi-style secrecy.[8] In this way solitary confinement was retrospectively legalized – 'a Third Reich practice', as *Stern* commented.[9]

The origin and content of this crucial law with its harmless sounding name are reminiscent of the 'Emergency Decrees' of the Weimar period. The new provision, which instantaneously turns fundamental guarantees for convicted prisoners and accused into waste paper,[10] gives the executive unrestricted powers and can be measured only by the standards of political and police expediency. The law, which bears a strong resemblance to a form of counter-kidnapping by the state, is a blanket authority to state security officials, 'after proper assessment' – as the empty restriction in the text puts it – to deny selected remand or convicted prisoners any oral or written contact with each other or with their lawyers. It even allows them, by appealing to a rapidly constructed suspicion of 'supporting a terrorist organization', to carry out arrests out of the public eye without allowing the victim to send for a lawyer of his choice. According to SPD deputy Coppik, one of the sixteen members of the Bundestag who dared to withhold approval from the emergency legislation:

Anyone who still says, 'what's it got to do with me? I'm not mixed up with terrorists,' must be told clearly that under the new law no one, however innocent, can be sure of not being imprisoned as a result of denunciation and vanishing into a prison for weeks and months without contact with a lawyer or even with his relatives. In terms of the rule of law I consider this intolerable.[11]

The 'contact ban' law forms the current peak of a political development which I would describe as the intrusion of police attitudes into all areas of social life and the generalization of an attitude dominated by ideas of 'security' and 'order'. Concepts deriving from police theory and methods are employed in an attempt to channel or quell political confrontations; they include 'order', orders', 'subordination', security' and 'prevention'. Police strategies of conflict management are used to defend 'normality' against any deviant political behaviour. Police institutions, following exclusively the logic of a campaign against an enemy, define what 'order' is and who 'disrupts' it.

An attitude deriving from such narrow views is increasingly dominating the content and application of legislation. So, for example, the general clauses of the proposed police law ignore, in the interests of a 'general defence against danger', the limits imposed by the Basic Law and the Code of Criminal Procedure on the state's exercise of its power: it is then proposed to eliminate this problem by bringing the laws in question into line with the forthcoming police law. The provisions of the new censorship law (§§88a, 130a, 140 StGB) are also modelled on provisions of police law, and refer to the 'likelihood' of words, pictures or written matter to 'disturb the public peace'. The central concept of police law, the 'responsible judgment' of an official, has been made the corner-stone of the 'contact ban' law. As a result of the campaigns against nuclear power stations there are calls for the law on demonstrations and assembly to be revised to meet police requirements – 'as a basis for the restoration of public peace and to ensure that decisions of the state can be carried out'.[12]

The procedures ensure that police ideas and demands will not only be listened to but also acted upon. Police experts with their science dominate the work of the ministries and committees, and this itself is increasingly concerned with finding ways of putting into practice political decisions already taken, if necessary, by using the power of the police. In this process the police have long since exchanged their merely instrumental strong-arm role for a share in the definition of policy. An important part in this is played by the conference of interior ministers and, more recently, the 'crisis committees', institutions for which there is no provision in the constitution – they may be unconstitutional organizations – and which are not subject to any public control. The Standing Conference of Interior Ministers of the Federation and the States is responsible for

a coordination of the joint security effort which is all the more effective for rarely attracting public attention ... The Standing Conference is sometimes criticized, but it discusses much more than you hear about in public, and we have no intention of changing this now ... [It is] not the job of political leaders to replace the experts. What we as the bearers of political responsibility have to do is simply to insist that what the experts think is right, where it is compatible with the rule of law, is given the necessary political backing.[13]

The initiatives for the main security measures of the recent past – the *Berufsverbot*, the tightening up of the criminal law, the militarization of the police – all came from this shadow cabinet of police ministers, which draws its experts from the Criminal Investigation Bureau, the secret services and the prosecuting staff of the Federal High Court.[14]

As the police's 'strategic assessments' become the main

influence on political decisions, citizens are coming to be seen only as potential 'trouble-makers'; they are always suspects. Suspicion is becoming generalized. When social conflicts are only 'translated into the practical logic of permanent latent threats and dangers . . . the motive force of which is suspicion',[15] it is also logical to compare the police to an 'osmotic filter'. The head of the Federal Criminal Investigation Bureau, Herold, who is the source of this image, has made his general attitude explicit:

Of all the organs of the state, the one most immediately and forcibly confronted with reality, the police force, has uniquely privileged access to knowledge which enables it to understand a multiplicity and diversity of socially deviant and antisocial forms of behaviour, structural defects in society and the laws governing social mass behaviour.

The police are in a position to recognize 'subliminal changes' at an early stage. They must therefore transform themselves 'from a subordinate object with merely executive functions into initiators of social change', which requires 'a firm move away from the restrictions of their traditional functions, a radically new intellectual start, the acceptance of a quite different self-awareness' – that of the police as 'a sort of institution of social hygiene'.[16]

The SPD, 'for the first time in history feeling really at home in its state',[17] has been an attentive partner to state security men like Herold. Hand-wringing about what is said to be the 'ill-fated role of the Social Democrats' misses the point that the party has not been allotted any role that it was not quite willing to play, that it is not the pathetic victim of a policy but its conscious creator. The SPD has for years striven – from the emergency legislation to the *Berufsverbote* – to clothe the whole area of 'internal security' in the forms of legality. The constitution is adapted as required to fit in with whatever 'security' laws are required at the moment.

It would nevertheless be too simple to interpret the state security measures exclusively in terms of their preventive role within West Germany; they also point to the role played by this state in Western Europe. 'The Federal Republic', declared CDU deputy Dregger in a 'security' debate in the Bundestag, was 'the strongest pillar of free Europe . . . If the Federal Republic of Germany falls, none of the other free states of Europe can be held. Lenin's remark, "Whoever controls Germany controls Europe", is even truer now than when it was first made.'[18]

The measures introduced by this state show typically German features. Their perfectionism and rigidity reflect the fears of change which have always dominated political life in Germany and can be appealed to especially in times of crisis. It is not just 'the capitalist system' which is the origin of all these measures, but the German way of dealing with this problem by 'over-reaction' and 'over-retaliation'. The German version of political crisis management has a history, a history which includes lack of a bourgeois democratic tradition, of a liberal public and of an aggressive labour movement, together with a surplus of submissiveness and respect for authority, a historical legacy which weighs on the political behaviour of citizens of this country no less than the forms in which political contradictions are dealt with here. It is important to bear in mind the history of the forms of political confrontation in Germany, which seems to have taken out a subscription to disaster. It is important to know who can be counted on, and whose resistance cannot be counted on as long as the memory of the rise of fascism remains obscured in the unions.

And yet there is no reason for despondency. After all, the state security measures expose the anxieties of those who introduce them; they indicate the points at which the system is politically vulnerable. The odd bomb doesn't frighten the state security men; on that level of force they are unbeatable, quite apart from the fact that this form of force only reproduces what has to be transcended. More of a worry are the first sparks which may ignite to create an alternative public and an alternative power in areas where their political weakness only becomes more obvious with every threat or use of open force, since government, police and judiciary continue to need cooperation as well as consent for the success of their measures. With the Red Army Faction, the current public enemy number one, this may still be a simple matter; it was already harder with the squatters, and it becomes a real problem for any action against a strike based on firm leadership. And lastly, the movement against nuclear power stations shows that the possibilities for 'asserting normality' are not unlimited, and that they narrow all the more as the 'political hinterland' of political activities broadens.

'The danger is people.' The interior minister's banal and yet nervous summary of the situation points to the fact that rules can only achieve their purpose as long as they are recognized and massively followed, as long as the real political movement does not create its own rules.

Notes

A list of Abbreviations is given on pp. 221–2.

Foreword

1. Cf. Franz-Josef Strauss's speech at the CSU party conference in Munich: 'those who are supposed to be fighting for the freedom of the people should be left to the people, then the police and the courts wouldn't have to bother any more about them' (F. J. Strauss, 'Rechenschaftsbericht auf dem Parteitag der CSU', Munich, 23/24.ix.77, duplicated MS, p. 47).

Cf. also the following reflections from the *Frankfurter Allgemeine*: 'The state must question and re-examine its legal and moral attitude to terrorists, as it has hitherto seen and practised it. Taboos must be cleared away . . . The question could be put something like this: Must terrorists continue to be allowed to torture, blackmail, murder and use the threat of any of these at any time, while the state has an obligation to preserve the lives and health of the members of the gangs and can't threaten them with anything that would really frighten them? Can nothing be done to change the depressing disparity in the survival chances of the gang members on the one hand and their targets and hostages on the other? There must be a meticulous examination of what the constitution allows in this area. If it should be found that all avenues are blocked, we must see how far the constitution is susceptible of amendment' (leading article, 18.x.77).

One day before the Stammheim prisoners were found shot and hanged in their cells, the celebrated historian Golo Mann had talked in similarly casual terms on the TV programme *Panorama* about possible state action against the prisoners.

2. The President of the Association of German Lawyers, quoted FR, 30.xi.77, p. 1.

On secure custody see Ch. 5. n. 35.

3. *Berliner Morgenpost*, quoted *konkret* 12 (1977), p. 10.

Notes

Introduction

1. SPD Press Service, 16.vii.75, p. 4.

2. Federal Prosecutor E. Träger, *Das Parlament* 3 (1976), 17.i.76, p. 3.

3. Federal Justice Minister Vogel, *Bundestag*, 16.i.76, pp. 14740–41.

4. H. J. Schwagerl *et al.*, *Der Schutz der Verfassung – Handbuch für Theorie und Praxis*, Cologne, 1968, p. 252.

5. FR, 30.vi.75, p. 4.

6. Bender (CDU), *Bundestag*, 24.x.75, p. 13558.

7. *Berufsverbot* judgment of the Federal Constitutional Court, 22.v.75 (Az.: 2 BvL 13/73), pp. 1 and 18.

8. Bender, loc. cit., p. 13559.

9. E. Benda, *Bundestag*, 10.v.68, p. 9257.

10. For example Vogel (CDU), *Bundestag*, 22.vi.72, p. 11424, and P. Lücke (ed.), *Verfassungsschutz – Beiträge aus Wissenschaft und Praxis*, Cologne, 1966, p. 119.

11. They talk about 'international terror' and 'gangs' while at the same time the newspapers are full of reports of arms sales, murder attempts, kidnappings, corruption, and the development of sinister weapons to wipe out the inhabitants of whole districts by internationally led gangs such as the CIA and the West German secret services, the latter permeated up to the highest posts by former SA, SS and Gestapo men. They preach about 'the defence of freedom', while the Bundeswehr trains Chilean officers, is said to keep in touch with Italian neo-fascists, and 'generals toy at least with the idea of breaching the constitution' (according to the SPD's army expert, Horn, FR, 19.x.75, p. 5, in a comparison with the Chilean army). Again, an old fascist like Filbinger is not just prime minister of the state of Baden-Württemberg, in which the *Berufsverbot* is operated particularly severely, but as late as 1975 was also going into print in a fascist paper for Italian workers in West Germany (FR, 27.xi.75, p. 4). The list of examples is endless.

12. 'Bismarck tackled the tragi-comic incident ... from the practical demagogic angle and cabled by return from Friedrichsruh to the first recipient of Hödel's revolver shots: "Emergency legislation against the Social Democrats!" A few days later the concoction was ready ... In six paragraphs it withdrew freedom of the press and freedom of association from the Social Democrats, in so far as it

still existed for the Party' (F. Mehring, *Geschichte der deutschen Sozialdemokratie*, Vol. 2, Berlin (DDR), 1960, p. 494).

13. *Reichsgesetzblatt* (RGBl), 1921 I, 1239. One result of the order was the banning of several papers. See G. Jasper, *Der Schutz der Republik*, Tübingen, 1963, p. 36ff.

14. *RGBl*, 1922 I, p. 521.

15. M. Weber, 'Parliament und Regierung im neugeordneten Deutschland' (1918), *Gesammelte Politische Schriften*, Tübingen, 1971, pp. 36ff.

16. This tactic was not always immediately successful.

Example 1: the attempt to get the emergency legislation passed together with the rearmament (setting up of the Bundeswehr) allowed by an amendment to the constitution. 'The Federal Government began the first preliminary work on emergency powers in 1955, but it was not possible to implement these ideas at the same time as the defence legislation of 1956' (E. Benda, *Die Notstandsverfassung*, Munich, 1966, p. 4).

Example 2: the enlargement, planned as early as the end of the 1950s, and extension of powers of the Federal Criminal Investigation Bureau and the secret services. The *'Spiegel'* affair', which was supposed to assist in getting the powers of the services increased, backfired: 'it did not exactly improve the climate for such a reorganization', as Eduard Kern wrote sadly (*Der Strafschutz des Staates und seine Problematik*, Tübingen, 1963, p. 52).

The plan had to wait until the 1960s, when it was put forward against the background of the anti-authoritarian movement by the then interior minister Ernst Benda in 1968: 'The general outline of events since 11 April [1968] is familiar to you all ... My short account will try to present a provisional assessment and provide a basis for a discussion of the conclusions which follow from it. In the period since the attack on Dutschke ... demonstrations took place in up to twenty-seven towns in five days. On particular days demonstrations in the Federal Republic involved between 5,000 and 18,000 people ... Between 4,000 and 11,000 people were involved in demonstrations leading to riots. Police investigations so far begun include 331 into offences involving unlawful assembly, 33 cases of riot, 215 of breach of the peace, 105 of resistance to state authority, 276 involving other offences such as damage to property, arson, personal injury and similar acts ... Of those charged, 87 are under eighteen years old, 210 between nineteen and twenty-one, 246 between twenty-two and twenty-five; 286 over twenty-five. A break-down by occupation gives the following picture. 92 are at school; there are 286 students, 185 white-collar workers, 150 manual workers, 31 in other occupations, 97 with no occupation, and occu-pation is unknown in the case of 26. Ladies and gentlemen, this breakdown seems to me to show how false it would be to describe the violent incidents as student unrest ... The events of Easter week raise a number of specific questions which require a rapid answer ... Some of the questions require careful thought. They may lead to the conclusion that some legal provisions need to be examined and possibly modified ... The lack of uniformity in police organization [makes] any general view and any possibility of coordination [more difficult]. If ever an emergency occurred in a number of regions which forced the Federal authorities to intervene, the diversity of police organization would very soon be shown up as a serious weak-ness, which might have very harmful consequences ... On the basis of an administrative agreement with the states, the Federal Govern-ment is involved in an equipment and training programme for the emergency police. Middle-term financial planning has led to a slow-ing down of further expansion. I intend to ask the minister of finance to examine the matter with me to see if it is not possible to speed things up' (interior minister Benda, *Bundestag*, 30.iv.68, pp. 8990–94).

What is also interesting here is that Benda argues for improved police coordination on the basis of a possible 'internal emergency', and does not – as is usual nowadays – talk about a general campaign against crime.

Benda put forward a proposal along these lines in June 1969, the 'plan for increasing the effectiveness of the Federal Criminal Inves-tigation Bureau' (Az: ÖS I 5-625 210/8), which envisaged a gradual introduction of electronic data processing together with 'an exten-sion of the executive activities' of the Bureau and an increase in its financial resources and staff. 'The target should be reached at the latest within a period of five years' (Benda, loc. cit.).

This plan was implemented by Benda's SPD and FDP successors sooner and more extensively than the present president of the Fed-eral Constitutional Court could have allowed himself to dream. An-nouncing his government's programme on 28 October 1969, Willy Brandt spoke of an extensive 'immediate programme to modernize and intensify crime prevention', which was presented a day later by his interior minister (Bundestag publication 6/1334 of 29.x.69). The

1969 immediate programme proposed the strengthening of the Criminal Investigation Bureau, the modernization of its equipment and the extension of its powers, the re-equipping and reorganization of the Federal Border Guard as a Federal police force, together with the setting up of a 'study group on the surveillance of foreigners' within the security service.

Example 3: The extension of preventive detention. Following the anti-Springer demonstration, Ernst Benda called for the introduction of this form of imprisonment (FR, 18/19.iv.76). The Berlin senator for internal affairs, Neubauer (SPD), supported him: 'The danger of repetition, which must be an automatic assumption in the case of such demonstrations, is unfortunately a ground for imprisonment only in the case of serious sexual offences ... I know that this legal position is regarded as unsatisfactory. The Berlin senate will see whether this legal gap can be closed by means of a proposal in the Bundesrat' (Neubauer, *Welt am Sonntag*, 10.xi.68, p. 43).

But the proposal, for which the only historical precedents in Germany are the Nazi 'protective custody' and preventive detention because of 'persistent danger', failed against the opposition of the remaining liberal deputies (the bill is reproduced in *Bundestag Publication* 5/3631 of 10.xii.68). Later, in 1972 (Law for the amendment of the Code of Criminal Procedure of 7.viii.72, in this case § 112a StPO), preventive detention was introduced for a number of offences, including 'serious theft' (which occurs when someone breaks into a kiosk and steals a couple of bottles of beer).

All along the CDU tried to have 'breach of the peace' (an offence often introduced by prosecutors and courts in connection with strikes and demonstrations) included as a ground for preventive detention, but failed. 'Ladies and gentlemen,' said their spokesman, 'I am sure that we shall have to consider this subject again in the foreseeable future, since developments are taking place in this field which have not been considered today.' ... '[I] have the impression that you [SPD and FDP – s.c.] have adopted this proposal retrospectively, that you have failed in what is normally your strength, developing forward-looking policies' (Vogel (CDU), *Bundestag*, 22.vi.72, p. 11424, and Lenz (CDU), ibid., p. 11412).

On 'terms like preventive detention', which aroused certain associations, Vogel said, 'I am glad that this rubbish – and it is rubbish – has been got out of the discussion.' And previously, 'I would only like to remind you of the almost pathological campaign against a stiffening of the imprisonment law [in the 1960s – s.c.] ... Without the false emotions ... this subject would have been dealt with years ago. We hope that this time the endurance of those who realize the need to stiffen the imprisonment laws ... will be great enough here in the house' (Vogel (CDU), *Bundestag*, 22.vi.72, p. 11423, and 7.vi.72, p. 10985).

It was great enough, and will be able to make the 'offences in connection with strikes and demonstrations', which the SPD/FDP excluded this time, the next ground for preventive detention.

17. Genscher, *Bundestag*, 22.vi.72, p. 11467.

18. A Stümper, 'Probleme der polizeilichen Führung in unserer Zeit', *Die Poleizei – Zentralorgan für das Sicherheits- und Ordnungswesen*, 11 (1975), p. 366.

The author occupies important posts. As ministerial director in the Baden-Württemberg interior ministry, he is head of the 'public safety' department, a member of the public safety working party of the interior ministers' conference, a member of the governing body of the Police Officer College at Hiltrup, a research adviser to the Federal Criminal Investigation Office, and teaches police methods at Mannheim University.

19. Heinemann, *Bundestag*, 16.v.68, p. 9267.

20. G. Schröder, 'Sicherheit heute', *Bulletin des Presse- und Informationsamtes der Bundesregierung*, 203 (1958), 31.xii.58, p. 2017.

21. ibid., p. 2020.

22. ibid., pp. 2018ff.

A year later, on the occasion of the tenth anniversary of the Basic Law, Schröder repeated the question 'whether the constitution made adequate provision for such times, when the ship of state has to be steered through stormy waters' (G. Schröder (ed.), *Das Gesetz für die Stunde der Not*, Bonn, 1961, p. 33).

The SPD speaker of the Bundestag also said on the radio on 22 September 1959 that there was to date no law 'providing for the use of the army in the event of an internal emergency ... a regrettable gap, which only creates uncertainty ... It is possible that normality will be threatened. I am thinking of crises on a catastrophic scale in the economic or social field and the resulting political radicalization' (quoted from Schröder, *Das Gesetz für die Stunde der Not*, p. 35).

The former vice-president of the Constitutional Court, Dr Rudolf Katz: 'We have a gap in our Basic Law ... It includes no provision for this possibility of a national emergency. This gap [is] not only worrying, but really threatening ... In my view it would be of enormous public benefit if the Bundestag and Bundesrat were to meet now, while the calm lasts, to draw up and pass this necessary additional article, the emergency article of the Basic Law ... I see, by the way, the constitutional and political difficulties arising not so much from an external emergency ... [but] in the event of a so-called internal emergency ... in the event of a transport strike, a general strike, supply difficulties in our industrial centres and so on ... These days it would probably be not so much the purely political as the economic and social situation which would give rise to an emergency. I am not sure whether Germany, as an exporting and industrial country, could take a complete strike of metal-workers, such as the United States has just experienced, without a crisis. A strike of such dimensions here might itself have produced a state of internal crisis and internal emergency' (Katz, 1959, quoted from Schröder, *Das Gesetz für die Stunde der Not*, p. 42).

23. H. D. Genscher, 'Auftrag und Aufgaben des Bundesgrenz-schutzes', *Bulletin des Presse- und Informationsamtes der Bundes-regierung*, 20 (1970), 13.ii.70, p. 190.

24. Genscher, *Bundestag*, 7.vi.72, p. 10976.

25. Koschnick at the SPD party conference in Mannheim during the discussion on the 'law for the protection of communal peace', Conference Report, 14.xi.75, pp. 188–9.

26. Schröder (ed.), *Das Gesetz für die Stunde der Not*, Bonn, 1961, p. 10.

27. 'Preventive counter-revolution' was Karl Korsch's term for this process in an analysis of German fascism made in 1939: 'In contrast to mere conservative and reactionary tendencies', this reflected, he said, an 'intensified consciousness'. Its aim was the creation of conditions 'which would make any future movement of the working class radically impossible for a long time' (K. Korsch, 'Staat und Konterrevolution', in *Politische Texte*, Raubdruck Wiener Neustadt, 1975, pp. 326–8).

28. *Bild*, 3.i.76, p. 2.

29. E. Benda at the CDU/CSU conference on legal policy in Karlsruhe in 1975, FR, 6.xii.75, p. 5.

30. G. Schröder, 'Sicherheit heute', BPIB 203 (1958), 31.x.58, p. 2017.

Chapter 1: The Crisis of Legitimacy in the State

1. Maihofer, in *Innere Sicherheit*, published by the Federal Ministry of the Interior, 30 (1975), 23.x.75, p. 5. Cf. Bundestag Publi-

cations 8/63; 8/1204; *Bundestag*, 10.ii.77, p. 648; *Bundestag*, 25.xi.77, p. 4530.

Maihofer was forced to resign as interior minister in June 1978 after severe criticism of his department from various quarters. The immediate cause was an official report which complained of a lack of co-ordination in the hunt for the kidnappers of Hanns-Martin Schleyer, for which Maihofer accepted political responsibility. Previously, however, he had been under attack from liberals after it had been revealed that the Federal Border Guard had a blacklist of 239 organizations and 287 newspapers and periodicals against which they had been checking the contents of West German travellers' briefcases at the country's airports. Maihofer claimed that the list had been issued without his knowledge.

2. Preamble to a draft amendment to the Criminal Code (Political Section), Bundestag Publication 1/1307 of 4.ix.50, p. 27.

3. Quoted from *Die Welt*, 18.vi.75.

4. Chancellor Schmidt in an 'Appeal to NATO for a joint attack on Recession and Inflation', FR, 31.v.75, p. 1.

5. Wörner, CDU defence expert, according to FR, 11.i.75, p. 2, and FAZ, 11.i.75, p. 4.

6. Schröder, 'Sicherheit heute', BPIB 203 (1968), 31.x.58, pp.2017 and 2020.

7. Kohl, *Bundestag*, 13.iii.75, p. 10777.

8. FR, 22.xi.73, p. 7.

9. Cf. FDP education expert Hildegard Hamm-Brucher, *Der Spiegel*, 53 (1975), 29.xii.75, pp. 18–19.

10. FAZ, 2.i.75, p. 4.

11. FAZ, 2.i.75, p. 4.

12. Schmidt, *Bundestag*, 20.i.76, p. 10583.

13. Apel, quoted *Der Spiegel*, 9.vi.75, p. 19.

14. FAZ, 4.vi.75, p. 1.

15. HB, 16.vi.75, p. 3.

16. *Der Spiegel*, 9.vi.75, p. 19.

17. Rohde at the SPD conference on 'Security through Social Democracy', quoted FR, 14.vi.75, p. 1.

18. FAZ, 22.i.75, p. 11.

19. Apel, quoted FR (evening edn.), 4.xi.75, p. 1.

20. Helmut Schmidt, quoted FAZ, 2.i.75, p. 4.

21. Apel, quoted FR, 15.xi.74, p. 1, and Schmidt, quoted DE, 16.vi.75, p 1.

22. Apel, quoted FR, 13.vi.75, p. 1.

23. Friedrichs, quoted FR, 2.vi.75, p. 1.

24. The Government's bill can be found in Bundestag Publication 7/4127 of 8.x.75, the 'budgetary structure' law finally passed in BGBl, 1975 I, pp. 3091ff.

25. 'A Clear Course', a series of advertisements by the Federal Ministry for Labour and Social Organization, Spring 1975.

26. W. Brandt, quoted DE, 2.iii.74, p. 1.

27. *Vorwärts*, quoted from FR, 8.ii.75, p 1.

28. Koschnick (SPD), *Bundestag*, 24.x.75, p. 13563.

29. W. Brandt, quoted FR, 3.vi.74, p. 4.

The Government had already had a study prepared with the title 'What's happening when nothing's happening?' (extracts in *Der Spiegel*, 5.xi.73, pp. 52ff.).

30. Helmut Schmidt, speech to the SPD group in the Bundestag, quoted FAZ, 26.iii.77, p. 6.

31. E. Lutz (SPD), quoted FR, 23.viii.77, p. 10.

32. FAZ, 20.iii.75, p. 1. The way the security service sees this development is illuminating: 'In spite of the difficulties which have affected large sections of the West German economy, and in spite of rising unemployment, the workers have so far shown little interest in the attempts of the extreme left to win their support for revolutionary goals' – note 'in spite of' and 'so far' (Security Service (*Verfassungsschutz*) report for 1974, Federal Ministry of the Interior, Bonn, 27.v.75, 'Extreme left-wing movements', p. 105).

33. Vogel (CDU), *Bundestag*, 12.vi.75, p. 12437, and 16.i.76, p. 14760. E. Benda, *Der Rechtsstaat in der Krise*, Stuttgart, 1972, p. 143.

34. J. Jeske (ed.), *Wie schütze ich meinen Betrieb?*, Düsseldorf and Vienna, 1973, p 11; *Jahresbericht des BDI 1972–1973*, Cologne, 1973, p. 125. On the growth of crimes at work and penalties for them, see G. Metzger-Pregizer and others, 'Betriebsjustiz und Betriebskriminalität', *Zeitschrift für Rechtspolitik* 7 (1974), pp. 167ff.

35. Cf. FAZ, 2.vii.75, p. 3.

36. von Weizsäcker, quoted HB, 18.iii.75, p. 3. For the detailed figures see *Polizeiliche Kriminalstatistik 1976*, Federal Ministry of the Interior, Bonn, 24.v.77. According to the yearbook for 1975, 'The general increase in crimes detected is mainly due to the growth in 'popular' offences such as theft, fraud and damage to property. For 1975 many of these show an above average rate of increase over the previous year. This group of offences alone accounts for 79·9 per cent of all crime recorded' (*Polizeiliche Kriminalstatistik 1975*, Federal Ministry of the Interior, Bonn, 27.v.76, pp. 1ff.).

37. E. Durkheim, *Regeln der soziologischen Methode* (1895), German edn, Neuwied, 1970, p. 160 ('On Criminality').

38. FAZ, 20.i.75, p. 3; HB, 30.iv.75, p. 3.

39. W. Wengler, 'Über die Unbeliebtheit der Juristen', in *Kölner Zeitschrift für Soziologie und Sozialpsychologie*, Supplementary Vol. 11, p. 241.

40. H. Herold, in E. Kogon (ed.), *Terror und Gewaltkriminalität – Herausforderung für den Rechtsstaat*, Frankfurt am Main, 1975, p. 49.

41. FR report of 4.viii.75, p. 4 on an empirical study, M. Kaase *et al.*, *Bedingungen unkonventionellen politischen Verhaltens in der Bundesrepublik*, University of Mannheim, 1975, reprinted in *Politische Vierteljahresheft*, special issue 7 (1976), pp. 179ff.

According to investigation carried out by 'infratest' into the same problem on behalf of the Federal Ministry of the Interior, 46 per cent of a representative sample of the population express a critical attitude 'to our system', and 33 per cent accept unconventional forms of political protest (FAZ, 19.vii.76, p. 10).

The study by the Frankfurt Battelle Institute mentioned in the text on the motives and potential for protest of community action groups against nuclear power stations was published by the Federal Ministry for Research: *Bürgerinitiativen im Bereich von Kernkraftwerken*, Bonn, 1975.

The study has since been extended. In order to reduce the continuing opposition of the action groups, the Federal Ministry of the Interior asked the Institute again in May 1975 to investigate 'the wishes for participation of those involved' and to produce 'concrete dialogue models'. The results of the Frankfurt social technologists' work, which cost a mere million DM, have now been submitted to the ministry. The action groups questioned described their experiences with officials as follows. 'The general view is that the elected representatives of the people have to take the decisions. But when a country's basic needs are involved, no one should be outvoted. No one has asked the so-called majority. Is the majority really informed? MPs don't represent the interests of the people involved or of a majority, but particular interests. Ideas must be judged by how far they really take account of the interests of the people involved. There is a danger that the impact of the action groups will be blunted. We must claim rights but not let ourselves be bought off . . . Participation could start straight away with a vote or referendum in the region. They don't do it because when you give the people information you get a straight no. The risk is too great for them. Then it's finished. Opponents are called left-wingers, politicians tell lies. We want honest politicians. Matthöfer's chats are a trick to get opponents off the street. They'd rather have yes-men, but the people are on their guard. We are ready to make any sacrifice for our existence in the fight against madness. We must fight for democracy, but first citizens must develop a sense of democracy. The older people are afraid because of their experiences in the Third Reich; most of the support for the opposition comes from young people. At the moment rights are being restricted by *Berufsverbote*, Section 88 and the swing to the right. Matthöfer has said: "In a democracy the majority decides. You people who oppose things are the minority. Worry about the majority, then we'll be able to look at all the other suggestions as well." Then I say is he really out of his mind? First, in a democracy there's also law. Law is something set up to oppose the idea of power. The powerful don't need law; it's always only the weak and powerless who need law. Obviously law was invented to protect the weak and the minority, and that means that even in a democracy what the majority says isn't the last word; it also has to be in accord with the law. But you don't find out what the law is about something just by reading the law codes; you have to look at the purpose of the law ... Parties are oligarchies and cliques ... What deputies do isn't so much what the people want ... Experts are tools ... They concentrate on the unpleasant side-effects and cure the symptoms, not the root of the trouble ... All real changes come from below' (S. van Buiren *et al.*, *Einstellungen unde Verhalten der Bevölkerung gegenüber verschiedenen Energiegewinnungsarten – Teil I: Gesellschaftliche Bedingungen für Kommunikation und Dialog in der Energiepolitik*, report of the Frankfurt am Main Battelle Institute (BF-R-62.919–1) for the Federal Ministry for Research and Technology (still unpublished), Frankfurt am Main, June 1976, pp. 94–5, 9, 89, 87.

42. E. Benda, *Der Rechtsstaat in der Krise*, Stuttgart, 1972, pp. 17 and 19. The same ideas appear in his party's 'offensive concept' towards these 'intrigues': 'Willingness to accept the social utopias put forward by the anarchists is encouraged by ... the loss of basic values, by the state's growing loss of authority as a result of a mis-understood liberalization, by carefully propagated doubts about ties of family, neighbourhood and religion ... It is intolerable that values and cultural achievements which grew up over centuries should be lightly called in question, that young people in schools

and universities should be given a world-view which makes the in-dividual person and the values he creates nothing and the pretended power of society and its 'evolution' everything ... It is one of the principal tasks of the state as an organizing force to ensure that the basic principles of our national order are not allowed to fall into disuse' (CDU *Offensiv-Konzept*, Bonn, 4.vii.75, p. 14).

Chancellor Schmidt has used similar language: 'It would be even more dangerous, and a threat to our existence, if the constitutional state were to lose the solidarity and self-identification of its citizens' (SPD conference on legal policy, quoted *Bundestag*, 12.vi.75,. p. 12435).

43. Vogel (CDU), *Bundestag*, 12.vi.75, p. 12435. Schmidt also be-lieves that 'too much constitutional liberalism has perhaps been practised' in some spheres (quoted FR, 2.v.75, p. 4).

44. Biedenkopf (CDU), quoted FR, 23.xii.75, p. 4.

45. Dregger (CDU), *Bundestag*, 13.iii.75, pp. 10739, 10743; Kohl (CDU), *Bundestag*, 13.iii.75, p. 10776. The Social Democrats think the same: 'Part of the concept of protecting the constitution ... [is] the strengthening of the people's capacity for intellectual resistance ... as a means of strengthening internal security ... Our state is only safe if ... the men and women of our country accept it as their own and stand up for it' (H. Schmidt as Hamburg senator in charge of the interior ministry, in P. Lücke (ed.), *Verfassungsschutz*, Cologne, 1966, pp. 15 and 33).

46. Krall (FDP), *Bundestag*, 7.vi.72, p. 10993.

47. Dregger (CDU), *Bundestag*, 13.iii.75, pp. 10742–3; Carstens (CDU), *Bundestag*, 24.x.75, p. 13589.

48. Dregger (CDU), *Bundestag*, 14.ii.74, p. 5005; E. Kern, *Der Strafschutz des Staates und seine Problematik*, Tübingen, 1963, p. 42.

49. Maihofer, *Bundesrat*, 20.ii.76, p. 25. The interior minister took care to avoid using the term *Berufsverbot* to describe the fact that 'an unsuitable applicant cannot realize his professional aim' (quoted, FR, 22.v.75, p. 2).

50. On 19 September 1950 the West German Government issued a 'Decision on political activity by members of the public service directed against the democratic basic order'. This includes the fol-lowing passage: 'The enemies of the Federal Republic are re-doubling their efforts to undermine the free, democratic basic order. Any involvement in such endeavours is incompatible with the duties of the public service ... The organizations support of which is in-

compatible with public duties include in particular [there followed, after the KPD and all its subsidiary organizations, the names of eight other left-wing groups, the 'Association of Victims of Persecution by the Nazi Regime' and two fascist bodies]. The Government calls on the heads of the service to take appropriate action against officials, clerical and manual workers who breach their obligation of loyalty to the Federal Republic by involvement in such organizations or activities. Without exception, those guilty [sic] are to be immediately removed from Government service, in the case of established officials by the opening of formal administrative proceedings, pending which they are to be suspended without pay, in the case of officials holding non-established appointments by the cancellation of the appointments, and in the case of clerical grades and manual workers by dismissal without notice. The Federal Government recommends the state governments to take corresponding action immediately.'

This so-called Adenauer–Heinemann decree (Gustav Heinemann, then not yet a member of the SPD, was at the time interior minister in the first Adenauer cabinet) was subsequently adopted by all the states and implemented on a massive scale.

'The service of a Federal civil servant as a KPD town councillor justifies the cancellation of civil servant status', it was ruled in a judgment of the Bavarian Supreme Administrative Court dated 20 December 1955 (NJW 1956, pp. 767–8). Or: 'The long-term membership of a civil servant in the Communist Party in every case constitutes a breach of his obligations to the service. Cancellation of an appointment for this reason is therefore neither unconstitutional nor an error of judgment', decided the Rhineland-Palatinate Labour Court on 11 December 1951 (*Recht der Arbeit* (1952), p. 196).

A third and final example: 'Under § 61 of the Federal Civil Service Regulations a non-established officer may be dismissed if by his behaviour he has given reason for doubt as to his suitability for acceptance as a permanent officer. The political activity of an officer may be justification for such doubts if it gives ground for concern that the officer would not fulfil his obligations to show, by his behaviour as a whole, loyalty to the democratic view of the state' (Federal Administrative Court, 10.iii.60, BVerwGE 10, 213ff.). This case involved a postman dismissed for political reasons (like the engine driver in 1976). This man went to the highest Federal administrative court because he rightly held it to be unconstitutional that his dismissal, which was justified on the ground of his membership of

163

the KPD, had taken place at a time when the KPD had not yet been banned by the Constitutional Court. The postman had to wait, as we saw, until four years after the ban on the KPD to be told the error of his ways. The court ruled that even before the 1956 judgment it had been apparent that Communists, at least, did not support the existing constitution. This finding, which had been made at the time of the postman's dismissal, had, said the Federal Administrative Court, subsequently been confirmed retrospectively by the Federal Constitutional Court in 1956 (BVerwGE, loc. cit., p. 216).

In its judgment on the *Berufsverbot* of 22 May 1975, the Constitutional Court attempts to justify present practice by presenting a pot-pourri of the history of German constitutional law since the founding of the Empire to show what benefits Germany has gained by looking after the 'body of officials'. It seems not in the least perturbed by the fact that these are the 1970s and the current constitution declares the Federal Republic to be a democratic state. The Constitutional Court, called upon to interpret the Basic Law, has made it clear in this judgment that the much-praised new democratic start, the break with the past said to have been made in 1949, never took place.

The judges of the Constitutional Court passed over National Socialism, specifically its 'Law for the restoration of the professional civil service' of 7 April 1933 (RGBl I, No. 34), in silence. This may have been out of personal consideration for Judge Willi Geiger, who took part in the judgment and who previously, in the 'Third Reich', had been heavily involved with issues of 'intellectual and moral rearmament' by keeping certain professions free of 'enemies'. In 1941 he published a study on 'The Legal Position of the Editor', which sought to reveal the reasons for the 'effectiveness of our press', 'the principles by which an editor is chosen, educated, appointed and guided', one 'of the greatest benefits of the National Socialist Revolution' (W. Geiger, *Die Rechtsstellung des Schriftleiters,* Darmstadt and Leipzig, 1941, p. v).

'Liberalism', according to Geiger in 1941, 'the outlook of the nineteenth century, also found its expression in press law. The general movement of the law in all European states until the early years of the twentieth century was towards "a liberation of the press from its fetters" and the establishment of legal protection to ensure its freedom. This reflected a fundamentally liberal attitude, the idea that there is a natural opposition between individual and state, which led to the belief that the human rights of citizens had to be protected against the omnipotence of the state' (op. cit, pp. 5–6).

'The editor in the new state must – and this clause of the new [press] law is particularly important – "possess the qualities required by the task of exercising moral and intellectual influence over the public" . . . The task of finding whether an editor fulfils this requirement is nothing other than the testing of personal suitability for the profession of editor, a test which is vitally important for the dignity of the profession and the correct influence of the press on public opinion . . . The lack of these qualities will not be concluded without special reason from previous membership of a political party, but is indicated by activity for the Marxist press continuing into the period of the National Revolution and must be regarded as proved if an editor has been guilty of persistent serious violations of his professional obligations or has shown himself, in his professional or his personal activity, to be harmful to the People and the State . . . An editor must be of pure Aryan descent . . . With a single blow this rule has put an end to the excessive influence of the Jewish race in the sphere of the press, where it was damaging the nation and undermining our culture. In doubtful cases there is provision for a certificate to be obtained; these are issued by the racial investigation expert attached to the ministry of the interior' (op. cit., pp. 38ff.).

In a fat 'Festschrift for his sixty-fifth birthday' this judge of the modern Constitutional Court is rightly declared to be 'a personality capable of making a striking impression in many offices' (G. Leibholz *et al.*, *Menschenwürde und freiheitliche Rechtsordnung – Festschrift für Willi Geiger zum 65. Geburstag*, Tübingen, 1974, p. ix).

51. Stoltenberg (CDU), *Bundesrat*, 20.ii.76, p. 20.

52. *Berufsverbot* judgment of the Federal Constitutional Court, 22.v.75 (2 BvL 13/73), p. 31, pp. 15 and 18.

53. Dregger (CDU), *Bundestag*, 24.x.75, p. 13547.

54. G. Gillesen, 'The Withering Away of the State', leading article, FAZ, 16.i.74, p. 1.

55. CDU, *Offensiv-Konzept*, Bonn, 4.vii.75, p. 19.

56. Willy Brandt, in a letter to the Chairman of the Dutch Labour Party, J. Van den Heuvel, dated 9 December 1974. Van den Heuvel had expressed concern to the West German Social Democrats about the measures in the field of 'internal security': 'It is very painful for us to learn of sudden changes to laws which were found satisfactory at the trials of the German war criminals.' The correspondence is reprinted in *Der lange Marsch*, 19 (Dec. 1975), p. 5.

Chapter 2: Channelling Emotions

1. Quoted FR, 10.iii.75, p. 4; West Berlin Senator Neubauer (SPD), in charge of police, on television (ARD), 1.iii.75, 8 p.m.; the mayor of Frankfurt, Arndt, during the West German trades union congress New Year reception – quoted FAZ, 12.i.76, p. 17. The nature of the threat is distorted whenever dangers are discussed. Now it is not nuclear power stations which threaten people and their environment, but 'Atom Centres Threatened by Terrorist Danger' (FR, 6.i.76, p. 1; FR, 21.ii.76, p. 12).

2. Maihofer, *Bundestag*, 13.iii.75, p. 10747.

3. FAZ, 14.iii.75, p. 1, and justice minister Vogel (SPD), *Bundestag*, 16.i.76, p. 14741.

4. G. Heinemann (SPD), quoted FR, 16.viii.75, p. 10.

5. Schneider (CDU), *Bundestag*, 7.vi.72, p.11017.

6. Maihofer, 'Rechtsstaat in der Bewährung', lecture at the Bitburg Dialogue, 8.i.76, MS, p. 10.

7. FR, 3.iv.74, p. 7.

8. C. Schmitt, *Der Begriff des Politischen*, Hamburg, 1933, pp. 28–9.

9. Vogel (CDU), *Bundestag*, 13.xi.74, p. 8802.

10. In order of the quotations: Vetter (TUC), quoted FR,10.iii.75, p. 3; Sabais (SPD), quoted DE, 8.ii.74; Brandt (SPD), quoted FAZ, 10.iii.75, p. 1 and FAZ, 21.v.75, p. 1; Wohlrabe (CDU), *Bundestag*, 7.vi.72, p. 10979; CDU/CSU Bundestag group, quoted FR, 28.ii.75, p. 2; FAZ, 26.iv.75, p. 1; FAZ, 28.v.75, p. 1; *Der Arbeitgeber*, No. 24–26 (1974), p. 1004; Kohl (CDU), *Bundestag*, 13.iii.75, p. 10777.

11. K. Schütz, in *Berliner Stimme*, 17.ii.68.

12. *Bunte*, No. 11 (1975), 6.iii.75, p. 30.

13. H. J. Vogel, quoted FR, 14.v.75, p. 4; FAZ, 30.iv.75, p. 1.

14 *Bild*, 5.xii.75, p. 2.

15. *Die Zeit*, 9.i.76, p. 4.

16. In order of the quotations: FAZ, 30.iv.75, p. 1; FR, 30.xi.7, p. 3; *Taschenbuch für Wehrfragen*, Frankfurt am Main, 1966–7, quoted P. Brückner and others, *Staatsfeinde*, West Berlin, 1972, p. 51.

17. In order of the quotations: H. Schmidt, quoted FR, 30.xii.75, p. 1; Strauss, Sonthofen speech, *Der Spiegel*, 11 (1975), 10.iii.75, p. 38; H. Herold (Federal Criminal Investigation Office) quoted *Der Spiegel*, 28.iv.75, p. 32; Spranger (CDU), *Bundestag*, 16.i.76, p. 14729.

18. H. Schmidt, quoted FR, 2.v.75, p. 2; *Bild*, 2.v.75, p. 1.

19. Strauss, in *Der Spiegel*, 28.vii.69, p. 20.

20. G. Löwenthal, quoted from *Stern*, 6.iii.75, p. 30; Strauss Sonthofen speech, *Der Spiegel*, 10.iii.75, p. 36.

21. *Bild*, 9.viii.73, p. 1.

22. K.-H. Krumm, in FR, 6.i.76, p. 3.

23. W. Maihofer, in *Innere Sicherheit*, Information from the Federal Ministry of the Interior, No. 31 (1975), 10.xii.75, p. 4. Interview with Buback, *Der Spiegel*, 16.ii.76, p. 38; cf. similar remarks in *Bild*, 3.i.76, pp. 1–2.

24. *Die Welt*, quoted from *Die Zeit*, 9.i.76, p.4.

25. FR, 27.xii.75, p. 1.

26. *Stern*, 8.vi.76, pp. 12ff.

27. Buback, FR, 28.x.74, p. 2.

28. Report on the Stammheim trial, FR, 29.iii.76, p. 13.

29. In order of the quotations: *Bild*, 24.ii.75, p. 1; *Welt am Sonntag*, 15.vi.75, DE, 14.iii.75, p. 1, FR, 14.iii.75, p. 24; *Bild*-Berlin, 2.v.75, p. 1; *Die Welt*, 16.v.75, p. 1; FR, 27.v.75, p. 18; FAZ, 4.xii.75, p. 1; FAZ, 20.i.76, p. 3; FR, 4.ii.76, p. 15; *Bild*, 21.vi.76, p. 1; FR, 22.i.76, p. 1; Buback, in *Bild*, 3.i.76, pp. 1–2 – *Bild am Sonntag*, 1.ii.76, p. 6; *Der Spiegel*, 5.i.76, p. 31; DE, 3.ii.76, p. 1.

30. Buback, quoted FAZ, 10.x.75, p. 5, and FR, 28.x.75, p. 2; Vogel (SPD), quoted FR, 14.v.75, p. 4.

31. 'Security circles in Bonn', quoted FAZ, 6.viii.75, p. 1; *Bild*, 22.xi.74, p. 1; FAZ, 19.vii.75, p. 3 and *Die Welt*, 8.x.75, p. 1.

32. FAZ, 24.x.75, p. 12.

33. *Quick*, 6.iii.75, p. 22.

34. W. Brandt, quoted FAZ, 10.iii.75, p. 1, and FR, 14.vi.75, p. 1.

35. H. Schmidt in an interview, DE, 7.ix.74, p. 3.

36. Maihofer, *Bundestag*, 13.xi.74, p. 8801.

37. *Bild*, 4.iii.75, p. 2.

38. Dregger, in *Neue Revue*, 10.iii.75, p. 11; *Bunte Illustrierte*, 6.iii.75, p. 11; *Quick*, 6.iii.75, p. 26; DE, 1.iii.75, p. 2; *Bild am Sonntag*, 8.xii.74; *Wort am Sonntag*, ARD television, 1.iii.75; FAZ, 1.iii.76, p. 1; Buback, in FR, 28.x.74, p. 2.

39. E. Benda, speech at the funeral of G. von Drenkmann, quoted FAZ, 22.xi.74, p. 2.

40. FAZ, 1.iii.75, p. 1.

41. Dregger, *Im Brennpunkt*, ARD TV programme, 5.iii.75; Schwarz (CDU), police minister of Rhineland-Palatinate, in *Bild*, 7.iii.75, p. 2.

42. FAZ, 1.iii.75, p. 10. Buback: 'I can only ask citizens as well to keep their eyes open and report to the police any incidents which strike them as odd' (*Stern*, 5.vi.75, p. 132), and Schmidt: 'I call on citizens to inform a police station immediately of any suspicious sights' (*Bild*, 12.x.74, p. 2).

43. In addition to normal warrant searches, in May 1975 the Criminal Investigation Bureau (BKA) began a new attempt to enlist auxiliary police. It called on all filling station attendants in West Germany to join the 'hunt for criminals on the run, especially anarchist terrorists'. 'We expect your observations to provide us with fresh clues for the search,' the Bureau told the 'dear operators' in a letter. 'Your knowledge puts you in a special position to help the police. The enclosed checklist will help you to notice suspicious features when attending to vehicles; please report them.' Suspicious features included 'large amounts of hard cash for coin-operated tanks', 'a striking amount of tools in the vehicle', 'inappropriate electrical equipment', 'large quantities of reserve petrol', 'bomb-like containers or parts', 'wigs and other items of disguise' (BKA letter of 9.v.75 to operators of West German filling stations, and 'Checklist for filling station personnel'). The plan to activate hairdressers – who were to report to the police who had their hair cut, dyed or restyled, who bought wigs, etc. – was later dropped.

44. DE, 31.v.75, p. 41.

45. Dregger (CDU), *Bundestag*, 13.iii.75, p. 8802.

46. FAZ, 7.iii.75, p. 1.

47. Carstens (CDU), in an interview with *Bild*, 6.iii.75. p. 3.

48. DE, 14.iii.75; the *Frankfurter Allgemeine* quoted the following figures produced by the Institute for Applied Sociology: 'Internal security the most important problem in Berlin: October 1974 37 per cent, November 49 per cent (Drenkmann), December 51 per cent, January 45 per cent, February 34 per cent' (FAZ, 4.ii.75, p. 2).

49. FAZ, 16.vi.75, p. 9.

50. 'In the light of their experiences of Weimar, the public of the time no longer regarded as spectacular or unusual the legal measures taken by the Nazi regime to bring about a permanent state of exception under their own regime' (H. Ridder, *Grundgesetz, Notstand und politisches Strafrecht*, Frankfurt am Main, 1965, p. 16).

51. 'Concerning Internal Security,' *Die Polizei*, 7 (1962), p. 219. The police minister of Rhineland-Palatinate takes an even gloomier view. He admitted that 'the public has developed a less

prejudiced and more factual view of internal security, but I see a danger that if spectacular violent crimes decline or people get used to them, large-scale public interest in the subject will slacken' (H. Schwarz, *Sicherheit oder Freiheit*, Stuggart, 1974, p. 45).

When the real nature and targets of the 'danger' are so openly stated, there can be no guarantee that it will remain confined to headlines. In Stuttgart, for example, press reports claimed that the Red Army Faction wanted to let off a bomb somewhere in the city on 2 June 1972. Some days previously the RAF had reacted by sending a letter, authenticated by the Criminal Investigation Bureau, to the editors of several newspapers stating that they had nothing to do with the alleged threat: 'The content, intention, spirit and style of the false statements makes them more likely to have come from the pigs themselves' ('Statement by the Red Army Faction', from K. Croissant and others, *Politische Prozesse ohne Verteidigung?*, West Berlin, 1976, p. 61).

The RAF statement was suppressed. On 2 June 1972 Stuttgart presented the appearance of a beleaguered city. Thousands of police checked all access roads, vehicles and 'suspicious persons'. By means of this 'threat', carefully launched by an interested party, the state security authorities had finally achieved the result said to be the necessary preliminary to the offer of a reward for Baader, Ensslin, Meinhof, Meins and Raspe in a discussion some months previously at the conference of interior ministers. 'At present', it was said at the interior ministers' conference at the end of January 1972, the offer of a reward could 'give the gang added psychological weight'. This undesired result could 'be avoided only if the reward were contrasted with a spectacular event which spontaneously justified it. In this way it would emphasize the particularly dangerous nature of the gang' (Proceedings of the Conference of Interior Ministers, reprinted in *The Baader–Meinhof Report–Documents of the Federal Criminal Investigation Office and the Federal Office for the Protection of the Constitution*, Mainz, 1972, p. 216).

Chapter 3: The Perfecting of Surveillance

1. *Verfassungsschutz* law of 27.ix.50 (*Bundesgesetzblatt* I, 682); BKA law of 8.iii.51 (BGBl I, 165).

2. 'Allied Police Letter' of 14.iv.49, reprinted in Huber, *Quellen zum Staatsrecht der Neuzeit*, Vol. 2, Tübingen, 1953–4, p. 216. This letter was in effect an order authorizing the use of the power given

to the Federal Government in the Basic Law to establish 'central offices for the police information and intelligence gathering service to collect data for purposes relevant to the protection of the consitution and for the criminal police' (Art. 87, Section 1, Para. 2 GG in the form approved by the parliamentary council on 8.v.49).

3. Von Thadden (DRP), *Bundestag*, 12.ix.50, p. 3133. During the celebrations for the twenty-fifth anniversary of the Federal Criminal Investigation Bureau, Horst Herold, its current head, complained about the shortsightedness of the Bundestag and the Allies in passing the 1951 law, and offered a new account, with some curious logic, of the background to the Nazi *coup d'état*: 'Barely six years after the capitulation the long and difficult discussions were still under the continuing influence of the terror which left the centrally administered police of the Third Reich graven on our memories. The fear of a possible misuse of police institutions prevailed. No attention was paid to the view that central police institutions would rather have prevented the trouble, given that the Third Reich did not inherit any but had to create its own' (H. Herold, '25 Jahre Bundeskriminalamt', address at the celebrations on 16.iii.76, MS, pp. 1–2).

4. Law on the Federal Criminal Investigation Bureau in the version of 29.vi.73 (BGBl I, 704); Law on the *Verfassungsschutz* of 7.viii.72 (BGBl I, 1382). The extension of the powers of the organizations was made constitutionally secure by the 'thirty-first Law to Amend the Basic Law' of 28.vii.72 (BGB1 I, 1305) which made important changes in Art. 7 No. 10 and Art. 87, Section 1, Para. 2 GG.

5. W. Maihofer, speech on the 25th anniversary of the BKA, MS, p. 1. 'As most people know,' Herold explained, 'our development has been literally explosive. Between 1968 and now budgets, office space, established posts and capital investment have increased four and five times, in some cases ten times,' a growth 'without parallel in the history of the public service' ('25 Jahre Bundeskriminalamt', MS, p. 5).

Tables 1 and 2 show the growth in personnel and expenditure on the BKA and the *Verfassungsschutz* (Source: *Innere Sicherheit im freiheitlichen Rechtsstaat – Leistungbilanz*, Federal Ministry of the Interior, Bonn, 1975, pp. 107–8):

1. Federal Criminal Investigation Bureau

Year	Posts	Total expenditure DM 000 000	Comparative figures
1965	818	13·9	
1966	832	16·0	Previous estimates
1967	843	16·6	(1968–72)
1968	893	17·8	19·4
1969	933	22·4	22·4
1970	1,211	38·9	24·8
1971	1,529	54·7	26·4
1972	1,585	75·2	40·0
1973	2,062	122·0	
1974	2,212	128·0	
1975	2,237	136·8	
1976	2,424	149·0	
% increase			
1969–76	159·8	565·2	

6. Herold, '25 Jahre Bundeskriminalamt', MS, p. 5. Helmut Schmidt wants to lay down new criteria: 'My personal opinion is that I don't believe things must always be like this. I do not believe that for the next twenty-five years of the existence of the Federal Republic of Germany we can totally rule out the setting up of a central detective force such as almost all our Western neighbours have – to say nothing of those in the East' (*Bundestag*, 13.iii.75, p. 1034). It ought to be made possible to have a 'centrally organized fight against crime reaching into the furthest village' (Schmidt, quoted DE, 24.iii.75, p. 1).

7. H. Herold, '25 Jahre Bundeskriminalamt', pp. 6–7.

8. W. Maihofer, Speech on the 25th anniversary of the setting up of the Federal Criminal Investigation Bureau, 16.iii.76, MS, p. 21.

9. Herold, loc. cit., p. 3.

10. G.-D. Schoen, P. Frisch, *Aufrechterhaltung der öffentlichen Sicherheit und Ordnung*, Bad Honnef, 1973, p. 11.

11. For the development and use made of the law on foreigners in West Germany since the recruitment of immigrant workers, see W.

2. Federal Office for the Protection of the Constitution (*Verfassungsschutz*)

Year	Posts	Total Expenditure DM 000 000	Comparative figures
1965	822	18·4	
1966	832	22·2	Previous estimates
1967	949	22·7	(1968–72)
1968	986	23·6	26·7
1969	1,016	29·9	28·0
1970	1,088	34·0	29·4
1971	1,186	37·3	27·2
1972	1,259	48·1	27·5
1973	1,459	62·1	
1974	1,559	74·5	
1975	1,585	76·9	
1976	1,628	80·8	
% increase 1969–76	60·2	170·2	

In Autumn 1977 the Federal Cabinet agreed on an increase in the budget for the Federal Criminal Investigation Bureau and the *Verfassungsschutz* of almost DM 1,000 million over a period of 5–10 years (FAZ, 15.ix.77, p. 1).

Däubler, 'Zur rechtlichen und sozialen Stellung der Gastarbeiter in der BRD', in *Demokratie und Recht* 1 (1974), pp. 3ff., and H. Heldmann, *Ausländerrecht – Disziplinarordnung für die Minderheit*, Darmstadt and Neuwied, 1974.

According to the Government, an explicit reference to the surveillance of foreigners in the new law on the *Verfassungsschutz* (§ 3, Para. 1, No. 3) was felt to be necessary because the law previously in force was 'doubtful' and revealed a 'gap in the definition of the powers of the service responsible for the protection of internal security' (Federal Government proposal for a law on the *Verfassungsschutz*, Bundestag Publication 6/1179 (22.ix.70), p. 3).

It appears from a reading of the *Verfassungsschutz* reports for the years before 1972 that these 'gaps' were either not noticed by the 'service responsible for internal security' or independently bridged without any legal justification: political groups formed by foreigners have always been kept under surveillance by the *Verfassungsschutz* (see the *Verfassungsschutzbericht 1971* published by the Federal Ministry of the Interior).

12. H. Emig, political policeman, Darmstadt police headquarters, in G. Wallraff, *Dreizehn unerwünschte Reportagen*, Reinbek bei Hamburg, 1975, p. 57.

13. L. Martin, former Federal Attorney-General, 'Die Rolle der Ämter für Verfassungsschutz bei der Strafverfolgung', in P. Lücke (ed.), *Verfassungsschutz – Beiträge aus Wissenschaft und Praxis*, Cologne, 1966, pp. 90ff. The 'Guidelines for criminal and Summary Procedure' (RiStBV) mentioned by Martin are administrative regulations, not law.

With regard to state security proceedings they run as follows: 'In state security cases (§ § 74a, 120 GVG) it is generally necessary to approach the offices of the *Verfassungsschutz* and the other intelligence services of the Federal Republic within the limits of their competence so that information and data collected by them can be assessed during the investigation. Attention is drawn to the central evidence collecting unit operated by the Federal *Verfassungsschutz*. In particularly important cases it is recommended that contact is made with the agencies mentioned before any action is taken . . . In state security cases members of the services listed in section 1 can be brought into interrogations or other aspects of the investigation (e.g. inspection of the scene of a crime, searches and confiscations) as experts or informants. Requests for their assistance should be noted in the file.' In state security cases the prosecutor sends a copy of the details of the investigation, charge and verdict to the Federal office of the *Verfassungsschutz* and to the office of the relevant state *Verfassungsschutz* 'if their content or the evidence mentioned in them make it important that they should be analysed' (No. 220, paras 1, 3 and 4 RiStBV in the version of 1.xii.70, reprinted in T. Kleinknecht, *Kommentar zur Strafprozessordnung*, 31st edn, 1974, Appendix F, p. 1617).

14. G.-D. Schoen *et al.*, *Aufrechterhaltung der öffentlichen Sicherheit und Ordnung*, Bad Honnef, 1973, p. 123.

15. In order of the quotations: FR, 14.vi.75, p. 1; FAZ, 19.vi.75, p. 1; *Bild*, 19.vi.75, p. 1; *Vorwärts*, 19.vi.75, p. 1.

16. Article 10, Section 2 GG, revised by the law of 24.vii.68 (BGBl I, 709). Article 19, Section 4 was also altered: the constitutional

Notes

guarantee of that section – 'if anyone's rights are infringed by a public authority, he shall have the right of redress through the courts' – was given a limiting postscript which allows the monitoring of mail and telephones in secret and without control by the courts: 'Art. 10, Sect. 2, Para. 2 is unaffected by this provision.'

Two months after this amendment to the Basic Law, which disregards central constitutional guarantees (Art. 79, para. 3 and so also Art. 1, para. 1 and Art. 20 and Art. 19, paras 2 and 4 GG), the Bundestag passed 'Law 10' (the so-called telephone tapping law of 13.viii.70, BGBl I, 949).

This law received the blessing of the Constitutional Court in spite of an objection from the state of Hesse, though this merely complained about the total withholding of information about surveillance from the subject, (judgment of 15.xii.70 – in BVerfGE 30, 1ff.). The Federal Government then proposed an addition which would allow the subject to be informed at the end of the surveillance if 'the purpose of the surveillance would not be endangered' (Bundestag Publication 72505, 27.vii.74). The first, and so far only, reading is reported in *Bundestag*, 18.i.74.

17. BVerfGE, loc. cit. Professor O. Kunze, chairman of the 'Law 10 Commission' on the telephone tapping law, in *Das Parlament*, 17.i.76, p 13.

18. § § 100a, 100b StPO, introduced by Article 2 of Law 10; cf. esp. § 100a, para. 1c with the commentary of T. Kleinknecht, *Strafprozessordnung*, 31st edn, 1974, No. 3 on 100a.

19. G.-D. Schoen *et al.*, *Aufrechterhaltung der öffentlichen Sicherheit und Ordnung*, Bad Honnef, 1973, p. 123.

20. R. Altmann and others, *Handbuch für Führung und Einsatz der Polizei – Kommentar zur PDV 100*, Stuttgart 1976, Note A on Point 2.1.2.2 PDV ('Observation Tactics').

21. *Kommentar zur PDV 100*, Note Db on 2.1.1.2 PDV.

22. H. J. Schwagerl *et al.*, *Der Schutz der Verfassung – Ein Handbuch für Theorie und Praxis*, Cologne, 1968, p. 91.

23. H.-U. Evers, *Privatsphäre und Ämter für Verfassungsschutz*, Berlin, 1960, p. 153.

24. The V-man also enjoys privileges in terms of court procedure – his reports count as the statements of a witness without his being required to appear, or even be named in court; someone else speaks for him, an official who, as a 'witness to hearsay', reports what the V-man has passed on to him. For reasons of police tactics the V-man, as the 'real witness' or alleged witness, deliberately stays in the

174

background, and the principle of direct evidence (§ 250 StPO) is abandoned. The Federal High Court was unable to see any problem here, even in state security cases (BGHSt,1.viii.62 (3StR 28/62), in NJW (1962), 1876). The practice has emerged as a result of decisions made in the High Courts.

25. H. J. Schwagerl, op. cit., p. 92, referring to an unpublished decision of the High Court (6.xii.74 – StR 17/54).

26. D. Posser, *Erfahrungen aus Vorverfahren, Hauptverhandlungen und Strafvollzug bei politischen Überzeugungstätern*, paper given at the 'Study meeting and general discussion of the enlarged amnesty initiative committee and defence lawyers in political cases, Frankfurt, 4 and 5 May 1975', report (ed. W. Amman), p. 19.

27. H.-J. Horchem, head of the Hamburg *Verfassungsschutz*, in E. Kogon (ed), *Terror und Gewaltkriminalität – Herausforderung für den Rechtsstaat*, Frankfurt am Main, 1975, p. 77.

Horchem here mentions the murder of Ulrich Schmücker in June 1974. Responsibility for the murder was claimed on leaflets by a group including a certain Jürgen Bodeux, who was charged with the crime together with former friends in West Berlin.

This was not the only trial in which Bodeux appeared as accuser for the political police; his information was passed on from prosecuting authority to prosecuting authority throughout West Germany, and introduced into various state security trials. Bodeux himself was soon sent on a tour, so that weight should be attached in as many political trials as possible to the statements of a man who not only denounced former friends but was also accused of committing the basest of crimes against one of them. It is doubtful whether the role of Bodeux's superiors in the security service in the murder of Schmücker can ever be established, particularly as Schmücker himself had close connections with the West Berlin security services. An important question is whether Schmücker was killed before the eyes of his police superiors and whether this crime was permitted by the security services to produce a blaze to illuminate the whole left.

Investigations into the case have come to a full stop – the security services invoke the 'obligation of secrecy in intelligence activity'. The secrecy in this case apparently went so far that even the state security department of the West Berlin detective force was groping in the dark. About Schmücker's involvement with the secret service they knew – officially, at least – nothing. The head of the West Berlin political police, Kittlaus, appealed for 'anyone who can give

175

us information about the recent movements of the dead man, Ulrich Schmücker, especially just before the crime'. Kittlaus's colleagues in the *Verfassungsschutz* could have done, but were not obliged to say anything and perhaps, for 'reasons of secret service tactics' really said nothing, even to the police. 'It should be noted', according to the *Verfassungsschutz* commentary on its law, 'that officials of the *Verfassungsschutz* are not obliged in every case to pass on relevant information to the judicial authorities or, for example, to the Federal Criminal Investigation Bureau in its role as central information centre for the criminal police' (Commentary on § 3, para. 3 of the law on the *Verfassungsschutz*, in G.-D. Schoen *et al.*, *Aufrechterhaltung der öffenlichen Sicherheit und Ordnung*, Bad Honnef, 1973, p. 122). In the Schmücker case the secret service no doubt thought it more expedient to keep out of any executive action though it does, as we have shown, take part in this in other cases. (Details from the ARD TV programme *Panorama*, 14.iv.75.)

28. FR, 19.iii.76, p. 24; statement by the deputy police commissioner for West Berlin on the 'legal basis', *Berliner Morgenpost*, 18.iii.76, p. 5.

29. T. Kleinknecht, *Kommentar zur Strafprosessordnung*, 31st edn, 1971, No. 1C, on § 163.

30. J. Bardenhewer, deputy head of the Federal *Verfassungschutz*, in *Das Parlament*, 3 (1975), 17.i.76, p. 2.

31. H. H. Bielefeld, Minister of the Interior for Hesse, in *Hessische Polizeirundschau* 10 (1975), p. 2, and quoted FR, 26.ix.75, p. 15.

32. According to the list in the judgment of the Tübingen Provincial Court, 18.iii.74, KJ 1974, 418ff.

33. ibid.

34. ibid.

35. Judgment of the criminal panel of the High Court, 12.viii.75 (NJW 1975, 2075–6). Administrative proceedings of this sort to compel the production or destruction of material collected during police investigations are, as events show, usually unsuccessful.

36. If the police are ever unable to take photographs themselves, they simply confiscate those of reporters or film-makers present. This happened in West Berlin, where newspaper editor Helke Sander had filmed a women's demonstration in front of the Kaiser Wilhelm Memorial Church with a video camera. They filmed women distributing leaflets against the anti-abortion law, talking to passers-by and using the forecourt of the church to produce plac-

ards, and the subsequent moving in of police and fire brigade to restore the 'disrupted order'. Helke Sander and a colleague were arrested and the video equipment confiscated as 'evidence', an action confirmed as legal on appeal by the courts. As an independent film-maker, Helke Sander could not invoke the right of a journalist not to give evidence, nor alternatively the constitutional guarantee of the freedom of art: a documentary film was nothing to do with art, according to the court (LG Berlin, 27.v.75 – 515 Qs 29/75).

The discovery was not new. This was not the first time journalists had been made tools of the police against their will, and their films and photos made the basis of police investigations. For similar confiscations against photographers of daily papers, see *Vorgänge* 2 (1969), p. 70, and 6 (1969), p. 222.

37. W. Maihofer (ed.), *Innere Sicherheit im freiheitlichen Rechtsstaat – Leistungsbilanz*, Bonn, 1975, p. 27.

38. H. H. Bielefeld, Hesse interior minister, *Hessische Polizeirundschau*, 11 (1973), p. 18.

39. BVerfGE of 22.v.75 (2 BvL 13/73, p. 28).

40. Figures from FR, 9.i.76, p. 4.

41. *Der Bundesminister des Innern teilt mit*, press release, 8.iv.76, p. 1.

42. Vogel (CDU), *Bundestag*, 14.ii.74, p. 5073.

43. There is now an abundance of material on *Berufsverbot* hearings. On the questioning of neighbours, see FR, 15.i.76, p. 1.

44. H. J. Schwagerl *et. al.*, *Der Schutz der Verfassung – Ein Handbuch für Theorie und Praxis*, Cologne, 1960, p. 90.

45. 'Radikalen-Suche: McCarthy auf deutsch?', *Der Spiegel*, 12.iv.76, p. 52.

46. Judgment of the Darmstadt administrative court, 8.i.76 (IV M622/75, pp. 5 and 6).

47. Letter from Amnesty International to President Walter Scheel; extracts printed in FR, 16.x.75, p. 1.

48. Von Thadden (CDU), *Bundestag*, 22.vi.72, p. 11428. The deputy cited Amnesty as an example of an organization which carried out 'a moral, humanitarian task' and therefore, unlike other organizations, was not an object of secret service concern or activity.

49. FR, 9.ii.76, p. 1; FR, 10.ii.76, p. 1; FR, 10.iii.76, p. 1; FR, 11.ii.76, p. 4; FR, 14.iv.76, p. 4; FR, 16.iv.76, p. 4.

50. FR, ibid.

51. *Berufsverbot* judgment of the Constitutional Court, 22.v.76 (2 BvL 13/73), p 24; Maihofer, *Bundestag*, 12.v.76, p. 16953.

52. FR, 13.ii.76, p. 1; FR, 9.iii.76, p. 15; FR, 12.vi.76, p. 4.

53. The sections of private police forces in industrial concerns described as 'responsible for security' are naturally not responsible for keeping an eye on the security of jobs, but on the insecurity which can be introduced into 'industrial peace' by employees.

'Industrial police' (*Werkschutz*) is therefore a clearer title for the men and women, currently about 100,000, in plain clothes and uniform, with weapons and without, who are employed to keep down 'industrial crime', strikes, and also – like the *Verfassungsschutz* – on front-line observation. In this work 'collaboration between industrial police, plant and departmental managers, and foremen' is vital. It 'must be so close that the industrial police are constantly informed about the feelings of the work-force. In this context the slightest sign of annoyance among certain members of the work-force with their superiors may be of significance.' Supervisors and foremen 'should for their part immediately inform the head of the industrial police of anything suspicious they notice among the members of the work-force under their authority, for example suspicious behaviour, radical political attitudes, unreliability at work . . .' (*Zivilschutz*, 5 (1963) pp.159–60, quoted from *Blätter für deutsche and internationale Politik*, 10 (1969), p. 1078). The 'Journal for Leadership Practice' – *Plus* – advises 'keeping workers or groups of workers known to be radicals under special observation. Keep a careful eye on all publications distributed in the firm. If unrest occurs, address the works council immediately to remove the basis of conflicts' (*Plus*, 10 (1973), pp. 37ff.).

The ratio to be aimed at is to have one observer per 100 subjects; as far as possible observers should be long-standing 'members of the firm' who know everyone and who are accepted.

Employers thankfully assured the inquirers that unions were 'concerned to regularize the relationship between work-force and industrial police' (ARD TV programme on 'Works policemen', 7.i.76). The West German TUC, whose member unions organize between 80 and 90 per cent of the 80,000 industrial police, works to improve the image of these members. They must qualify for their job, and after being examined by an 'Employer-Employee Commission' are awarded certificates by the Chamber of Trade and Industry designating them 'trained industrial police officers' (*Spiegel*, 3.ii.75, p. 38).

178

Cooperation also goes on above the level of the factory. The umbrella organization 'Association for the Protection of the German Economy', founded in 1951 by the West German Federation of Employers' Associations, the Association of German Industry and the German Conference of Trade and Industry, has since changed its name to 'Coordinating Centre for Security Questions in the Industrial Economy', with headquarters in Bonn and four regional offices (see *Die Polizei*, 1 (1976), p.14).

Outside the factory contacts are excellent with the Federal and state Criminal Investigation Bureaux, local police stations and the *Verfassungsschutz*. Following the example of the latter, the industrial security service constantly records the results of its observations and the information it receives. It keeps the famous blacklists: 'A file should be kept on all a company's personnel, and should include information about who is a union member and who would probably be prepared to continue working in the event of an unofficial strike. If necessary the file should be kept off the premises' (*Plus*, pp. 37ff. On the history of the use of such lists or files see, 'Arbeitgeber und Arbeitskampf', in H. Maus (ed.), *Gesellschaft, Recht und Politik – Wolfgang Abendroth zum sechzigsten Geburtstag*, Neuwied and Berlin, 1967, pp. 277 and 285).

Dossiers of this sort can be passed from firm to firm. A recent development is to do this quite openly in the form of coded testimonials (see 'Millionen Arbeitszeugnisse in Geheimcode abgefasst', FR, 22.xi.74, p. 8, and 'Arbeitszeugnisse – Tricks mit schönen Worten', *Stern*, 10.x.74, p. 202).

54. Parliament of Lower Saxony Publication 8/922 (30.vi.75): the law was passed on 24.vi.76 with the agreement of all the parties (FR, 25.vi.76, p. 4). Cooperation with managements is dealt with in § 6 of the law (see also the preamble in the Publication cited).

55. Lower Saxony *Verfassungsschutz* law § 5 (and preamble).

56. Holtfort, member of the council of the West German Chamber of Notaries, quoted *Die Zeit*, 18.vi.76, p. 33.

57. FR, 2.iv.75, p. 13; *Quick*, 11 (1975), 6.vii.75, p. 30.

58. *Polizei – bürgernah!* published by the West Berlin police commissioner, 1974.

59. H. Herold, interview in *Wirtschaftswoche*, 14 (1972), 7.iv.72, p. 20.

60. 'Der Schutzmann, der auch mal ein Bierchen trinkt – "Kontaktpolizisten" kennen sich im ihrem Viertel aus – Pläne der SPD' – report in FAZ, 14.ii.76, p. 42.

61. From the 'Information Service for the Circulation of unreported News', Frankfurt am Main, 119 (3.iv.76), p. 10.

62. Stümper, 'Problem der polizeilichen Führung in unserer Zeit', in *Die Polizei*, 11 (1975), p. 368.

63. H. J. Schwagerl, *Verfassungsschutz*, p. 96.

64. H. Herold, interview with *Wirtschaftswoche*, 14 (1972), p. 22.

Another important aid for the security services is the file set up at the Federal Attorney-General's headquarters under the 'Federal Central Register Law' (BZRG), which is available to all official bodies (law of 18.iii.76, BGBl I, 243). This contains information collected from courts and other official bodies, with full personal details, of all confirmed convictions (except minor offences punished by fines), suspended sentences, decisions of administrative bodies such as expulsion orders against foreigners, absence without leave from the forces, *Berufsverbote* for 'unreliability, unsuitability or discreditable behaviour', withdrawal of passports, information about warrants and searches, and convictions by foreign courts of Germans or foreigners living in Germany. Information from the register is provided to foreign authorities within the framework of bilateral agreements (§ § 4, 5, 8, 11, 20, 22, 25, 52, 53 BZRG).

In order to keep better check on the population, on arrivals and removals, it is planned to introduce a 'Federal Registration Law' and a 'subsidiary duty of registration for providers of accommodation', 'obligatory registration in the hotel and accommodation industry combined with an identity check', and a new system of personal numbers (see the Federal Government's proposal for a 'law on the registration system', Bundestag Publication 7/1059 of 4.x.73 and the details given by CDU deputy Schneider, *Bundestag*, 7.vi.72, p. 11020). The registration law, 'which could make an important contribution to internal security' (Schneider, loc. cit.) is intended to replace the provisions of the Reich registration system, which dates from the Nazi period.

65. *Stern*, 37 (1975), p. 34. On the BKA's data-processing system, see the pamphlets, *Betrifft: bundeskriminalamt*, published by the Federal Ministry of the Interior, Bonn, 1975, and *Gesucht wird . . . Elektronische Datenverarbeitung im Dienste der Verbrechensaufklärung und Verhütung*, Federal Criminal Investigation Bureau, Press and Public Relations Section, Wiesbaden.

66. Quoted, *Deutsche Polizei* 12 (1972), p. 357.

Chapter 4: Criminal Law as a Weapon

1. E. Kern, *Der Strafschutz des Staates und seine Problematik*, Tübingen, 1963, p. 5.
2. By Control Commission Law No. 11 of 30.i.46.
3. Preamble to the Government proposal for a political criminal law. Bundestag Publication 1/1307 (4.ix.50), p. 28.

No gap existed. At the time, the Basic Law contained in Article 143 wide-ranging provisions for 'high treason', though farsightedly this had only been envisaged as a transitional arrangement which would lapse when new criminal provisions relating to state security were passed, and duly lapsed at the end of 1951.

4. The quotation is taken from the Government bill cited in n. 3 above. The SPD proposals can be found in Bundestag Publication 1/563 (16.iii.50).
5. The three readings of the bill took place in the Bundestag on 12.ix.50 and 9.vii and 11.vii.51.
6. Dehler, *Bundestag*, 12.ix.50, p. 3108.
7. Dehler, ibid. The law came into force on 30.vii.51. (BGBl I, 739). The KPD's criticism that this was a 'lightning bill' being whipped through was not contradicted by the Government: 'Yes, I am in a hurry. I admit it,' was Dehler's reply to a heckler from the KPD parliamentary party (*Bundestag*, 12.ix.50, p. 3105) before he went on to appeal to his colleagues from the bourgeois parties: 'Ladies and gentlemen. You will be helping our democracy and helping our young state, if you pass this draft of mine quickly' (*Bundestag*, loc. cit., p. 3110).
8. In order of the quotations: *Bundestag*, 12.ix.50, p. 3107; E. Dreher, *Kommentar zum Strafgesetzbuch*, 35 edn, 1975, No. 4 on paragraph 83 ('Planning an act continuing high treason'), BGHSt, 4.vi.56, in BGHSt 9, 290; von Merkatz (CDU), as Federal Minister of Justice, *Bundestag*, 8.ii. 57, p. 10933.
9. *Bundesrat*, 23.vi.50, and 16.vi.60, quoted from BGHSt 9, 289, 291.
10. Government proposal for a political criminal law, Bundestag Publication 1/1307 (4.ix.50), p. 34; *Bundestag*, 8.ii.57, p. 10931; *Bundestag*, 9.vii.51, p. 6305.
11. Dehler, *Bundestag*, 12.ix.50, p. 3109.
12. *Verhandlungen des 38. deutschen Juristentages – Abteilung E*, Tübingen, 1951, E 10.
13. Government proposal cited above in n.10, p. 34.

14. Dehler, *Bundestag*, 12.ix.50, p. 3105.

15. R. Freisler, 'Das neue Strafrecht als nationalsozialistisches Bekenntnis', in F. Gürtner, R. Freisler, *Das neue Strafrecht*, Berlin, 1936, p. 136. See also R. Freisler, 'Der Volksverrat', in C. Schmitt (ed.), *Deutsche Juristen-Zeitung* (1935), p. 302.

16. G. Dahm, 'Verrat und Verbrechen', *Zeitschrift für die gesamte Staatswissenschaft* (1935), p. 302.

17. ibid., p. 291.

18. Dehler, *Bundestag*, 12.ix.50, p. 3108; also BGHSt 9, 291.

19. Federal Constitutional Court judgment of 14.i.69 on a constitutional objection to a judgment of the criminal panel of the High Court, in BVerfGE 25, 56–7.

20. Von Merkatz (CDU), *Bundestag*, 8.ii.57, p. 10916.

21. *Verhandlungen des 38. deutschen Juristentages – Abt. E*, op. cit., E 78.

22. E. Dreher, *Kommentar zum Strafgesetzbuch*, op. cit., No. 4 on Paragraph 83. The relevant extension of the provisions governing high treason was first introduced by the 'Law to Amend the provisions of the Criminal Law and the Code of Criminal Procedure', the so-called treason amendment of 24.iv.34 (RGBl I, 341), and was taken over in essentials in 1951.

Josef Schafheutle, in 1951 Ministerial Director in the Federal Ministry of Justice and before 1945 Ministerial Counsellor in the Reich Ministry of Justice, was one of the authors of the political criminal law passed in 1951 and a leading figure in the legal committee of the Bundestag. In 1934 he wrote as follows in support of the newly created crime of 'subversive high treason': 'Subversive high treason [§ 83 StGB, new version] is dangerous because it is an attempt to undermine the loyalty and reliability of the bodies established to defend the Reich and preserve internal order. The mass propaganda of high treason seeks to create a readiness among the mass of the people to follow the commands of the ringleaders when the moment for action arrives. Its main form hitherto has been the production and distribution of pamphlets. By such means an avalanche of agitation is set in motion from a safe hiding-place' (J. Schafheutle *et al.*, *Die Strafgesetznovellen von 1933 und 1934 mit Ausführungsvorschriften*, Berlin, 1934, p. 140).

23. BGHSt, 4.vi.56, in BGHSt 9, 288; BVerfG, 14.i.69, in BVerfGE, 25, 56ff.

24. R. Maurach, *Deutsches Strafrecht – besonderer Teil*, Darmstadt, 1952, p. 494.

25. H. Schmidt, *Bundestag*, 13.iii.75, pp. 10732–3. Schmidt's speech simply attached the highest court to the executive as an appendix, alongside the *Verfassungsschutz* and the Criminal Investigation Bureau.

26. Former Federal prosecutor D. W. Wagner, Federal Judge G. Willms, in *Fünfundzwanzig Jahre Bundesgerichtshof*, Munich, 1975. The book claimed that criticisms of decisions of the Sixth Criminal Panel (from 1.x.56 renamed the Third Criminal Panel) had come from 'distinguished quarters' through 'reputable channels' – but always in 'crude', 'tendentious' and 'petty' forms (pp. 267–8, 272).

27. BGHSt, 2.viii.54, HuSt I, 67.

28. BGHSt Index, Vol. 1, p. 550.

29. BGHSt, 2.viii.54, in HuSt I, 55/6.

30. BGHSt, 4.vi.55, in HuSt I, 180.

On a general strike, which in the High Court's view is regularly to be regarded as force in the sense of the provisions on high treason, the Court said: 'A strike restricted in area, or limited to a particular, non-vital branch of industry or activity will not normally constitute the use of force against organs of the constitution, since compulsion cannot be achieved in this way. With mass or general strikes, however, it is different. In a highly industrialized and thickly populated country like the Federal Republic the provision of the necessary goods and services for the population requires the smooth interaction of the most diverse institutions, enterprises and activities. If essential parts of this complicated mechanism are put out of action over a large area or for any length of time, or if, as with a general strike, there is a paralysis of the whole of public and economic life, the orderly functioning of the governmental system becomes impossible, and chaotic conditions must necessarily result' (BGHSt, ibid.). The general ban on political strikes is based on § 105 StGB, 'The exercise of compulsion against organs of the constitution'.

31. L. Martin, former Federal Attorney-General, 'Zur strafrechtlichen Beurteilung "passiver Gewalt" bei Demonstrationen', in *Fünfundzwanzig Jahre Bundesgerichtshof*, Munich, 1975, pp. 216, 219.

The Federal High Court said of sit-downs against fare increases that 'the decision whether an incident is to be regarded as force in the sense of a specific criminal act' could not be made by considering it in isolation. 'The incident must always be judged in association with the goal of the enterprise, which is implicit in its component acts, and in its relation to the person or persons it is designed to affect or influence' (BGHSt, 8.viii.69, in JZ (1969), p. 638, with explicit reference to the 'discussion of new methods of political revolt and their place in the concept of force' quoted in FN 30).

32. 'Strafrechtsangleichungsverordnung' of 29.v.43 (RGBl, I, 339).

33. 'Bereinigungsgesetz', of 4.viii.53 (BGBl I, 735).

34. O. Schwarz, *Kommentar zum Strafgesetzbuch*, 17th edn, 1954, No. 1a, on § 240.

35. E. Dreher, *Kommentar zum Strafgesetzbuch*, 35th edn, 1975, No. Bb, on § 240.

36. BGHSt, 8.viii.69, in JZ (1969), 638.

37. BGH, 30.v.72, in NJW (1972), 1573.

Some examples from the judgments of superior courts: 'A demonstration (a sit-down) is violent which has it as its aim to bring traffic to a halt for a longer or shorter period of time in order in this way to obtain a hearing for a particular view.' The right to demonstrate gives 'no one a right to have attention paid to them, and in particular to be given a hearing, by others' (Bavarian Supreme Court, 14.iv.69, in JW (1969), 1127).

'Any sort of aggressive action arising out of the disorder, whether merely in the form of pulling away a police officer or overturning an object, is violent activity and fulfils the requirements for a breach of the peace' (BGHSt, 8.viii.69, in JZ (1969), 639).

38. BGHZ, 30.v.72, in NJW (1972), 1366ff.

39. BGHZ, loc. cit. This judgment concerned the picketing of the Springer publishing firm in West Berlin after the attack on Rudi Dutschke. For a judgment in the same terms on the incidents at the Frankfurt Sozietät press, see BGH in NJW (1972), 1572–3.

40. W. Wagner, Preface to HuSt I, p. 16.

41. Supreme Court, Stuttgart, 9.vii.69, NJW (1969), 1543. Bavarian Superior Provincial Court, 7.x.55, in NJW (1955), 1806–7. The Federal High Court agreed: 'Encroachments' during a strike come under § 125 StGB – 'No action in a strike which goes beyond the cessation of work and violates interests protected by law is justified by the so-called strike law. [This also applies] to disruptions of public order, in other words breaches of the peace' (BGHSt, 19.x.54, in MDR (1955), 144).

42. Superior Provincial Court, Hamm, 15.i.51, in NJW (1951), 206. BGHSt, 2.x.53, in NJW (1954), 439.

43. Superior Provincial Court, Cologne, 7.i.70, in NJW (1970), 261.

44. Provincial Court, Frankfurt am Main, quoted from *Rote Robe* 1 (1975), p. 30.

45. Munich District Court, quoted from *Vorgänge* (1969), 266.

The Federal High Court attempted still further to increase the deterrent effect of sentences by making orders for damages against demonstrators. At the request of the Springer Company demonstrators picked out at random were ordered to pay crushing damages to the firm. Their argument, that 'the individual demonstrator's liability [must] be limited to the damage which he himself can be shown to have caused, unless we are to encumber the right to demonstrate with unacceptable risks', was not accepted. The demonstrators ordered to pay damages could of course appeal to the other demonstrators – 'The law leaves it to them to settle among themselves according to their contribution to the damage.' This 'is particularly appropriate in cases of damages arising out of demonstrations' (BGHZ, 30.v.72, in NJW (1972), 1366ff., and BGHZ of the same date, in NJW (1972), 1571ff.).

By this decision the Federal High Court quietly took back through civil procedure what the SPD/FDP majority had been forced to agree in 1970 under pressure from the extra-parliamentary opposition. An amendment to the law on breaches of the peace sought to eliminate the possibility of bringing charges against any participant in a demonstration deemed to be violent simply because he or she was there (Third Penal Code Reform Law, 20.v.70, BGBl I, 505).

Although this reform changed nothing in the fundamental definition of criminal force and violence, the law was criticized by the CDU/CSU and conservative jurists as an over-generous concession to students opposed to authority. They argued that more than enough had been done to win back the loyalty of the students in the law passed at the same time giving an amnesty to those convicted of 'crimes arising out of demonstrations' (BGBl (1970) I, 509), and that it was superfluous and dangerous, because shortsighted, also to alter the law on demonstrations in this way. The reform law, wrote Eduard Dreher, then still Ministerial Director in the Federal Ministry of Justice, 'is, like so many that our parliament passes, an *ad hoc* law, that is, in this case, one designed for the demonstrations of rowdy young people in recent years ... Although warning voices were raised, too little thought was given to the need to make provision also for phenomena sociologically and politically very different from student demonstrations' (E. Dreher, 'Das Dritte Strafrechtsänderungsgesetz und seine Probleme', NJW (1970), 1155).

These ideas were brought up again by the CDU/CSU in connection with the discussion on the 'Law for the protection of communal peace'. With references to 'demonstrations for the introduction of free transport' and 'incidents at the occupation of the nuclear power station at Wyhl', the CDU called for the law on demonstrations to be toughened, and put forward a suitable bill (Bundestag Publication No. 7/2772, 11.xi.74, pp. 7–8). The CDU accused the Social Democrats of talking a lot 'about the front-line campaign against crime', but doing nothing about it: 'Both now and in the past you have allowed the front line and the whole field to be taken over by violent mass demonstrations' (Spranger (CDU), *Bundestag*, 16.i.76, p. 14725).

46. Filbinger (CDU), quoted FR, 28.ii.75, p. 32.

It is well known that charges for 'breaches of the peace', 'breaches of privacy' and breaches of anything else breachable were handed out to the citizens of Wyhl. They also received demands for compensation, which the hard-pressed state government subsequently had to withdraw.

The much-feared mass demonstrations, notably manifestations of popular solidarity with demonstrators, resulted from demonstrations against fare increases in Heidelberg. 'The events of the last ten days in Heidelberg cannot be described as the work of "political rockers". The steady increase in the severity of police action resulted in an increase not only in the number of demonstrators but also in popular sympathy with the protest demonstrations' (FR, 30.vi.75, p. 3).

The statement: 'In 1969 the citizens of Heidelberg learned that successful defence is possible. The Council found itself forced, as a result of massive protests, to withdraw the fare increases it had already decided on' (FR, loc. cit.).

This time the Heidelberg city authorities tried to intimidate the people. A planned 'red spot campaign', in which the paralysed tram service was to be replaced by lifts in private cars, brought a warning from police to motorists. Anyone taking part, they said, would be guilty of 'an offence against the passenger transport law' (FR, 30.vi.75, p. 4). This produced even greater indignation among many Heidelbergers, who literally fell on the police from behind as they used water cannon, batons and gas against the demonstrators. 'In the old quarter especially, refuse bags, ashtrays, bottles and bags of paint and water rained down on the police. "It was hell," said the commander of a unit summoned from Constance'(FR, 28.vi.75, p. 4).

47. See § § 87, 88, 88a, 89, 90, 90a, 90b, 92 StGB.

48. H. J. Schwagerl *et al., Der Schutz der Verfassung – Ein Handbuch Für Theorie und Praxis*, Cologne, 1968, p. 68.

49. BGHSt, 6.ii.63, in BGHSt 18, 246ff.

50. BGHSt, 2.viii.54, in BGHSt 7, 228. So also BGHSt, 25.vii.63, BGHSt 19, 55.

51. Former Federal prosecutor D. W. Wagner, Preface to HuSt I, pp. 10–11.

52. SPD parliamentary group, Bundestag Publication No. 5/102 (8.xii.65), p. 7, and Publication No. 5/2860 (9.v.68), p. 1.

53. BGHSt (14.x.52), in BGHSt 3, 346.

The 'defamation' lay in the 'implication of cheapness contained in the word 'stall' and in the charge that the Federal Republic is in unworthy dependence on American capitalism' (BGH, op. cit., p. 347).

54. BGHSt (10.vii.74), in DuR 1974, 434ff.

The main object of this decision was a piggy bank painted in slightly unusual colours; it was not pink, but had black, red and mustard stripes, with a swastika on its belly. [Black, red and gold are the West German national colours. *Translator.*] Several of these were produced by a man who offered them for sale to art and craft galleries and art dealers until the public prosecutor's office confiscated the pigs and brought charges. The producer, who invoked the artistic freedom granted by the Basic Law, was convicted of 'insulting the state and its symbols' on the ground that even artistic freedom was subject to 'limitations imposed on it by the criminal law as part of the constitutional system' (State Security division of the Cologne Provincial Court).

This judgment was quashed by the High Court on appeal for the reasons quoted in the text: while the 'expression of opinion embodied in the plastic pigs' was 'clearly an insult to the colours of the Federal Republic', the 'circle of possible viewers ... was limited in advance to people with a general interest in art'. There was no attempt to produce 'an effect on a scale large enough to be important'. 'In these circumstances ... the need to protect the state gives way to artistic freedom' – note the qualification: 'in these circumstances' (BGH, op. cit.).

55. President Scheel, address at the swearing in of emergency police in Münster, in *Die Polizei*, No. 1 (1976), p. 33.

56. On the solidarity shown by many policemen with the occupiers of the nuclear power station site in Wyhl, see *FR am Abend*, 26.ii.75, p. 28, and N. Gladitz (ed.), *'Lieber aktiv als radioaktiv – Wyhler Bauern erzählen'*, West Berlin, 1976, pp. 97ff.

An above average rate of absence through sickness was found in the Frankfurt police by an empirical study of officers' expectations from the satisfaction with their work. The findings of this survey, carried out by the police in Autumn 1974 – considerable discontent and dissatisfaction with routine duty, and especially about frequent operations against demonstrators ('major public order duties') – were initially suppressed by the police administration, but extracts were subsequently published after pressure from the unions. The answers about squatting were particularly interesting. To the question, 'Are you basically in agreement with squatting, as far as the situation in Frankfurt is concerned, provided it takes place peacefully?', more than half the sample (51·1 per cent) answered 'Yes'. 25·5 per cent of those questioned were even prepared to take part in a squat themselves, 7·3 per cent even 'if disorder were likely to occur'. These results were obtained even though the survey was carried out explicitly 'under the immediate impact of the evictions at Kettenhofweg 51 and the associated violence' (*Das 'Betriebsklima' bei der Schutzpolizei in Frankfurt/Main*, Frankfurt am Main, October 1973, pp. 39ff.).

The timing of the survey was of course not accidental, but nonetheless the criticism of the police administration it revealed was harsher than senior officers had feared. Comments included: 'dangerous tensions', 'alarming findings', 'individual findings ranging according to the reader's point of view, from unpleasant to depressing' (study, pp. 23, 42, 51).

At all events, according to the police sociologists, 'it must be accepted that the proportion of dissatisfaction revealed by the statements about the 'senior administration' must be regarded with great probability as being no longer normal and unimportant, but as deviating very significantly from the expected or desired norm' (study, p. 52). An 'important factor' in this was probably 'the relatively large social distance between the top and bottom of the hierarchy' (p. 20).

The study admitted that 'even with the greatest possible openness in the administrative process, individual officers find it hard to ignore the way the decision-making process of the administration operates in detail, and the way and extent to which it is subject to political influence' (*Hessische Polizeirundschau*, 10 (1974), special issue on the study, p. 3), but the police sociologists then dismissed this as 'obsessional' or prejudice among the ranks. 'The dissatisfaction – particularly with the senior administration – appears not to be objective. Quite clearly, many of those questioned are hardly in a position to assess the problems with which the administration has to deal and which produce a particular attitude in the adminstration' (study, p. 20).

57. Judgment of the Berlin Provincial Court, 6.iv.76, quoted FAZ, 7.iv.76, p. 2. The chances of the appeal to the High Court can be counted on the fingers of one hand. In 1964 this court convicted a speaker of 'subversion of the security organs' because he had complained about the presence of police informers in the room. The officers, according to the High Court, were 'engaged in defence against subversive activity directed against the constitution', and had been ordered to the meeting for that reason. The speaker must have known when he made his hostile remarks about the police 'that a reduction in police surveillance would result in increased communist infiltration, a consequence he was at least prepared to countenance' (BGHSt, 4.vi.64, in NJW, 1964, 1680).

58. Wahl (CDU), *Bundestag*, 9.i.51, p. 6304, and BGHSt, 2.xii.55, in BGHSt 9, 145–6.

59. Von Merkatz (CDU), *Bundestag*, 8.ii.57, p. 10934.

60. BGHSt, 6.ii.63, in BGHSt 18, 256.

61. BGHSt 18, 255.

62. BGHSt, 18.ii.64, in NJW 1964, 1084. The defendant's constitutional objections against such methods of securing a conviction were rejected as unfounded, and the High Court decision upheld: BVerfGE, 14.i.69 and 15.i.69, in BVerfGE 25, 44ff; 87ff.

63. BGHSt, 4.vi.55, in HuSt I, 113; BGHSt, 28.vii.55, in HuSt I, 257; BGHSt, 2.xi.56, in HuSt II, 57.

See also the Constitutional Court judgment on the ban on the KPD (BVerfG, 17.viii.56) in BVerfGE 5, 277.

64. C. Schmitt, *Der Begriff des Politischen* (1932), new edn, Berlin (West), 1963, p. 47.

65. P. Schneider, *Schon bist Du ein Verfassungsfeind*, West Berlin, 1975.

66. Schafheutle, Legal Committee 26.i.51, Proceedings, p. 1; cf. *Bundestag*, 9.vii.51, p. 6308.

'The stability of the state's internal order also requires protection against attacks not deriving from intentions of high treason or attacks where such intentions cannot be proved' (*Proceedings of the 38th Conference of German Jurists – Section E,* Tübingen, 1951, E 15).

67. T. Maunz *et al., Kommentar zum Grundgesetz,* 4th edn, 1974, marginal number 9c on Article 91.

68. T. Maunz, 'Gestalt und Recht der Polizei,' in E. R. Huber, (ed.), *Idee und Ordnung des Reiches,* Hamburg, 1943, p. 57.

69. BGHSt, 8.v.64, in BGHSt 19, 317. The same view was expressed by the former head of the *Verfassungsschutz,* Hubert Schribbers, in a *Spiegel* interview: 'On the one hand there is the written constitution, the Basic Law, and on the other the reality of the constitution. It is the second which we have to protect.' The interview is reprinted in W. Busse (ed.), . . . *wir danken für dieses Gespräch,* Munich, 1970, p. 238.

70. BGHSt, 9.iii.56, in BGHSt 9, 101.

On the other hand, there is no mention of any parliamentary forms either in the 'core articles' or the Basic Law which are exempt from any amendment (see Art. 79, Section 3 GG) or in an interpretation of these by the Constitutional Court. In the Court's list of the 'principles of the constitution' the basic rights are explicitly mentioned in first place with 'equality of opportunity of all political parties and the right to form and exercise opposition in accordance with the constitution', alongside the 'division of powers', the 'responsibility of the Government', 'government in accordance with the law', 'the independence of the courts' and the 'principle of a plurality of parties' (BVerfG, 23.x.52, in BVerfGE 2. 1).

The fact that, in contrast, in the legal definition of 'the principles of the constitution' for the purposes of offences which 'endanger the state' (§ 92 StGB) there is not a word about the basic rights has a very good reason: since 'the basic rights laid down in the Basic Law, with the exception of the basic right to life, are not absolute', since of course 'a situation may very well occur in which the basic rights are less important for the preservation and security of the state than the limitation of basic rights', 'no attempt was made to include the basic rights in the catalogue of entrenched constitutional principles contained in the Criminal Code' (Kopf (CDU), *Bundestag,* 9.vii.51, p. 6309).

In other words, the political section of the criminal code (§ 92) ignores the basic rights – the only important consideration is the security of the state. The implied neglect of the connection between the principle of the constitutional state and human rights was sharply criticized by Werner Maihofer as late as 1968 on the ground that it 'sets up what exists and prevails here and now as an absolute', and 'implicitly infringes the fundamental decision of Article 1 of the Basic Law that people do not exist for the sake of the state, but the state for the sake of people' (W. Maihofer, *Rechtsstaat und menschliche Würde*, Frankfurt, 1968, p. 58).

Of course in 1976 Interior Minister Maihofer no longer wanted to know anything about all this. He now had a different view of § 92 StGB, which he once regarded as 'infringing' the Basic Law: the 'unalterable core of our liberal constitution' was 'spelt out in detailed provisions in § 92 StGB' (Maihofer, *Bundestag*, 12.v.76, p. 16952).

71. Thereby 'undermining' and 'subverting' the decisions of the High Court: BGHSt, 2.viii.54, in BGHSt 7, 222ff.; BGHSt 4.vi.56, in BGHSt 9, 286–7; BGHSt, 25.vii.63, in BGHSt 19, 54–5; BGHSt 2.xi.56, in HuSt 11, 57–8.

72. 14th Criminal Law Amendment Law, 22.vi.76 (BGBl I, 1056).

73. Vogel (SPD), *Bundestag*, 16.i.76, p. 14742, and Special Committee for Criminal Law Reform (subsequently cited as *Legal Committee*), report of proceedings for 2.x.75, p. 2293. The proposals and arguments for the Criminal Law Amendment Law discussed here (which was approved by the Bundestag on 16.i.76) are published as Bundestag Publication 7/2772 (11.xi.74, CDU/CSU), Bundestag Publication 7/2854 (28.xi.74, Bundesrat), and Bundestag Publication 7/7030 (23.xii.74, Government).

In addition to providing penalties for the 'advocacy of force', the proposals of the CDU/CSU and of the Bundesrat included a tightening of the law governing demonstrations and the right of assembly (especially in the case of foreigners). The last two proposals were rejected by the Government and the SPD/FDP parliamentary parties.

The preamble to the CDU/CSU amendment to the law on assembly included the following passage: 'The law on assembly at present contains no provisions specifically related to foreigners. At the time it was passed the number of foreigners in the Federal Republic was relatively low, and special regulations for foreigners seemed unnecessary. Since then this situation has altered considerably. The large number of foreign workers and their sometimes lengthy periods of residence in West Germany has increased the awareness of many foreigners of the problems of the economic, social, and also general political situations of their countries of origin. It has also encouraged their tendency to give forceful expression to their critical views, and demonstrations suggest themselves as a particularly effective means.

'These activities on the part of particular groups of foreigners are concerned predominantly with alleged abuses in their states of origin. However, they are on occasion also directed against the liberal democratic basic order of the Federal Republic of Germany . . . This development must be dealt with by means of legislative measures' (Bundestag Publication 7/2772, pp. 9–10).

74. Article 1b of the Spanish emergency legislation of 27.viii.75 reads as follows:

'Terms of imprisonment of between six months and six years with fines for

– anyone who preaches or supports violence,

– anyone who shows solidarity with terrorists charged under the new law,

– anyone who criticizes courts dealing with terrorist cases.'

75. The tightening of the provisions of § § 145d 241 StGB ('Using the threat of a criminal offence against an official' and 'threatening another person') took place against the background of a rapid increase in the number of threats by telephone or letter to commit a criminal offence against officials or private individuals such as judges, prosecutors, supervisors and teachers. The threats, not seriously intended, came from manual and white-collar workers, schoolchildren and pensioners (see 'Terror und Telefon', *Stern*, 21.vi.62, p. 144, and NJW (1972), 1789ff.) The people involved are described in legal jargon as 'typical imitative individual offenders' (NJW, loc. cit.), and it is this copying, the imitative effect, which worries the lawmakers. In the period 1971–4, between 2,700 and 3,000 cases of 'threats to officials' were recorded annually, and there were around 1,400 convictions under § 145d StGB in 1973 alone. In the case of 'threatening another person' as defined in § 241 StGB, the number of convictions annually lies between 450 and 750; the number of threats made but not brought to court is considerably higher (figures from *Legal Committee*, 2.x.75, pp. 2297–8).

The expensively arranged publicity campaign about 'violent criminals' evidently has an unwanted byproduct in a more widespread readiness to use at least threats of violence; it encourages this method of giving vent to anger and discontent about working or living conditions. The worried question asked at the height of the campaign against the Red Army Faction – 'In certain situations isn't it perhaps possible to help things along a bit with reporting slanted in a particular way?' (Schulze-Vorberg (CDU), *Bundestag*, 7.vi.72, p. 10999) – has been answered: it is. This is the value of the indispensable press and television campaign.

It was not so much the fact that Lorenz had been kidnapped which worried his friends, but the fact that negotiations had to be carried on with the kidnappers – and in full public view. 'The humiliation of the state was completed in the nation's electronic Valhalla,' said the *Frankfurter Allgemeine*, and Dregger talked about dangerous signals being given: 'Citizens have the impression that alongside the legitimate civil power there now also exists an illegitimate power, which, at least on occasion, can make the power of the state submit to it, an illegitimate power which has become a negotiating partner of the state power in the full glare of television publicity. This means we must expect further attempts at kidnapping and blackmail' (*Bundestag*, 13.v.75, p. 10740).

76. FR, 17.i.76, p. 4: 'Im Wortlaut: Der Gewaltparagraph'. See also *Der Spiegel*, 16.ii.76, p. 38.

77. Typical of many speeches were those of the deputies von Schoeler (FDP) and Müller-Emmert (SPD) during the final reading of the bill in the Bundestag: *Bundestag*, 16.i.76, pp. 14731, 14722–3.

78. § § 37, 53 of the Weapons Law in the version of 2.iii.74 (BGBl I, 469).

79. As early as 1962, in the Bundesrat's 'Proposal for a Criminal Code', a section on 'Offences against communal peace' was suggested including new provisions under which 'invitations to commit offences' (§ 291) and the 'rewarding and approval of offences' (§ 293) would become offences.

The 'means' – a new provision this, only finally introduced in 1976 – were meetings and publications; their potential was deemed to include the 'disruption of communal peace' – and this is now the law. (The Bundesrat's proposal is printed in Bundesrat Publication, No. 200/62, Bonn, 1962.)

80. Constitutional Court decision, 22.v.75 – 2 BvL 13/73, pp. 42, 21.

81. K. Härtzschel (ed.), *Die politischen Notverordnungen*, Berlin, 1933, Preface, p. 7.

On 22 October 1878 'with the agreement of the Bundesrath and the Reichstag, We, Wilhelm by the grace of God Emperor of Ger-

many and King of Prussia,' proclaimed the 'Law against the danger
to the community from the activities of Social Democracy' (RGBl
1878, No. 34). The law was directed against 'associations which, by
social democratic, socialist or communist activities aimed at the
overthrow of the existing order of the state or society, act in a
manner dangerous to the public peace and in particular to the harmony between the different classes of the population' (§ 1, Anti-
Socialist Law).

The preamble to this law says: 'The activities of social democracy
are directed towards the implementation of the radical theories of
modern socialism and communism. According to these theories, the
present mode of production must be rejected as uneconomic and an
unjust exploitation of labour by capital ... Their aim, in other
words, is nothing less than a break with the whole line of development of law in civilized states, a radical transformation from below
of the existing relations of ownership and property ...

'These aims are matched by socialist agitation and its methods,
which are well organized and pursued with passionate energy in
speech and writing. The agitation seeks to spread among the poorer
and less educated classes of the population a dissatisfaction with
their condition and a conviction of the hopelessness of that condition under the existing legal system, and to incite them, as the
'disinherited', to envy and hatred of the other classes of bourgeois
society. The moral and religious convictions which hold society
together are shattered, reverence and piety are ridiculed, the sense
of justice of the masses is confused and respect for the law destroyed ... The descriptions given, in speech and writing, of revolutionary events of the past, the glorification of famous
revolutionaries and the deeds of the Paris Commune are of such a
sort as to stimulate revolutionary appetites and passions and to in-
cline the masses to acts of violence ... The constant disturbance and
disruption of the public peace brought about by social democratic
agitation does serious damage to the general welfare and prevents
successful and normal development in both the economic and the
political field. The duty of self-preservation incumbent on state and
society therefore requires limits to be placed on socialist agitation
... The state must do this if it is not to surrender or allow the
populace to believe either that it is powerless or that the revolutionary activities of social democracy are justified ...

'For this extraordinary legal powers are required which will place
the authorities responsible for internal security and order in a posi-

tion to meet their constitutional obligation to protect state and society from internal dangers in the face of social democracy . . .

'Extraordinary and diseased conditions which endanger the state indicate the need for defence by means of special laws which would be directed exclusively to averting the immediate danger and would automatically lose their efficacy when this aim was achieved . . .

'These measures (alone however) provide the conditions necessary for curing the evil, not the cure itself. This requires the active participation of all the sound elements of bourgeois society to remove the roots of the evil both by strengthening the sense of law and morality and by further economic reforms' ('Prologue to a law against the dangers to the community from the activities of social democracy', *Die Sozialdemokratie vor dem Deutschen Reichstag*, Vol. 1, Hamburg, 1878, pp. 10ff.).

If we ignore the formulation, and the fact that this law was directed at the very people who are today bringing in comparable laws, the striking feature is the similarity of the arguments. In both cases we hear of 'sickness and healing', of fear of the awareness which could be created by agitation linked to experience and interests. In both cases there are appeals to the 'elements of security', talk of the 'defence of normality', emergency situations and emergency legislation, of 'constitutional obligations' and the 'state's duty of self-preservation'. Other key phrases are 'internal peace' and 'internal security', the 'loss of values', the 'influence of events abroad' (the role of the Paris Commune then is played now by the liberation movements in the so-called Third World), 'incitement and efforts to promote class war', and finally the carrot and the stick – the combination of reform and revolution.

The Nazis, notably in the 'Reich President's Decree for the Protection of the German People' of 4 February 1933, penalized 'publications whose content is likely to threaten public safety or order'. These could be confiscated by the police (the so-called press police) 'if they contain invitations or incitements to acts of violence or if they glorify acts of violence after they have been committed' (§ § 7ff, RGBl I, 35).

However, in one point the Nazis went further. 'Anyone who receives reliable information about the presence of a supply of publications the content of which seeks to justify the performance of one of the above-mentioned criminal acts, and receives the information at a time when the authorities are unaware of the presence of this supply of publications, is obliged to inform the police immediately. Copies of the publication which come into a person's possession or charge must be immediately surrendered to the police authorities. Anyone who fails to give information or surrender publications promptly will be punished by imprisonment for up to one year' (op. cit., § 21).

82. *Bundestag*, 12.vi.75, p. 12461.

83. *Legal Committee*, 18.ix.75, p. 2243, and 19.ix.75, p. 2246.

84. *Bundestag*, 24.x.75, p. 13547, and p. 13546.

85. 'The preservation of communal peace is the concern of the national community and of every individual as its member' (Decision of the Superior Administrative Court of Saxony, 18.i.35, in *Jahrbücher des Sächsichen Oberverwaltungsgerichts*. Vol. 39, Leipzig, 1936, p. 10).

The 'new German criminal law' was directed particularly against 'attacks on the order of the community', against ' "peaceful" destruction of the basic order, intellectual subversion and literary propaganda', against 'the weakening of state power', against the 'annihilation of the community', against 'the destruction of the moral foundations on which national defence rests, the destruction of the power and will to resist' (G. Dahm, 'Verrat und Verbrechen', *Zeitschrift für die gesamte Staatswissenschaft* (1935), pp. 301–2, 309, 310; see also G. Dahm, *Gemeinschaft und Strafrecht*, Hamburg, 1935).

The 'public peace' constantly mentioned in the provisions of the 'New Communal Peace Law' is defined in West German law as follows:

'It means the "internal security" of the community. It has to do with the stabilization of collective arrangements, reliability and confidence in the existing social order, a generalized attitude of confidence among the people in the formally existing situation, and with the prevention of a general lack of confidence' (NJW, 1972, 1791).

86. E. Dreher, *Kommentar zum Strafgeseztbuch*, 35th edn, 1975, No. 3A, on § 130.

This was also the line of Nazi commentary on § 130 StGB: 'Taken literally, the measure deals with incitement to class war. In its interpretation, however, account must be taken of the change brought about by the National Socialist revolution. The division of the German people into classes has been ended, and its return is inconceivable. It is therefore more correct to speak of stirring up one section of the population against another ... The forthcoming code

196

will develop this measure to cover a crime of agitation (*Volks-verhetzung*)' – this change of title, as we have seen, did not take place until 1960. Quotation from A. Schönke, *Kommentar zum Strafgesetzbuch für das deutsche Reich*, Berlin, 1942, Nos. 1 and VII, on § 130.

87. *Legal Committee*, 18.ix.75, p. 2243.

88. Bundestag Publication 7/2854, p. 15.

89. Bundestag Publication 7/3030.

90. *Legal Committee*, 2.x.75, p. 2293.

91. Bundestag Publication 7/3030, p. 8.

92. Bundestag Publication 7/3030, p. 5.

93. Vogel (SPD), *Bundestag*, 16.i.76, p. 14742.

94. SPD party conference in Mannheim, *Report* (14.xi.75), pp. 180–81.

95. Bundestag Publication 7/2772, pp. 8–9.

96. FR, 22.i.75, p. 7.

97. For examples of criminal proceedings against left-wing alternative media, see KJ (1972), 369ff.

98. Bommi Baumann's book, *Wie alles anfing* ('How it all began'), published by Trikont publishers in Munich, was confiscated in November 1975 in an elaborate police operation in West Germany and Berlin for allegedly 'giving approval to violence' (§ 140 StGB). In the book Baumann describes the reasons which led him and other young workers and students to join groups such as the Red Army Faction in the late 1960s. Baumann describes his political experiences in these would-be 'urban guerrilla' groups and ends by criticizing their ideas and actions very sharply. The winner of the Nobel Prize for Literature, Heinrich Böll, vigorously recommended the book as suitable for schools on the ground that here for once was the voice of an 'insider', an authentic account of experience. The prosecuting authorities reacted in their own way; as was mentioned above, they had the book confiscated in every possible bookshop and brought charges against Trikont.

The publishers replied to this censorship with a new edition of the book, this time published jointly by several hundred academics, writers and publishers. A passage in the 'Publishers' foreword' to the new edition says, 'We will not let ourselves be forbidden to have thoughts or to express them. We will not let ourselves be forbidden to conduct discussions or to make them public. Michael 'Bommi' Baumann's *Wie alles anfing* will appear again and again and again.'

The authorities' attempt to make an example of Trikont, a com-

Notes

mitted socialist firm, by intimidating, convicting and isolating it was
frustrated by this new edition. Against the background of these
events the directors of Trikont were acquitted of the charges against
them by the Munich Provincial Court on 27 October 1976. However, the judgment was quashed by the Federal High Court after an
appeal by the prosecution, and a new trial was ordered.

The High Court judgment contains three particularly note-
worthy and significant features. First, the High Court extends the
law by introducing the concept of 'sympathizer' into the theory of
guilt and complicity. It describes Bommi Baumann as 'partly an
accomplice of and partly an avowed sympathizer with those responsible' for the actions described in the book, who had 'not explicitly dissociated himself from the acts' of which his friends were
accused, which, said the court, was equivalent to the offence of
'advocating an offence'. Secondly, continued the High Court,
Bommi Baumann did 'not in principle reject acts of violence', which
constituted 'approval' in the sense of 140 StGB. With this argument,
as it were by the back door, the High Court builds up 'approval'
into an offence of omission: anyone who does not explicitly dis-
sociate himself from particular actions gives approval to them. And
thirdly and finally, the High Court claims that there is a distinction
between the appearance of a book like Baumann's with a firm like
Trikont and its appearance among 'value-free background material'.
It was true that the passages objected to had also been published in
other places, such as the magazine *Der Spiegel*, but there the 'prim-
ary aim had been the journalistic function of reporting' by a publication 'which did not identify itself with the text'. The case was to
be retried before a different criminal panel of the Munich Provincial Court (BGH decision of 9.viii.77, NJW (1978), pp. 58–9).

99. *Legal Committee*, 18.ix.75, pp. 2238ff., and 1.x.75, p. 2246.

100. *Legal Committee*, 18.ix.75, pp. 2239–40.

101. *Legal Committee*, 24.ix.75, p. 2267.

102. FDP Bundestag group, *Vermerk zu Fragen des* § 130a StGB,
Bonn, 4.xi.75, p. 2.

103. BGHSt, 22.xii.76, in BGHSt 10, 170.

104. Bundestag Publication 7/4559, 7.i.76, p. 9.

105. H. Ule, *Streik und Polizei*, Cologne, 1972, p. 42.

106. The reference in § 126 StGB to a 'serious breach of the
peace' should not be a problem. Quite apart from the fact that the
boundary between a 'breach of the peace' (§ 125 StGB) and a
'serious breach of the peace' (§ 125a) is fluid, the 'other weapons'

198

referred to in § 125a are not only weapons in the technical sense or as defined by the weapons law, but – so courts have ruled – 'suitable objects', which might include banner poles, cars placed across roads or other 'deliberate obstacles' (cf. Superior Provincial Court, Cologne, in NJW (1970), 260).

According to the commentary on 'serious breaches of the peace', it was necessary to extend the notion of a weapon in this way because 'all experience shows that a crowd is more likely to equip itself for disturbances with these sort of home-made implements than with less easily obtainable technical weapons. If the law ignored this and did not include these objects, which can be so dangerous in the hands of a crowd, it would fail seriously in its duty' (LK, marginal No. 4, on § 125 StGB).

As well as the advocacy of actions described legally as 'breaches of the peace', the advocacy of the obstruction of transport services or road traffic is an offence ('Dangerous interference with rail, water or air transport' under § 315 StGB and 'dangerous interference with road transport' under § 315b StGB). This would cover the advocacy of a strike in which private railway lines or access roads were blocked to obstruct the movement of goods, strikebreakers and police.

107. Dreher (JZ, 1953, 426) already emphasized that the intention of § 140 StGB ('the approval and rewarding of offences already committed'), which was not included in the Penal Code until 1953 (BGBl I, 735ff.) and was made much more severe by the 'communal peace' law, was to make the advocacy of political activities a crime.

In 1871 concern about interference with freedom of opinion made the Reichstag refuse to include a law equivalent to § 140 StGB in the Penal Code. This was not done until the 'Law for the Protection of the Republic' was passed in 1922.

108. The new § 130a StGB appears in the Penal Code in the place occupied until 1953 by a clause which also made words intended to guide action a criminal offence, the famous 'misuse of the pulpit' law: 'A clergyman or other minister of religion who in the exercise of or arising out of the exercise of his profession publicly before a group of people or in a church or other place set aside for religious gatherings makes affairs of the state the object of a sermon or discussion in a way which endangers the public peace will be punished by imprisonment' (repealed by the Third Criminal Law Amendment Law of 4.viii.53).

It remains to be seen whether the churches, who at present punish the 'misuse of the pulpit' with *Berufsverbote*, will call for the revival of this offence.

109. BGHSt, 17.xii.68, in BGHSt, 22, 285.

110. Bundestag Publication 7/3030, 8.

111. The 'social utility clause [of § 86, para. 3 StGB] is uncertain in its legal nature'; making a decision in individual cases a matter for the courts (E. Dreher, *Kommentar zum Strafgesetzbuch*, 35th edn, 1975, No. 6, on § 86).

112. *Legal Committee*, 10.xii.75, p. 2380.

113. Decision of the Federal Administrative Court, 12.i.66, in BVerwGE 23, 108 and 106.

'The freedom of art,' says another decision of this court, 'does not include the right to disseminate works of art in any way at all' (BVerwG, 16.xii.71, in BVerwGE 39, 208).

114. Müller-Emmert (SPD), *Bundestag*, 16.i.76, p. 14722.

The Federal High Court has already given its opinion on 'camouflaged' publications: 'If a work presented as a factual report shows, even if in disguised form, attitudes hostile to the constitution, Article 5 of the Basic Law is not an obstacle to a ban on its distribution, even if the apparent or real purpose of the report is only 'information (BGHSt, 28.ii.64, in BGHSt 19, 52).

The wording is significant. We no longer check to see whether a criminal law might possibly conflict with the basic rights contained in the constitution, but whether the constitution 'is an obstacle' to a law.

115. BVerfG, 26.v.70, in BVerfGE 28, 292 (referring to the 'Lüth judgment' of 15.i.58 – in BVerfGE 7, 209–10).

116. BVerfG, 17.viii.56 (the ban on the KPD), in BVerfGE 5, 85.

117. SPD Bundestag motion, 8.xii.65 (Bundestag Publication 5/102, p. 7).

118. BGHSt, 28.ii.64 (BGHSt 19, 247).

119. In the sitting of the Legal Committee on 1 October 1975, FDP deputy von Schoeler objected that he was 'still not sure what the formula "in a manner likely to" is really supposed to mean'.

The Government spokesman replied, 'Under current law the public peace must actually be disturbed. Establishing this fact presents considerable difficulties, as we know from experience. This is one reason why the Government proposal abandons this requirement.'

Nevertheless, the committee agreed, at Schoeler's suggestion, to delete the elastic addition of 'likelihood'; only what actually caused a 'disturbance' would be an offence (*Legal Committee*, 1.x.75, pp. 2276, 2277, 2280).

Three weeks later SDP deputy Penner moved 'the restoration of the Government proposal in the 'likelihood' clause. Deputy Dr Eyrichs (CDU/CSU) did not support the motion.' Deputy von Schoeler (FDP) 'stated that he had no objection to Deputy Penner's motion', which – as the text finally approved shows – was carried: 'The committee agreed by a majority to restore the Government wording' (*Legal Committee*, 22.x.75, p. 2313).

120. BGHSt, 14.i.64, in BGHSt 19, 221–2.

121. BGHSt, 8.v.64, in BGHSt 19, 308.

122. BGHSt, 28.ii.64, in BGHSt 19, 247.

123. BGHSt 21.iv.61, in BGHSt 16, 53.

124. Schmude, Parliamentary Secretary in the Federal Ministry of the Interior, address to the Police Officer College at Hiltrup, in *Innere Sicherheit – Informationen des Bundesministeriums des Innern*, 13.iv.76, p. 27.

125. BVerfG, 14.i.69 (BVerfGE, 25, 27). Nevertheless it was quite possible to imagine 'cases in which even an individual, by virtue of his abilities and the resources available to him, creates a danger which must be fought on the ground of the constitution's right to self-preservation' (BVerfGE, loc. cit.).

126. Proposal for a political criminal law, preamble to the Government bill, Bundestag Publication 1/307 (4.ix.50), p. 27.

Cf. Dregger: 'We are not concerned with the threat of an anarchist bomb planter ... It is quite clear that it is not individual fighters who constitute the danger to liberal democracy in our country, but the organized enemies of the constitution, and the disciplined ones more than the disorganized' (*Bundestag*, 24.x.75, pp. 13543–4).

127. For the history of § 129 StGB in the period up to the First World War, see G. Bernstein, *Geheimbündelei und Teilnahme an staatsfeindlichen Verbindungen in ihrer Strafrechtlichen Bedeutung*, Leipzig, 1914, p. 35.

128. § 129, para. 4 StGB. 'A ringleader is anyone who as a member or covert organizer or as an outsider giving intellectual or material support has an influential role in the organization' (E. Dreher, *Kommentar zum Strafgesetzbuch*, 35th edn, 1975, No. 2B, on § 84).

The criterion for an 'influential role' is 'not the amount of activity but the importance the assistance given has for the organization ... It can be, and often is, indirect, in that the person in question may perform important functions of a more material or technical nature (printers, suppliers of materials, etc.)' (BGHSt, 2.x.63, in BGHSt 19, 110 and BGHSt, 1.xii.64, in BGHSt 20, 122–3).

129. 'At its discretion the court may reduce the sentence or not impose a penalty if the accused makes a serious effort of his own accord to prevent the continuance of the organization or the committing of an offence for the furtherance of its aims or if he places his knowledge at the disposal of an official agency in time to enable offences of the planning of which he has knowledge to be prevented' (§ 129, para. 6 StGB).

This so-called 'active regret' clause was appropriately described by the Nazis as 'Preferential Treatment for informers and rogues' and recommended for inclusion in the Penal Code (F. Gürtner, R. Freisler *et al.*, *Das kommende deutsche Strafrecht – Besonderer Teil*, Berlin, 1935, p. 206), though it was not in fact included until 1951 by the first Criminal Law Amendment Law. A number of SPD and CDU/CSU politicians had suggested that it be supplemented by a procedural measure on 'state's evidence', but after much toing and froing the idea was dropped. The provisions quoted from the law itself for a reduction or suspension of sentence are just as good as a 'state's evidence' provision, though this has long operated in practice. 'Witnesses' of this sort are called in state security cases without any special regulation. Examples are many. Ruhland, a crucial witness against the accused in an RAF trial in Berlin, said that he was in contact with the secret service (FR, 7.xi.74, p. 4). Hoff was pulled out of the hat by the prosecution at the Stammheim trial to fill gaps in their evidence and presented as an 'RAF bomb-maker'. After a faultless performance he named his prompters: 'He said that he had spent every evening on the days of the hearing, including the evening before his appearance, with the officers who had previously interrogated him. He would discuss the day's events with them, and the contents of his evidence. Once he had been praised for doing well' (Trial report, FAZ, 30.i.76, p. 2).

130. § 153d StPO in conjunction with § 5b 7a, 120, 146, 147 GVG.

131. S. G. Flatow, 'Der heutige Stand des Arbeitsrechts', in H. Sinzheimer *et al.*, *Grundfragen des Arbeitrechts*, Berlin, 1927, p. 11.

132. The Düsseldorf Provincial Court made this clear in 1976 in a case involving the 'National Socialist Task Force "Greater Germany"'. A gang of fascists were charged with offences under § 129 StGB and minor offences against the 'Military weapons law'. They had been found in possession of explosives and light infantry

weapons – hand grenades, pistols, rifles, ammunition – which were to be used 'to defend Germany against the Reds'.

Without any of the press reaction which normally follows trials under § 129, the fascists were given light, suspended prison sentences of between six and twelve months, in keeping with the presiding judge's markedly friendly words at the opening of the trial. The political views of the accused, he said, were not on trial, and the words from Dante's *Divine Comedy*, 'Abandon hope', did not apply to this trial (FR, 22.i.76, p. 4, and FR, 20.ii.76, p. 4).

133. Most recently BGHSt, 12.ii.75 (3 StR 7/74I) and 14.v.75 (3 StR 9/75), p. 7, a judgment against squatters (see below). In these decisions the High Court explicitly cites its decisions of the 50s and 60s and basic interpretations of § 129 by the Reich Court, even though the law has been twice altered since 1964.

134. BGHSt, 9.x.64, in NJW (1965), 55–6.

135. BGHSt, 22.xii.56, in BGHSt 10, 170.

136. § 298, para. 1 of the proposed Criminal Code of 1936; see Bundestag Publication 1/1307, 4.ix.50, preamble to § 129 StGB.

137. BGHSt, 30.x.64, in BGHSt 20, 89. Cf. the Government spokesman in the Legal Committee, 28.i.76, pp. 2441–2.

138. Schmude, secretary of state in the Federal Ministry of the Interior, quoted FR, 24.iii.75, p. 4.

139. Police Commissioner Hübner in an interview with the *Berliner Morgenpost*, 28/29.iii.75.

140. Buback, justifying the conduct of the search carried out after the seizure of hostages at the Vienna OPEC conference, quoted FR, 29.xii.75, p. 1.

141. Report and proposal of the Legal Committee on Changes in the Penal Code, in Bundestag Publication 5/2860 (9.v.68), p. 6.

142. The Government spokesman in the Legal Committee commenting on the present legal position under § 129 StGB, 28.i.76 (pp. 2442, 2443).

143. Berlin Provincial Court, judgment of 28.v.74 (KJ, 1974, 406ff.).

144. Stuttgart Superior Provincial Court, decision of 22.iv.75 (1 ARs 27/75), citing BGHSt 20, 89; the same court, decision of 30.xii.74. On the provisions of § 138 StPO allowing the exclusion of defence counsel, see the chapter on political defence.

145. Stuttgart District Court, warrant against Klaus Croissant, 23.vi.75.

146. Karlsruhe Provincial Court judgment of 5.vi.75 (I KLS 9/75 – IV AK 3/75), pp. 21, 25ff.

147. BGHSt, 29.x.75 (3StR 369/75), pp. 3ff.

148. BGHSt, 12.ii.75 (3StR 7/74 I) and BGHSt, 14.v.75 (3StR 9/75), pp. 4ff.

As the High Court said in an order for damages against Hanover squatters, the accused had 'announced their alliance' with the initiators of the squatting operation, and 'made the planning and execution of active resistance psychologically easier'. They had 'done nothing to produce calm'. 'By their presence in the illegally occupied house and by remaining there in the increasingly tense situation' of the police eviction, 'they voluntarily contributed to strengthening the courage of the participants and their will to resist' (BGHZ, 29.x.74, VI ZR 182/73, pp. 11, 5).

149. Bielefeld District Court, judgment of 27.v.74 (KJ, 1975, 190).

150. These are the titles suggested for the new § 129a StGB by the Government, and the SPD/FDP and CDU/CSU parliamentary groups.

151. Vogel (CDU), *Bundestag*, 12.vi.75 p. 12437.

152. SPD/FDP group proposals for § 129a StGB, Bundestag Publication 7/3739 (4.vi.75), p. 7.

153. ibid.

154. ibid. In addition informing was made a duty for everyone: the 'formation' of or 'acts of support' for 'gangs' were to be reported to the state security authorities 'forthwith' (§ 138 StGB, new version).

Chapter 5: Political Trials

1. W. Wagner, Preface to HuSt I, p. 11.

During the discussion of the political criminal law in 1951 the Legal Committee was told, 'The Federal Interior Ministry stresses that there should be no exaggerated nervousness over the definition of offences, since this would make the task of the Interior Ministry unduly difficult. Even if definitions are not framed precisely and do not in all points satisfy the criteria for precise legality, and if they make large demands on judicial interpretation, this deficiency can always be eliminated in a less dangerous period' (*Legal Committee*, 26.vi.51, pp. 14–15).

2. 'In my view,' wrote Maihofer in 1963, 'here too, in our zeal to defend our freedom with the weapons of unfreedom, we ourselves

have left the ground of our free system. This distinguishes itself from arbitrary regimes by refraining, even when making use of political justice, from any arbitrary act. It refrains from a retrospective drawing of the boundaries between criminal and non-criminal behaviour which the normal citizen could not predict or anticipate. Here we have a simple alternative. Either we abolish these so-called offences endangering the state completely or we change them into specific offences of causing danger framed and applied according to strict criteria of legality' (W. Maihofer, 'Staatsschutz im Rechtsstaat', in W. Amman (ed.), *Protokoll der 10. Arbeitstagung des 'Initiativausschusses für die Amnestie und die Verteidigung in politischen Strafsachen'*, Frankfurt am Main, 1963, p. 14).

Maihofer subsequently brought about the exact opposite.

3. BVerfG, 30.xi.55 (BVerfGE 4, 358) and BVerfG, 22.vi.60 (BVerfGE 11, 237). Cf. BGHSt, 15.ii.58 (BGHSt 11, 37) and BGHSt, 3.v.63 (BGHSt 18, 362).

4. Federal prosecutor E. Träger, 'Strafrechtlicher Staatsschutz', in *Das Parlament*, 17.i.76, p 3.

5. Federal Attorney-General Bader, *Verhandlungen des 38. Deutschen Juristentages – Abteilung E*, Tübingen, 1951, E 29.

6. Rotberg, Federal Ministry of Justice, *Verhandlungen des 38. Deutschen Juristentages*, op. cit., E 73.

7. ibid.

8. The remarks quoted were made in debates about the setting up of special criminal courts (§ 74a GVG): von Weber, 'Das Strafrechtsänderungsgesetz', in MDR (1951), 645; Rotberg, Government spokesman in the Legal Committee, 29.vi.51, p. 2; O. Schwarz, 'Zuständigkeitsfragen im Strafprozess', in NJW (1956), 1305; Penner (SPD), Legal Committee, 10.xii.75 (p. 2377) – debate on § 88a StGB.

Under § 74a GVG the competent courts of first instance for state security cases are the state security courts of Provincial Courts in whose area a Superior Provincial Court exists. If, 'because of the special importance of the case', the Federal Attorney-General takes over the investigation and the prosecution, the courts of first instance are the state security panels of the Superior Provincial Courts of the relevant state (§ 74a, para. 2 GVG with § 120, para. 2 GVG). This – for example – was the case in the trial of the Red Army Faction in Stammheim (Stuttgart Superior Provincial Court).

Appeals in all state security cases are heard by the Federal High Court. The Legal Committee is at present discussing changes in the Code of Criminal Procedure and the law on the organization of the courts to make possible 'faster, more efficient and simpler trials' (Jahn, SPD, *Bundestag*, 7.vi.72 p. 11038), to increase the powers of the Federal prosecutor's office in political trials, and to concentrate trials 'of particular importance' in a few Superior Provincial Courts (see Bundestag Publication 7/5267, 28.v.76).

9. Eyrich (CDU), *Bundestag*, 16.i.76, p. 14753.

10. Federal Prosecutor E. Träger, 'Strafrechtlichen Staatsschutz', in *Das Parlament*, 17.i.76, p. 3.

SPD deputy Gnädinger openly admitted in the Bundestag that the important changes in procedural law in 1975 (the exclusion of lawyers, hearings without the accused, etc.) were made in order to give the prosecuting counsel in the Stuttgart Red Army Faction trial, who were finding difficulty in proving their case, the necessary means to bring this trial to the planned conclusion at any price: 'It is clear to anyone in the know,' said Gnädinger, 'that without the changes in procedure already agreed the trial of the Baader–Meinhof terrorists in Stammheim would have got into even greater difficulties. It might even have had to be abandoned. Only a change in the law made last year . . . made the continuation of the trial possible. I therefore ask all the critics to consider for a moment what disastrous consequences for our citizens' sense of law and order would have resulted if the trial in Stammheim had had to be abandoned without a verdict' (*Bundestag*, 24.vi.76, p. 17990).

11. § § 161a, 163a, para. 3 StPO.

12. § 10 StPO.

13. Government bill to reform the criminal law, Bundestag Publication 7/551 (2.v.73), p. 72.

14. Bill cited in note 15, pp. 38 and 75.

15. Although, according to § § 112, 119ff StPO, only judges and courts have the power to determine the use, form and length of a remand in custody, an 'internal notice' from the prison administration in Cologne-Ossendorf dated 2.viii.73 on the condition of the political prisoners detained there included the following passage: 'Prisoners may only be allowed out – even in the gravest emergencies (i.e. danger to life) – when the Bonn security group has given instructions to that effect' (see also the report in FAZ, 23.vi.75, p. 4).

This practice of giving judicial powers to the secret services and the political police was already familiar in the 50s. Posser mentions cases from his time as a lawyer in which the *Verfassungsschutz* decided whether or not political prisoners should be released from custody (D. Posser, in W. Amman (ed.), *'Initiativausschuss'*, op. cit., report of proceedings on 4/5.v.57, p. 18). This is confirmed by former FDP deputy and lawyer Diemer-Nikolaus: 'frequently control over whether a case is brought to trial no longer lies with the public prosecutor at all, but with the offices of the *Verfassungsschutz'*, *Bundestag*, 7.ii.68, p. 7788.

On the other procedural resources available to the prosecution which are mentioned in the text, see § 153d StPO with § § 74a, 120, 146, 147 GVG.

§ 54 StPO with § 39 paras. 2–3 BRRG allows an official body to forbid its staff – say *Verfassungsschutz* officers – to make statements to a court 'if the statement would prejudice the welfare of the Federation or of a German state or seriously endanger or impede the performance of public duties'.

16. D. Posser, op. cit., p. 19.

17. Karlsruhe Provincial Court, 5.vi.75 (IKLS 9/75/IV AK 3/75), p. 5.

18. The institution of 'common knowledge' as defined in § 244 StPO was first introduced by a law of 28.vi.35 (RGBI I, 844).

'Common knowledge', according to the High Court, 'must include facts known to the court ... "Known to the court" in this sense means reliably learned by the judge in connection with his official activity ... The status of a fact as common knowledge has the consequence that no evidence needs to be heard about it ... Whether a fact is a common knowledge must be decided by the judge in the court of first instance ... There is no objection to the assumption that facts are known to the court in areas which form the background to the events and, as it were, leave the field free for the perpetration of a larger number of identical crimes' (BGHSt, 14.vii.54, in BGHSt 6, 292ff.). The remarks were made at a trial of the Western Freie Deutsche Jugend.

19. FAZ, 9.vi.75, p. 8.

20. Exclusion of the accused from the hearing: § § 231a, 231b StPO; exclusion of defence lawyers: § § 138a-d StPO; prohibition of joint defence: § 146 StPO – in the Stammheim trial lawyers Schily and Heldmann were even forbidden under this clause from speaking in the courtroom to accused they were not defending (FR, 12.iii.76, p. 4). Surveillance of defence correspon-

dence: § § 148, 148a StPO (BGBl 1976 I, 2181); the right of accused and defence lawyers to issue statements lapsed with the deletion of § 275a StPO, which had been in force until the end of 1974.

21. F. J. Strauss, Sonthofen speech, *Der Spiegel*, 10.iii.75, p. 36.

22. Buback, quoted *Stern*, 25.vi.72, p. 141.

23. Hesse Criminal Investigation Bureau, quoted DE, 30.viii.74, p. 7.

24. The term 'procedural sabotage by the defence lawyers', which was tossed into the debate by the CDU, appears among the Nazis in this form: 'The presence of a vigorous defence counsel can only act as a brake on the process of justice if the position is occupied by someone inspired not by the desire to work for the law but by the intention of sabotaging the law' (R. Freisler, *Deutsches Strafrecht*, 1937, p. 115).

On obstacles put in the way of defence, its dependence on the state's interest in a conviction and the exclusion of politically undesirable lawyers in the 'Third Reich', see F. Ortlieb, *Der Verteidiger nach nationalsozialistischem Recht*, Tübingen, 1940.

25. W. Otto, *Die Festungshaft*, Magdeburg, 1938, pp. 297ff.

Formally the Nazis left § 17 RStGB in existence, but its exercise was abolished by a rewording of § 20 RStGB: 'Where the law allows a choice between penal servitude or imprisonment and fortress confinement, fortress confinement should only be imposed when the act is not directed against the well-being of the nation and when the accused has acted exclusively from honourable motives' (§ 20 RStGB, as part of the 'Law to amend penal provisions' of 26.v.33 (RGBl I, 295)). 'The act is directed against the national well-being when it either has led to prejudice to the national well-being or is objectively likely to produce such prejudice ... Motives are honourable when the accused's action was influenced by the adoption of moral values regarded as worthy of esteem by general sound national sentiment' (A. Schönke, *Strafgesetzbuch für das Deutsche Reich*, Berlin, 1942, No. II 1 and II 2, on § 20).

26. § 94 StGB in the form in force until 1968 not only provided for an increase in penalties for actions performed with 'deliberate hostility towards the constitution', but also changed the status of the offence from minor to major, with all the procedural consequences this entailed. Offences where prosecution had been left to the injured party, such as bodily harm, violation of privacy and damage to property, now became offences requiring official prosecution. Remands in custody became easier to obtain, attempts were made

offences, and changes were made in the time limits for prosecutions
and the ease with which proceedings could be abandoned.

This device was first used in Nazi law, for example in the 'Order
against elements harmful to the nation' of 5.ix.39 (RGBl I, 1679).

27. BGHSt, 18.iii.52 (BGHSt 2, 208) and BGHSt, 28.vii.55
(BGHSt 8, 163), basic judgments on the problem of the convinced
offender.

What this means was explained by two Federal prosecutors with
reference to the prohibition of abortion under § 218 StGB: 'Convinced offenders typically act from political or economic motives,
and the offence is a direct means of securing goals seen as
right. The motives of the offender may be honourable or reprehensible, but are subject to the determination of the judge . . . A case in
point would be that of a doctor who, to give 'help', sets himself
above the law and carries out abortions because he personally
regards the prohibition of the termination of a pregnancy as out of
date. On the other hand, only the doctor who, on conscientious
grounds, refuses to take an active part in abortions takes a decision
protected by the basic right contained in Article 4, Paragraph 1 of
the Basic Law (Freedom of Conscience and Belief). Apart from
cases of generally accepted medical grounds, the killing of a foetus
cannot be a dictate of conscience. A person who from profound
moral conviction regards abortion as simply immoral, however, is
following his conscience' (Federal Prosecutors Schulte and Träger,
'Gewissen im Strafprozess', in *25 Jahre BGH*, Munich, 1975, pp.
252–3).

28. BGHSt, 28.vii.55 (BGHSt 8, 163); High Court president R.
Fischer, quoted FR, 4.vi.75, p. 4.

29. Two more examples. In a judgment against a member of the
West German section of the communist youth organization Freie
Deutsche Jugend, the High Court justified the heavy sentence as
follows: 'Another factor is his unreasonableness, which gives reason
to fear that he will continue on his present course. His behaviour at
his trial showed clearly that he was capable of reasoned discussion
and not just dependent on slogans learned by heart. But at the same
time it was also clear that he is not prepared to tolerate other points
of view . . . He did not even learn from the year and more he spent
in custody before trial, and immediately after his release in May
1954 he resumed criminal activity in the Association for German-
Soviet friendship. Under these circumstances a harsh sentence was
necessary' (BGHSt, 28.vii.55, in HuSt I, 282).

Notes

The judgment on a participant in an anti-Springer demo ('breach of the peace') said in part: 'In fixing the sentence regard had to be paid to the character of the accused. The accused plays a not unimportant role in the extra-parliamentary opposition ... During the trial the accused attempted to bully the court by unseemly and disgusting behaviour. This, together with his offence and his membership of the extra-parliamentary opposition, which is known to be hostile to law and order, indicates that the accused is motivated by a dangerous hostility towards the laws, and is likely to commit further offences. These were all proper grounds for imposing a heavier sentence' (Munich Provincial Court, 27.v.69, in *Vorgänge*, 1969, p. 266).

30. Düsseldorf Provincial Court, 24.v.74 (II–27/73), pp. 32–3.

31. BGHSt, 25.vi.75, 3 StR 119/75.

32. Düsseldorf Provincial Court, 12.iii.76 (XV 35/75S – 5 Ks 22/73), pp. 50–51.

33. The 'danger' from the writer Zahl against which the 'public' are to be protected is shown by the conditions under which he has been kept in prison since 1972. He may write anything he likes, but not everything he writes may be published. The manuscript of a book on isolation was confiscated by the security authorities, and this act of censorship was backed by the Constitutional Court when Zahl appealed to it. There could be no constitutional objection to the refusal of permission to publish, said the court, 'even if the book were a work of art as defined in Article 5 of the Basic Law'. 'The manuscript includes many direct or indirect insinuations of a grossly defamatory nature, such, for example, as the claim that prisoners are generally and purposely subjected to inhuman and degrading treatment by police officers and prison staff, bullied, threatened, beaten and even killed either deliberately or by neglect. The book also seeks to produce the impression that conditions in prisons today are similar to the terror and arbitrary methods of the Nazi period. These insinuations and comparisons are such a serious violation of the personal rights of the officials working in the police and prison service, which are constitutionally safeguarded by Articles 1 and 2 of the Basic Law, notably their right to social status and respect, that the complainant's freedom of literary activity must in this case be overridden ... This decision is unchallengeable' (BVerfG, 12.ii.76 (2 BvR 151/75), p. 2). The highest court in the land says nothing about the personal rights of the victims ill-treated and killed by the police and the law – these are all 'gross insinuations'

about which those most affected have to keep quiet – they might be reporting something disruptive of 'communal peace'.

34. *Verhandlungen des 38. Deutschen Juristentages – Abteilung E*, Tübingen, 1951, E 20.

35. F. Vogel (CDU), in E. Kogan (ed.), *Terror und Gewaltkriminalität – Herausforderung für den Rechtsstaat*, Frankfurt am Main, 1975, p. 105.

The death penalty was demanded by the CDU politicians Windelen (FR, Easter 1975, p. 1), Dregger (FR, 14.iv.75, p. 4) and Jaeger (SZ, 5.iii.75, p. 1). The scene of Jaeger's remarks was significant; it was a press conference in Fürstenfeldbruck, where in 1972 the Federal Border Guard, in the presence of the Federal Minister of the Interior, brought about a blood-bath among the Palestinian guerrillas and their hostages, instead of letting them leave the country as had been agreed.

The CSU proposed 'secure custody' for political offenders in cases where 'there is a high probability of further offences' (FR, 24.iv.75, p. 8). This insidious device, which is already available for use on 'active persistent offenders' (BGHSt, in NJW, 1971, 1416) at the end of long sentences (§ 66 StGB, with § 48 StGB), was introduced by the Nazis in 1933 by the 'Law against dangerous habitual criminals and on measures for security and correction' (24.xi.33, RGBl I, 995).

According to Roland Freisler, 'the National Socialist Government introduced secure custody' in order to have in its possession 'a sharp sword'. 'In every nation there is a certain percentage of degenerate or depraved individuals who cannot be reformed by punishment ... Secure custody helps the campaign against crime by preventing the formation of new criminal gangs by isolating the crystallization points of professional crime and drying up the breeding and training sites of the new brood of criminals' (R. Freisler *et al., Dringende Fragen der Sicherungsverwahrung*, Berlin, 1938, p. 7).

The CSU suggestion that secure custody should also be used for political offenders is even discussed in the commentary under § 66 StGB (detention in secure custody'). It is suggested for 'symptomatic offenders', 'in cases of involvement in criminal organizations, where imprisonment has proved ineffective, unreasonableness and so on' (E. Dreher, *Kommentar zum Strafgesetzbuch*, 35th edn, 1975, No. 4A, on § 66).

During the Stammheim trial the defence revealed that a section had been constructed some time previously in Bruchsal prison containing eight separated and specially soundproofed isolation cells. The prosecution described this as 'pure myth', but one day later the Stuttgart ministry of justice admitted that the cells had been built, and said that they were being kept for 'troublesome prisoners serving life sentences' (FR, 27.viii.75 p. 4; FR, 28.viii.75, p. 4).

36. Professor W. Rasch in an interview with *Stern*, 20.v.76, p. 74. On the even stricter isolation imposed at certain periods, see the relevant decisions of judges and courts in *Kursbuch Nr. 32*. The fact that this unusual treatment is incompatible with the prohibition of torture contained in the constitution and in ordinary law (Art. 1, 104 GG, and its application in § 136a StPO and § § 233, 343 StGB) and with Article 3 of the Human Rights Convention, which in West Germany has the force of domestic law and is binding on administrative bodies, does not seem to have impressed the security authorities.

37. The most comprehensive definition of torture to date is that made by the General Assembly of the United Nations on 9 December 1975.

Asked about the treatment of political prisoners in Iran, the Shah, speaking as an expert on all forms of torture techniques, commented on the increasing sophistication and scientific nature of torture in Europe and America: 'Torture? In your countries you have much more sophisticated methods of torture – you do it by psychology' (*Le Monde*, 25.vi.74, p. 3).

On the Gestapo's use of psychological techniques in interrogation, see Stefan Zweig, *Schachnovelle*, Frankfurt am Main, 1959, pp. 47ff.

38. Henck, quoted FR, 13.vi.75, p. 2.

39. Professor Rasch's report of 10.ix.75, pp. 4ff.

The state of health of prisoners in Zweibrücken, who are also being kept in strict isolation, was described in a specialist opinion as follows:

'The following identical symptoms were found in the three prisoners on remand:

1. Marked vegetative regulatory disturbances, with hypotonic circulatory disturbance.

2. Psychophysical exhaustion.

3. Underweight.

. . . I would here like to make a few comments which seem to me important. They are based on my experience in diagnosing and treating psychosomatic symptoms, which is also part of a physician's task. The accused in their present condition feel unable to cope with either the mental strain or the intellectual demands placed on them by their imprisonment and trial. This leads to uncontrolled outbursts of aggression, as can be seen repeatedly in the trial. During the medical examination, on the other hand, they remained calm, showed no signs of aggression and – an important feature in this context – also no additional symptoms. Their mood veered between resignation and activity. Their resignation is a result of their conviction that they are in the hands of a 'power machine' which will not allow them to receive 'fair treatment'. The accused see proof of this conviction in the prison conditions in which they live. As a result they alternate between phases of bitterness and phases of resignation and loneliness, which also show marked depressive features. In this connection, a constant theme of the accused is that the worst thing they have to bear is the strict isolation . . .

'Next a comment on the question of how far the disorders revealed are the result of the prison conditions, the accused's hunger strike or factors independent of both. There follow details of some series of medical tests . . . When all the data cited are taken into account it seems to me that there is nothing to show that the hunger strike, which ended ten months ago, played any great part in bringing about the prisoners' present state of health. Since, as has been explained many times already, there are no signs of other organic or mental illnesses – either inherited or contracted before imprisonment – it is my view that the cause of the medical disorders revealed by the examination lies overwhelmingly in the prison conditions. The accused have now been in custody for periods between forty-one and forty-five months. Since then they have been kept in unusually strict isolation. Their contact with other people is limited to the relatively rare visits of relatives and defence lawyers. The communication with other remand prisoners usual in other prisons is missing, and they are not allowed to take part in communal events or to attend religious services.

'Possibilities for physical movement and activity are limited.

'In order to improve the prisoners' mental state and intellectual capacity, a number of steps must be taken, primarily involving their isolation. If one accepts that human life can only develop and take on meaningful shape in communication and association with other human beings, it is then a medical requirement that the strict isolation of the accused practised up to now be ended. The accused should in future be able to take part in communal activities within the prison, and they should at intervals be allowed contact with other remand prisoners. An important result of this will be to make possible a confrontation with basic political attitudes different from the uniform view which prevails in the group. The range of possible visitors should be widened to include people other than relatives.' (Report by Dr Kreiter, 10.xii.75, p. 7ff.)

40. BGHSt (22.x.75), in StR 1/74 – STB 60–63/75, pp. 12, 13, 15.
41. ibid., pp. 4, 9, 18.
42. ibid., p. 19.

The last urgent appeal for the ending of the solitary confinement was dated 14.iii.77. A letter from the Stammheim prison doctor, Dr Henck, to the relevant court contains the following unambiguous passage:

'Almost eighteen months have passed since the last opinions of the expert assessors were given and the continuance of the remand custody under practically identical conditions has certainly resulted in no improvement in the mental state of the prisoners. In view of this, the recommendations of the doctors referred to (Prof. Rasch, etc.) must be emphatically reiterated ... Consequently it is, in my opinion, urgently necessary to correct the present prison conditions along the lines suggested by the experts, who regard the most important curative measures as consisting in a modification of the prison conditions to allow greater social interaction. It would be hard to imagine any attempt to treat the effects of isolation visible in the accused without a fundamental change in the existing prison conditions. The carrying out of treatment while the present prison conditions are maintained would seem to be impossible.'

As is well known, the judicial authorities ignored these requests by the doctors. The prison conditions were even made more severe after the attacks on Federal Attorney-General Buback and Schleyer, the president of the employers' association (see the discussion of the 'contact ban' law in the last chapter).

Chapter 6: Military State Security

1. A. Stümper, in *Die Polizei* 11 (1975), p. 370.

The 'State Development Programme 1985' produced by the former SPD/FDP government of Lower Saxony, said: 'The growing complexity of social life and its problems, which in a democracy can only be solved by lengthy processes, and the increasing political consciousness of the population will probably result in an increased readiness to engage in public confrontations. The police expect that a considerable number of operations in the next decade will result from demonstrations ... The situation we have outlined will become more acute in times of crisis ... Consequences. The aim of the present measures is to put the police in a position, both personal and professional, in which they can deal with any dangerous situation flexibly and effectively before it develops. They must be able to provide the necessary help anywhere, at any time and in any circumstances' (*Landesentwicklungsprogramm Niedersachsen 1985*, Hanover, 1973, pp. 447 and 446).

2. From the programme for 'internal security' produced by the Conference of Interior Ministers of the Federation and States in February 1974, supplement to *Gemeinsames Ministerialblatt*, 16.iv.74.

3. U. Wegener, commander of the Border Guard unit GSG9 in M. Tophoven (ed.), *Politik durch Gewalt*, Koblenz and Bonn, 1976, p. 148; *Der Spiegel*, 18.ix.72, p. 25.

Hesse Interior Minister Bielefeld (FDP) added, 'Terrorists are human beings too. Killing them is something that has to be learned' (*Spiegel*, loc. cit.).

4. The new administrative agreement between the Federal Government and the states which came into effect on 1 January 1971 is reprinted in G.-D. Schoen, P. Frisch, *Aufrechterhaltung der öffentlichen Sicherheit und Ordnung*, Bad Honnef, 1973, pp. 150ff. There is a commentary on it in *Innere Sicherheit – Informationen des Bundesministeriums des Inneren*, 13.iv.76, p. 10.

The quotation from the Constitutional Court about the Emergency Police comes from a decision of this force: BVerfGE 17, 332.

5 § § 1 and 2 of the Federal Border Guard Law of 16.iii.51 (BGBl I, 201).

The maximum strength of 10,000 men was agreed between the parties in the Bundestag, and was to be raised only with their consent (*Bundestag*, 15.ii.51, p. 4516). In 1953 its strength was raised to 20,000 men against the opposition of the SPD and KPD (*Bundestag*, 19.vi.53, p. 13608), and in 1956 it went back to the old figure because around 10,000 men were withdrawn to strengthen the Bundeswehr, which was at that time being formed (see § 1 of the Second Federal Border Guard Law of 30.v.56 (BGBl I, 436)). The present figure is 21,000 men.

6. Article 91 of the Basic Law (introduced by the emergency laws

of 24.vi.68 (BGBl I, 709)) and Article 35, para. 2 of the Basic Law (introduced by a law of 28.vii.72 (BGBl I, 1305) with the Third Federal Border Guard Law of 1972). This Third Border Guard Law is in BGBl I, 1834.

SPD deputy Schäfer, chairman of the Interior Committee, commented on the new BGS law: 'To set up the Federal Border Guard quite legally and properly as a crack reserve for key tasks ... that is the decision we have been waiting for since 1956' (*Bundestag*, 7.vi.72, p. 10990'.

7. Konrad (SPD), *Bundestag*, 22.vi.72, p. 11459.

Joint manoeuvres between the BGS and the emergency police were being mentioned as long ago as 1958 by Interior Minister Schröder in his speech on 'Security today', in *Bulletin des Presse-und Informationsamtes der Bundesregierung*, 31.x.58. Such joint exercises were eventually allowed a little later by the second Federal-state agreement on the emergency police of 1.v.71, § 5.

8. W. Maihofer, address on the twenty-fifth anniversary of the creation of the BGS, 18.vi.76, in *Der Bundesminister des Innern teilt mit*, Federal Ministry of the Interior press release, 18.v.76, p. 14.

9. § § 9, 10 of the Federal Border Guard Law.

10. G.-D. Schoen and P. Frisch, commentary on the Federal Border Guard Law, in G.-D. Schoen and P. Frisch (ed.), *Aufrechterhaltung der öffentlichen Sicherheit und Ordnung*, Bad Honnef, 1973, pp. 91–2.

11. ibid., p. 39.

12. Federal Government report on the development of the BGS, Bundestag Publication 7/3170, 24.i.75, pp. 13 and 3.

13. According to a study by the 'Bundeswehr Social Science Institute', DE, 8.iii.75, p. 2.

The extent of disaffection within the Bundeswehr is revealed by the preamble to the bill brought in by the Federal Government in 1975 to tighten up the law on military discipline: 'Absence without leave is a serious breach of discipline. It endangers the internal structure of the armed forces and is a challenge both to constant readiness and to military order and discipline. The growing number of offences in the last few years involving unauthorized absence and desertion' was said to approach the strength of a division each year! The number rose from 3,614 cases in 1968 to 11,395 in 1974, and in 1973 there were 13,901 (Bundestag Publication 7/4027, 16.ix.69, pp. 14–15).

14. Naturally internal operations are also part of the Bundes-wehr's duties under the emergency laws (esp. Art. 87a, para. 4 GG). The fact that internal crises as well as foreign conflicts could result in the use of the army was demonstrated by the 'Hilex 1975' manoeuvre mounted in December 1974 – at the height of the 'energy crisis'. The imagined context was described by *Der Spiegel*:

'In Chile workers opposed to the junta have been occupying the copper mines for months. African and Asian raw material pro-ducers have imposed a ban on deliveries to the Western industrial countries. The oil countries would rather carry on keeping their oil under the desert than sell it for daily depreciating Western cur-rencies. Europe's economy, dependent from the beginning on raw materials from other continents, is faced with collapse. Inflation and stagnation on an unheard-of scale are destroying in a few months the complicated machinery of the economy. Very soon the countries of Europe will be unable to keep to the social obligations they assumed in times of prosperity. The funds are empty. Governments can no longer provide for the growing army of the unemployed. In Italy, France and even in West Germany, there have been outbreaks of disorder. Hungry workers engage in bloody street battles with the police . . .' (*Spiegel*, 14.vii.75, p. 64).

The new manpower structure law for the BGS was passed by the Bundestag on 9.vi.76. On the Federal-state agreement on transfer-ring long-serving Border Guards to the ordinary police, see W. Maihofer (FN 8), p. 21.

15. Bundestag Publication 7/3170, p. 2.

16. ibid., pp. 6ff.

17. E. Benda, as a member of the Bundestag Internal Affairs Com-mittee, in the BGS magazine *Die Parole* 4 (1971), p. 6.

18. Benda, ibid. (see also Bundestag Publication 7/3170, pp. 8–9, and the 'security programme' produced by the Conference of In-terior Ministers in 1974, in *Gemeinsames Ministerialblatt* 9 (1974), point 4.2.2).

19. H.-G. Pries, Hamburg police commander, FR, 5.vi.74, p. 4.

20. For example § 6, para. 2 of the Hesse law on the use of direct force by police officers. The police laws of the other states contain similar provisions.

21. Ruhnau, address at a swearing-in ceremony for police officers, *Polizeimagazin*, September 1972, p. 525.

22. The most comprehensive study I know is in a dissertation by

Notes

R. Buchert, *Zum polizeilichen Schusswaffengrebrauch*, Lübeck, 1975. Buchert also reports having considerable difficulty in getting access to the official statistics (op. cit., pp. 63–4).

23. According to Buchert's figures, in the period 1945–74 288 policemen were shot on duty, 205 of these in the five years just after the war! In the next twenty-four years 83 policemen died of gunshot wounds, while an equal number of civilians were shot by police in only eleven years (1962–72). Figures are not available for the period before 1962.

On the general issue and the legend of the dangerousness of a policeman's job, see A. Funk, F. Wekentin, 'Der Todesschuss der Polizei', KJ 2 (1976); G. Wettschereck in *Die Polizei* 7/1971, pp. 202ff.; and *Stern*, 10.vi.76, p. 45.

24. Suttinger, quoted *Der Spiegel* 6 (1974), p. 51.

25. K. Müller, FR, 29.v.74, p. 9.

26. BGHSt, 20.iii.75, in NJW (1975), p. 366.

27. A. Stümper, in *Die Polizei*, 11 (1975), p. 366.

28. The 'German Judges' Association', quoted FR, 7.ii.76, p. 1.

29. *Hessische Polizeirundschau* 10 (1973), p. 12; the quotation is from an expert opinion on a fatal shooting (NJW, 1972, p. 1822).

30. 'Model for a standard police law' – preamble to § 36, para. 3. Cf. also the 'security programme' of the Interior Ministers Conference (n. 2 above), p. 16; H. Schwarz, *Der Spiegel* 32/1976, p. 31.

31. Schmitz (CDU), Berlin House of Deputies, 11.vi.70 (p. 373).

32. W. Siedschlag, 'Zur Diskussion um die Bewaffnung der Polizei', *Die Polizei* 7 (1971), p. 209.

33. *Vorwärts*, 5.ii.76, p. 3.

34. See the expert on police weapons and police adviser H. J. Stammel, *Polizeiwaffen von heute and morgen,* Stuttgart, 1974.

35. W. Weyer, former Interior Minister of North-Rhine-Westphalia, *Westdeutsche Allgemeine Zeitung,* 2.i.72.

36. On police measures, see the FR report (7.iii.75, p. 3) and the following two reports: Georg-von-Rauch-Haus and Thomas-Weissbecker-Haus, *Police Raids on 5 March 1975*, West Berlin, 1975, and Humanistische Union Landesverband Berlin, *Demokratischer Rechtsstaat zwischen individuellem Terror und Polizeigewalt*, West Berlin, 1975.

37. Frankfurt police, quoted FAZ, 27.xi.74, p. 35.

38. § § 10 ('Checking of Identity'), 17 ('Searches of Persons'), 19 ('Entry into and Searches of Dwellings') of the model standard police law proposed by the Conference of Interior Ministers. The

introduction to this general authorization says that its purpose is to create 'a clear legal basis for so-called 'raids' whereby 'under the conditions described no specific suspicion will need to exist against the persons to be investigated'.

The new police law for Baden-Württemberg, operative since 19 February 1976, is published in Baden-Württemberg Parliament Publication No. 6/9104.

Conclusion

1. H. J. Vogel (SPD), quoted FR, 9.v.75, p. 1.

2. Bubank in an interview, *Der Spiegel*, 16.ii.76, p. 34.

3. § § 31ff of the Introductory Law to the Law on Judicial Organization (EGGVG) of 30.ix.77 (BGBl I, 1877ff.).

4. Federal Press Office, *Dokumentation zu den Ereignissen und Entscheidungen im Zusammenhang mit der Entführung von Hanns Martin Schleyer und der Lufthansa-Maschine 'Landshut'*, Bonn, November 1977, Appendix 6, 'Bulletin der Bundesregierung Nr. 88/1977', p. 820. [Background material to the kidnapping of Hanns Martin Schleyer and the Lufthansa hijack.]

5. See the decisions in NJW (1977), pp. 2157–8, 2172ff., 2177.

6. Bundestag Publication 8/935, 28.ix.77; 8/943, 29.ix.77; 8/944, 29.ix.77.

7. West German Government statement in its collection of background material (n. 4 above).

8. Bundestag, 29.ix.7, pp. 3366ff.; Bundesrat, 30.ix.77, pp. 226ff.

9. *Stern*, 6.x.77., p. 269.

10. The law, under which prisoners selected by the executive can be held responsible and punished for the actions of various unknown persons outside the prison, contravenes in particular the following articles of the Basic Law 1 (human dignity), 2 (inviolability of the person), 17 (right of petition), 19, section 4 (right to legal process), the principle of the separation of powers (art. 20, Sect. 2), the guarantee of a lawful judge (101, Sect. 1), the guarantee of a hearing in accordance with law (103, Sect. 1), and the guarantees connected with deprivation of liberty (104), as well as the relevant provision of the International Agreement and of ordinary law.

11. Coppik (SPD), Bundestag, 29.ix.77, p. 3372.

12. Bundestag Publication 8/322, 26.iv.77, p 1 (CDU/CSU motion calling for a stiffening of the law on demonstrations).

Notes

13. Genscher (FDP) and Ruhnau (SPD), *Bundestag*, 7.vi.72, pp. 10976 and 10998.

14. The increasing influence of considerations of police tactics on legislation is also shown by the events of the first reading of the CDU/CSU Opposition bill to alter the law on demonstrations (see n. 12 above). The FDP said that agreement to the proposal should depend on the views of the police experts: 'The Police Officer College at Hiltrup, which is supported by all the Federal States, is engaged in an analysis of events so far (the confrontations over nuclear power stations) and the police handling of them. If it is necessary to translate the findings into legislation, this will be done' (Hirsch (FDP), *Bundestag*, 5.v.77, p. 1698).

15. U. K. Preuss, 'Ein Skandal findet nicht statt', *diskus* (Frankfurt student newspaper), 1/77, p. 4.

16. H. Herold, 'Gesellschaftlicher Wandel – Chance der Polizei?', in H. Schäfer (ed.), *Grundlagen der Kriminalistik*, Vol. 11, Hamburg, 1973, pp. 13ff.

17. SPD executive, quoted HB, 24.ii.75, p. 1.

18. Dregger (CDU), *Bundestag*, 28.x.77, p. 4099.

List of Abbreviations

AG	District Court *(Amtsgericht)*.
BGH	Federal High Court *(Bundesgerichtshof)*.
BGHSt	High Court Decisions in Criminal Cases, official collection, cited by volume and page.
BGHZ	High Court Decisions in Civil Cases, official collection, cited by volume and page.
BGS	Federal Border Guard *(Bundesgrenzschutz)*.
BGSG	Federal Border Guard Law *(Bundesgrenzschutzgesetz)*.
BGBl	Federal Law Gazette *(Bundesgesetzblatt)*, cited by volume and page. The volume numbers refer to the year in which the law was published.
BKA	Federal Criminal Investigation Bureau *(Bundeskriminalamt)*.
BRRG	Legislation for Federal Civil Servants *(Bundesbeamtenrechtsrahmengesetz)*.
Bundesrat, Bundestag	Official record of proceedings, cited by day and page.
BVerfG	Federal Constitutional Court *(Bundesverfassungsgericht)*.
BVerfGE	Decisions of the Federal Constitutional Court, official collection, cited by volume and page.
BVerwG	Federal Administrative Court.
BVerwGE	Decisions of the Federal Administrative Court, official collection, cited by volume and page.
BZRG	Federal Central Records Office Law *(Bundeszentralregistergesetz)*.
CDU	German Christian Democratic Union *(Christlich-Demokratische Union Deutschlands)*.
DE	*Darmstädter Echo*.
DGB	West German Trades Union Congress *(Deutscher Gewerkschafts-Bund)*

List of Abbreviations

DuR	*Demokratie und Recht.*
FAZ	*Frankfurter Allgemeine Zeitung.*
FDP	Free Democratic Party (*Freiedemokratische Partei*).
FR	*Frankfurter Rundschau.*
GG	Basic Law (*Grundgesetz*).
GVG	Law on Judicial Organization (*Gerichtsverfass-ungsgesetz*).
HuSt	Decisions of the Federal High Court in Political Cases (*Hochverrat und Staatsgefährdung*), Vols. I and II, Karlsruhe 1957 and 1958.
JZ	*Juristenzeitung.*
KJ	*Kristische Justiz.*
KPD	German Communist Party (*Kommunistische Partei Deutschlands*).
LK	Leipzig Commentary on the Penal Code, 9th edn., 1974.
LG	Provincial Court (*Landgericht*).
MDR	*Monatsschrift für Deutsches Recht.*
NJW	*Neue Juristische Wochenschrift.*
OLG	Superior Provincial Court (*Oberlandesgericht*).
Legal Committee	Proceedings of the Special Committee of the West German Bundestag on Penal Law Reform, cited by day and page.
RAF	Red Army Faction (*Rote Armee Fraktion*).
RGBl	Reich Law Gazette (*Reichsgesetzblatt*).
RG	Reich Supreme Court (*Reichsgericht*).
RGSt	Decisions of the Reich Supreme Court in Criminal Cases.
SPD	German Social Democratic Party (*Sozialdemo-kratische Partei Deutschlands*).
StGB	Penal Code (*Strafgesetzbuch*).
StPO	Code of Criminal Procedure (*Strafprozessordnung*).

Glossary

Berufsverbot	Refusal to employ (or retain) people in public service jobs on the ground that they are 'hostile to the state' or 'hostile to the constitution'. See pp. 33–6, and p. 162 n. 50.
Bundesrat	Upper house of the Federal parliament, composed of representatives of the *Länder* or states of the Federation. Many laws can come into force only after approval by the Bundesrat.
Bundestag	Lower house of the Federal parliament, comparable with the British House of Commons.
Bundeswehr	The West German armed forces.
Federal Border Guard	Paramilitary force, originally formed to guard the frontier, especially along the border with the GDR, and subsequently developed into a Federal police force for large-scale internal operations.
Federal Criminal Investigation Bureau *Verfassungs-schutz*	Central Federal detective police. (Lit. 'Office for the Protection of the Constitution'). Secret service organization responsible for keeping political organizations and activists under observation. It is not concerned with classical 'counter-espionage', which is the task of another secret service organization, the Federal Intelligence Service (*Bundesnachrichtendienst*).